THE ROMANCE OF INDIVIDUALISM IN EMERSON AND NIETZSCHE

Series in Continental Thought

The Romance of Individualism in Emerson and Nietzsche

DAVID MIKICS

Ohio University Press
ATHENS

Ohio University Press, Athens, Ohio 45701

© 2003 by David Mikics

Ohio University Press books are printed on acid-free paper ⊖

12 11 10 09 08 07 06 05 04 03   5 4 3 2 1

Library of Congress Cataloging-in-Publication Data

Mikics, David, 1961–
　The romance of individualism in Emerson and Nietzsche /
David Mikics.
　　p. cm. — (Series in Continental thought ; 31)
　ISBN 0-8214-1496-8 (alk. paper)
　1. Individualism. 2. Nietzsche, Friedrich Wilhelm, 1844–1900.
3. Emerson, Ralph Waldo, 1803–1882—Philosophy. 4. Emerson,
Ralph Waldo, 1803–1882—Influence. I. Title. II. Series.
　B824 .M54 2003
　141' .4—dc21
　　　　　　　　　　　　　　　　　　　　　　　2003040572

To K. V.
und hörte fremd einen Fremden sagen:
Ichbinbeidir.

CONTENTS

ACKNOWLEDGMENTS

For their helpful and generous readings of my work on Emerson and Nietzsche, I am grateful to Charles Altieri, Leslie Brisman, Gerald Bruns, Charles Dove, Randall Havas, William Kerrigan, Joshua Leiderman, Daniel Price, and Rei Terada.

Among my students, Ronnie Yates, Clayton Alexander, and Carol Quinn, along with several others, contributed significantly to my understanding of Nietzsche. Talking about Nietzsche with Sheridan Hough, and with the Rice University Continental Theory Workshop, was also important.

John Hollander, Perry Meisel, and Stanley Cavell lent support to this project at an early stage. I am especially thankful for Stanley Cavell's grace and generosity.

For administrative support I owe much to Lois Zamora and Harmon Boertien.

I would also like to thank the following friends: Richard Armstrong, Glenna Bell, Wendy Scheir, and Edward Schiffer. And I am grateful to the staff and owners of Café Brasil, in Houston, Texas, where much of this book was written.

I owe a special debt to Steven Crowell for his interest in this project.

KEY TO ABBREVIATED REFERENCES

BT   Nietzsche, Friedrich. *The Birth of Tragedy*. Trans. Shaun White-
        side. London: Penguin, 1993.
BGE   Nietzsche, Friedrich. *Beyond Good and Evil*. Trans. R. J. Holling-
        dale. London: Penguin, 1990.
D   Nietzsche, Friedrich. *Daybreak*. Trans. R. J. Hollingdale. Cam-
        bridge: Cambridge University Press, 1982.
E   Emerson, Ralph Waldo. *Essays and Lectures*. Ed. Joel Porte. New
        York: Library of America, 1983.
EH   Nietzsche, Friedrich. *Ecce Homo*. Trans. R. J. Hollingdale. Intro-
        duction by Michael Tanner. London: Penguin, 1992.
GM   Nietzsche, Friedrich. *On the Genealogy of Morality*. Trans. Carol
        Diethe. Cambridge: Cambridge University Press, 1994.
GS   Nietzsche, Friedrich. *The Gay Science*. Trans. Walter Kaufmann.
        New York: Vintage, 1974.
KSA   Nietzsche, Friedrich. *Sämtliche Werke (Kritische Studienausgabe)*.
        Ed. Giorgio Colli and Mazzino Montinari. 15 vols. Berlin: de
        Gruyter, 1967–77.
PTAG   Nietzsche, Friedrich. *Philosophy in the Tragic Age of the Greeks*.
        Trans. Marianne Cowan. Washington, D.C.: Regnery Gateway,
        1962.
UM   Nietzsche, Friedrich. *Untimely Meditations*. Trans. R. J. Holling-
        dale. Cambridge: Cambridge University Press, 1983.
WP   Nietzsche, Friedrich. *The Will to Power*. Trans. Walter Kauf-
        mann and R. J. Hollingdale. New York: Vintage/Random
        House, 1968.
WWI   Schopenhauer, Arthur. *The World as Will and Idea*. 2 vols. Trans.
        E.F.J. Payne. New York: Dover, 1958.
Z   Nietzsche, Friedrich. *Thus Spake Zarathustra*. Trans. R. J. Hol-
        lingdale. Harmondsworth: Penguin, 1961.

For convenience, *Daybreak, The Gay Science,* and *On the Genealogy of Morality* (or *Toward the Genealogy of Morals,* as I here translate Nietzsche's
title *Zur Genealogie der Moral*) are referred to by section number. The
other texts listed above are cited by page number.

INTRODUCTION

FRIEDRICH NIETZSCHE DISCOVERED Ralph Waldo Emerson in the 1860s, as a schoolboy immersed in the committed scholarly environment of his boarding school, Schulpforta. Introduced to Emerson's essays by a friend, Carl von Gersdorff, Nietzsche became an immediate and, as it turned out, lifelong enthusiast of the American's work. Nietzsche quickly discovered his crucial philosophical affinity with Emerson: a dream of individual power set against what Emerson called conformity, the common or official beliefs that surround us. Both Emerson and Nietzsche insist on the individual's free, searching evaluation of culture. They assume as a starting point that both cultures and individuals are not-yet-achieved entities. For both these writers, the self can be startled into action, into the labor and joy of critical power, by its meeting with an unexplained impulse. This impulse, or sharp presence, is the self's desire to be transformed and to be fully created for the first time.

Among the other concerns Emerson and Nietzsche shared are the wish to be perfected and to be guided by the allure of the exemplary (Emerson's central or representative man, Nietzsche's *Übermensch*); the paradoxical connection between necessity, or fate, and freedom; the need to take the measure of the demystifying habits of a skeptical modernity, in order to pass beyond demystification; the role of mood, and more generally of the transitory and ephemeral, in our collective and individual lives; the importance of provocation as a means of instruction; the decisive potency of the oblique, unconscious, and random; the sense of life as an illusion, at once isolating the individual and interweaving him with the cosmos; and the importance of living both dangerously and cheerfully. Nietzsche's *Heiterkeit,* or joyousness, like Emerson's abrasive geniality, aims to transform tragedy into comedy, a goal that will occupy much of my attention in this book.

To speak more broadly, Emerson and Nietzsche are both, as Dilthey named them, philosophers of culture. They are critics of the unthoughtful busyness and philistinism that obstruct genuine thought. They detect a potential opposition between life-serving and merely sterile or unuseful knowledge. Their vitalism, which emphasizes the development of an instinctive or spontaneous moral life rather than one imposed from without, bases itself on a spiritual sympathy between human and cosmic *viriditas,* or growth-force. This sympathy takes, in their work, an experimental or risky and, at the same time, a necessary form.[1]

Both Emerson and Nietzsche challenge us to become who we are, to undertake the task of identity on our own. But in Nietzsche, unlike Emerson, identity remains (at times promisingly, at times maddeningly) subject to the other person who, we hope, might unlock the mystery of the self for us. This other person takes on different forms in Nietzsche's work: true reader, neighbor, father, sister, beloved, friend, and foster-father Wagner. The relation to the other involves Nietzsche in the problem of asceticism; Emerson, by contrast, remains a stranger to the ascetic impulse.

George Stack has addressed the resemblance between Nietzsche and Emerson in his *Nietzsche and Emerson: An Elective Affinity.* In this book, I follow in particular Stack's important remark that Nietzsche "inherited the problem of Fate" from Emerson.[2] But I depart from Stack's inclination to assimilate Emerson and Nietzsche instead of tracing the differences between them. For example, he sees Nietzsche's will to power as "a creative tendency towards form, expression, and life" analogous to Emerson's term "power."[3] Surely this is partly right, but Nietzsche's understanding of the will to power also includes a reflection on the ascetic impulse, and the human perversity and self-destructiveness that asceticism entails. This Nietzschean meditation on the ascetic's dangerous allure remains foreign to Emerson.

Stack's comment that "Nietzsche expands, develops, and dramatizes insights that Emerson presents in an almost casual way" is representative of his sense that the two thinkers' "doctrines and themes" are "overlapping."[4] In contrast to Stack's emphasis, I wish to outline a dynamic relation in which Nietzsche struggles with Emerson's influence and example in order to develop his own path.

In this book, I understand Nietzsche in part through Jacques Lacan's reading of Freud, because Lacan places fundamental emphasis on the self's subjection to the other. For Lacan, the self is a hermeneutic puzzle or labyrinth whose contours can only be discovered truly if we recognize the (impossible) demand we place on the other: that he reveal us to ourselves.

Lacan explores the fascination we feel for the other, as beloved or master, in dual terms. The other, Lacan explains, is both a figure that promises to unlock and explain the secrets of the self (the big Other) and an independent mystery that cannot be seen into, a cynosure for our sense of the obscurity of desire (the other as *objet petit a,* or object *a* as I will translate it in this book). (I supply a broad definition of the object *a* near the beginning of chapter 2.)

Emerson is not, as he has often been accused of being, tone-deaf to such entanglements. Rather, he is from the start free of the temptation to see the connection between self and other as Nietzsche does (and as Lacan will), as a mutually implicating puzzle or detective story. Emerson believes in a Gnostic self capable of communion with other selves. For him, illuminated moments of power or self-reliance authenticate us, even in our aloneness, with a clarity that shines through our meetings with others. Even when these encounters are warring ones, they still bear witness to a hermeneutic peace.

This is not to suggest that the Emersonian pneuma or spark offers itself as definitive, revolutionary liberation from a fallen state of things, as in authentic Gnosticism. Emerson asserts the innocence of the world against the accusations of its guilt and fallenness that the Gnostics share with normative Christianity—and with Schopenhauer.[5] If an idea of fallenness can be ascribed to Emerson, the fall would be our characteristic habit of lapsing into inertia and unthinking, rather than our wickedness.

Yet the Christian (or Gnostic, or Schopenhauerian) accusation against life elicits a profoundly sympathetic response from us, as Nietzsche explains most fully in his *Genealogy of Morals.* This response is familiarly known as asceticism. Although Nietzsche shares Emerson's urge to redeem existence from the claims of *ressentiment* that it is inherently corrupt and defective, he understands these claims more fully than Emerson can. As a result, Nietzsche lives through, as Emerson does not, the ascetic impulse that takes pleasure in ruining existence. (In chapter 5 I associate the ascetic's morbid pleasure with Lacan's notion of drive as fundamentally oriented toward repetition, and therefore toward death.)

The question of asceticism bears on Nietzsche's fear of and his attraction to transformation, to becoming other, since the ascetic aims at resisting such otherness. Asceticism wants a purity of consummation, an overthrow of whatever otherness remains within the self. The ascetic dreams of erasing the disturbing stimulus that confronts him in the form of other persons, and of personal history itself. But the ascetic also wants to be other, to be elsewhere (Nietzsche's definition of asceticism in the *Genealogy of Morals*). For Emerson, unlike Nietzsche, this otherness takes a stabilizing, harmonious form; it is an influx rather than an escape. In a passage selected by Harold Bloom to illustrate the essence of the Emersonian illumination, Emerson writes in his notebooks, "Were you ever instructed by a wise and eloquent man? Remember then, were not the words that made your blood run to your cheeks, that made you tremble or delighted you, — did they not sound to you as old as yourself? . . . It is God in you that responds to God without, or affirms his own words trembling on the lips of another."[6] This passage, I suggest, sums up Emerson's view of the relation between self and other. In our strong moments, we have no need and no desire to defend the self against its impulse to identify with the other, for this impulse simply marks the basic, shared character of illumination: "It is God in you that responds to God without." (Emerson's worries about influence, about yielding too much to a powerful other, address a weak self, one captive to illusions of its insufficiency; that weakness, he argues, can be shed.) For Nietzsche, by contrast, the urge to identify, which is also a theatrical impulse to wear the mask, to speak through an assumed persona, threatens our balance, because it implies a serious escapism: a deeply creative, but also potentially dangerous, and even corrupt, wish to be other and elsewhere. Nietzschean individualism involves both experimental *Maskenfreiheit* (the freedom of the mask), a living out of variant possibilities for the self, and the necessary reaction against such freedom, the architectonic construction of a self that can be defended against fluidity.

Yet, once again, Emerson and Nietzsche share a common aspect, or view. The Nietzsche who urges experiment, the discovery of new possibilities for the self through impulsive action, owes a debt to Emerson, as does the Nietzsche who steps back and sees how these possibilities fit together within the greater, impersonal action of the will to power. For Emerson as for Nietzsche, the impersonal view from outside reduces to insignificance the differences we cannot stop feeling from the inside: between fate and freedom, between the compulsive and the creative. My argument is that Emerson in his Gnosticism integrates, as Nietzsche cannot, inside and outside, the perspective of the experimental self — dispersed and Dionysian in its nature, given to theatrical or musical play—and the perspective of the architectonic or Apollonian self, which can see and settle its place within a cosmos ruled by necessity.

NIETZSCHEAN PLURALISM AND JUSTICE

> *Those who are evil or unhappy and the exceptional human being, all these should also have their good right, their philosophy, their sunshine. What these people need is not confession, conjuring of souls, and forgiveness of sins; what is needful is a new justice.* (GS #289)

In this passage from *The Gay Science,* which I will return to later in this introduction, Nietzsche calls for a "new justice" that would acknowledge the infinite variety of human individuals, each one a planetary entity swinging beyond the scope of our usual moral judgments. Nietzsche calls for an end to the morality that works by imposing our perspective, our own world's terms, on another person's radically different world.

Yet Nietzsche does not merely invoke a plurality of individual perspectives. He does not just ask us to recognize, as in the *Genealogy of Morals,* the alluring-yet-repulsive otherness of the blond beast or the Dostoyevskian criminal. He also argues for the separation and hierarchical positioning of perspectives. The new justice he demands is not merely a promiscuous recognition of difference. It means discernment, selection, a philosopher's dividing of health from sickness, the future-directed from the past-obsessed, the living from the dead.

A persistent question for Nietzsche's readers has been how to relate these two aspects: his impulse to explore and exploit otherness, to urge us to try on perspectives radically different from our own, and his drive to show that the other already inhabits us, asking to be judged or placed, as a proper part of the soul. The latter aspect is insistent in Nietzsche. Can one really become radically other to oneself? For Nietzsche, masculine and feminine, slave and master, decadent and ascendant life, secretly imply each other's place at the heart of human identity. Even as we give ourselves over to experiment and play, we do not simply surrender to the freedom of the mask. Instead, we depend on a defining structure, the antipodes that wait to be discovered, from inside, by the philosopher-psychologist. And this structure, when seen from outside by the philosopher-judge, can be understood as the work of the will to power.

One way of mapping the terrain of Nietzsche studies is to separate those commentators who describe a Nietzsche demanding new justice, a judgment that would overturn our customary moral valuations and engender an innovative and definitive way of seeing the world, from those who embrace a Nietzsche welcoming a plurality of worlds, each of them with its own health and happiness, its own moral sun. Broadly speaking, there are those who, like Heidegger, see Nietzsche as the purveyor of a new justice and therefore as the last metaphysician, announcing a Copernican revolution that wants to replace the old gods of reason, truth, or historical progress with the new one of will to power. Then there are those like Derrida who invoke an exfoliant and uncentered Nietzsche, the philosopher who not only welcomes difference, the variant perspectives that bring us to new worlds and new ways, but *lives through* difference, suffering these perspectives in his own person and writing. The two poles of Heidegger's and Derrida's Nietzsche suggest the division between Apollo and Dionysus, the sun-god who asserts judgment as the founding moment of a planned, built world, and the dark god of ecstasy who undergoes *sparagmos,* the tearing apart of all such structure.

Between these extremes, many interpretive paths beckon. In this book, I emphasize the polarity itself as it is enacted in Nietzsche's development: the division between an Apollonian or architectonic image of self and a Dionysian or musical one. (This dynamic, if we attend to it carefully, implies the limitation of either an exclusively Heideggerian or an exclusively Derridean reading of Nietzsche.) In the course of his writing career Nietzsche lives out the difference between Apollo and Dionysus, between a definitive and fortified self and one that gives itself over to the mask, to the role that occupies it at the moment. Nietzsche often describes this separation as that between the architect and the musician or actor, the self that builds and the self that plays.

Both the architectural and the theatrical mode, I argue, develop as responses to the fundamental Nietzschean problem of ascesis, the radical self-punishment that Nietzsche associates with the will to truth. The grounding involved in Nietzsche's architectural image, which as Heidegger writes "clears the way and decisively erects," implies a distinction between *Urtext* and interpretation, between nature and the ascetic project that works over this nature and transforms it—builds on it, so to speak.[7] But the theatrical metaphor involves no such discrimination of a primitive *Ur*-nature. For it, all the world's a stage—or a text, as it is for most of the French commentators in David Allison's influential anthology *The New Nietzsche* (1976). Although Jean Granier, for example, asserts that "Nietzsche himself can distinguish a text from its interpretations" and that Nietzsche's project of diagnosing his age relies on such a distinction, Granier goes on to write: "Since the interpreter and the act of interpretation are already the life of being, it is being that interprets itself within its own self-dissimulation . . . being *is* mask, it *is* phenomenon."[8] In an account like Granier's (or Derrida's), then, the inevitable outcome of the theatrical or masking metaphor is the dissolution of the Nietzschean ambition for a critical, centered self, an ambition stated most clearly in "On the Use and Disadvantage of History for Life": the striving for a sensibility grounded on a sense of historical location, as well as the fundamental law of its individual being. Granier, like Derrida, fails to emphasize that the surrender to play, to the endlessness of text, is dangerous for Nietzsche (as it is not for Emerson), and that he defends himself against the allure of the mask as often as he gives in to it.[9]

EMERSON AND NIETZSCHE VS. LIBERAL INDIVIDUALISM

I see Nietzschean individualism as a concept fractured by the division between play and ground, but all the more important because of this fracture: because it presents a more divided, and therefore more profound, sense of individualism than is present in contemporary liberal thought. Nietzsche's emphasis on the individual as contested or split derives from the thinking of Emerson, but Nietzsche sees the split as a wound in existence, which only asceticism confronts fully.

The more resilient Emerson does not suffer the Nietzschean strife between the architectonic and the musical/theatrical self, since he is not tempted by ascesis as Nietzsche is. A characteristically strong Emerson can write that, "when his mind is illuminated, when his heart is kind," a man "throws himself joyfully into the sublime order, and does, with knowledge, what the stones do by structure" (*E* 1076). This wholesome strength offers a reconciliation of impulse and poise, instinct and calculation, based on the Emersonian gospel of continuity between human work and the work of nature. According to Emerson in *The Conduct of Life*, "the art of the surgeon," like all our *tekhnai*, rests on such sympathy. "In replacing the broken bone," it "contents itself with releasing the parts from false position; they fly into place by the action of the muscles. On this art of nature all our arts rely" (*E* 1008). By contrast, Nietzsche in *The Birth of Tragedy* suspects that there is an original brokenness or *sparagmos* in existence (which the ascetic exposes, in later Nietzsche). In the *Birth*, this brokenness can be healed or corrected only by the antithetical discipline of art, not by a natural completion like the one Emerson envisions.

The difference between the two forms of selfhood that are conflated in the *Gay Science* passage I have cited (*GS* #289), the one that wants a new justice reigning over a new world and the one that wills surrender to a multitude of worlds, bears on our contemporary situation, as does virtually everything in Nietzsche. The current ideology of multiculturalism may sound like Nietzsche when it insists on a plurality of worlds to be discovered, each to be respected and admired by the sophisticated academic (or politician, high-school teacher, etc.). But Nietzsche, like Emerson, sees an otherness within the self that the multiculturalist remains blind to. As Slavoj Zizek has recently pointed out, "Multiculturalism is a racism which empties its own position of all positive content": the multiculturalist is "the privileged *empty point of universality* from which one is able to appreciate (and depreciate) other particular cultures properly."[10] Multiculturalist appreciation might more precisely be called a depreciation, since the "other" culture's otherness has been reduced to a commodity, rendered incapable of challenging the appreciator's own position. For the multiculturalist, consumption of a commodity, otherness, is the only possible activity. The otherness he procures for him- (or her-)self does not alter or shape his consciousness, but rather signals his own distance from culturally located identities.

Part of the problem with the current enthusiasm for multicultural studies is its definition of identity as culturally located situation. In terms of the current debate, such identity politics, as Charles Altieri notes, is difficult to coordinate with the "ideals of heterogeneity" that twentieth-century art forms have handed down to us. When Altieri describes the work of those poetic heirs of Emerson, Frank O'Hara, and Robert Creeley, for example, he conveys the pliability of a mode that is hard to combine with multiculturalist assertions that identity must be based on one's firm place in a community or culture.[11] In fact, as Emerson and Nietzsche teach us, the individual's place is always open, yet to be determined, and not to be limited by public definitions of the surrounding culture.

Nietzsche's idea of discovering new worlds differs from the multiculturalist's because he assumes that we become foreign to ourselves when we encounter the foreign: otherwise no true encounter can occur. The Western feminist who visits an Indian village to raise the consciousness of her oppressed sisters must prepare to have her own consciousness shaken. The oppressed may be divided just as the liberal crusader is, between (for example) an attachment to local customs and an attention to universal human rights, so that the strict multiculturalist division in which the other represents local custom, whereas "we" bear universality, is disturbed. Each new world we travel to has a local fascination for the traveler: its own law, its own health and happiness. For Nietzsche this means that these worlds tempt us, even as they may repel us, by the sheer brave fact of their existence. The cruelty of Renaissance Italy, the barbarous severity of the laws of Manu, the savagery of the blond beast: these cultural phenomena speak for themselves, and to see them at all we must enter into them, take imaginative part in them. In our strongest moods, Nietzsche suggests, we want such participation because we want to be shaken by an otherness that, if we fully or actually assumed it, would destroy us, and maybe others too. Nietzsche's architectonic image of self, in *The Gay Science* and elsewhere, aims to ward off such destruction, even as the dispersed self depicted in *Ecce Homo* and his last letters invites it.

The problem I have outlined with multiculturalism is also the problem with liberalism's idea of the individual. Nietzsche takes otherness seriously, in a way that liberal individualism generally does not, even though liberals often share the Nietzschean (and Emersonian) goal of becoming what one is, of owning the self. J. S. Mill expresses such an impulse to self-realization when he writes in "On Liberty" that "a person whose desires and impulses are his own—are the expression of his own nature, as it has been developed and modified by his own culture—is said to have a character. One whose desires and impulses are not his own, has no character, no more than a steam-engine has a character."[12] According to Mill, our desires should be modified and developed by culture, not driven by that culture in mechanical, steam-engine fashion. Mill does not want culture to animate us by force, to flow through us like steam or electricity; rather, he wants culture to lead us along into proper selfhood—to educate us (*educere,* to draw forth). Yet Mill's idea for the educating of the self by culture relies on the model of commodity exchange, in such a way that the commodities—interesting styles of selfhood—come to appear, like all commodities, expendable and even, from a certain perspective, useless. In the following passage, from a few pages earlier on in "On Liberty," Mill fails to illuminate our assumption of power, the attaining of achieved selfhood, because he overestimates its ease. He sees the self as a consumer of intellectual goods, a discerning blank (Zizek's "privileged empty point of universality"):

> That mankind are not infallible; that their truths, for the most part, are only half-truths; that unity of opinion, unless resulting from the fullest and freest comparison of opposite opinions, is not desirable, and diversity not an evil, but a good, until mankind are much more capable than at present of recognizing all sides of the truth, are principles applicable to all men's modes of action, not less than to their opinions. As it is useful that while mankind are imperfect there should be different opinions, so is it that there should be different experiments of living; that free scope should be given to varieties of character, short of injury to others; and that the worth of different modes of life should be proved practically, when any one thinks fit to try them. It is desirable, in short, that *in things which do not primarily concern others, individuality should assert itself.*[13]

Like Milton foreseeing the building of a temple of truth in his *Areopagitica,* but more tenderly and evasively, Mill starts from the hope for what we have not yet achieved: a situation of cognitive unanimity in which "all sides of the truth" will be recognized through "fullest and freest comparison of opposite opinions." The individualist's opposition to social norms, the expression of our current partiality and polemical inclinations, might eventually disappear, according to this model. Once become more perfect, we might piece together our partial views into a unified whole. Until that point, individualism is the very process of comparison among "different experiments of living," a process whose point is to make itself obsolete, since eventually truth—so we hope—will appear as union rather than contention. But in Mill's model contention (unlike Milton's war) has already, in effect, disappeared, since he posits the individual as a fully formed and assured connoisseur of difference. "The worth of different modes of life should be proved practically," Mill writes, "when any one thinks fit to try them." Here practical proof of worth means plausible exchange value in the eyes of normative society, a value that can only be estimated by a prospective buyer who is already an autonomous, fully established, neutral judge, rather than an individual in the process of formation. One "thinks fit to try" a mode of life, Mill implies, because one supposes it might prove useful or profitable.

Mill's is an utterly different notion from Nietzsche's and Emerson's of how and why we give style to our character. For Mill, profit can only be assessed in terms of the eventual prospect of broad social acceptance. In Mill extremes must be policed, rather than fostered as in Emerson and Nietzsche: difference is desirable "short of injury of others." But without injury difference becomes indifferent, a fact given away by Mill's final sentence: "It is desirable in short, that in things which do not primarily concern others, individuality should assert itself." This indifference may at first appear puzzling, since Mill's myth of concern esteems individuality only insofar as it contributes toward a normative wholeness, adding one more piece to the collective wisdom. The seeming contradiction in Mill's passage can only be explained if we understand that a consumerist model has covertly triumphed over the myth of common concern. The larger and more various the safe area of individual preference that does not concern others—an area whose creation is central to capitalism—the less these preferences mean, and the less value they have for our collective lives. The authority that would stand behind the individual's decisions and endow them with what Mill calls "character," and what Emerson calls "self-reliance," melts away when an antagonistic or socially contestatory inclination, an impulse to challenge the social order, is replaced by the consumer's desire for satisfaction.

In Mill's paragraph, then, what he calls "the worth of different modes of life" is subjected to consumerist appetite. This worth becomes "alternative" in the current marketing sense of the term, a "lifestyle" designation (for pop music, clothing, and so forth) that is designed to have the widest possible appeal to a college audience. Like Apple with its "Think Different" campaign featuring the Dalai Lama and other celebrities, the music and fashion industries target with the notion of the "alternative" the exact center of their traditional demographic, while flattering it for being outside the mainstream. Individualism within late capitalism invariably designates the most customary form of otherness with the broadest possibility of acceptance, the injunction to "let U B U" (Reebok). Obviously, wearing Reeboks rather than, say, Nikes is truly a thing indifferent, and therefore a choice in which, according to Mill, individuality should assert itself. But late capitalism seems to have exhausted individual choice of its significance, often in aggressive fashion. By endowing the choice of buying Apple rather than another computer with the symbolic weight of the Dalai Lama's resistance to Chinese domination (which is implicitly made analogous, in the ad, to the tyranny of Microsoft), Apple deprives a truly political event of its character by analogizing it to a consumer's decision.[14]

At this point it becomes necessary to ask a hard question: if the consumerist reduction of individual choice is in fact a reduction, if we can recover a more powerful version of individualism from writers like Emerson and Nietzsche, what will that power free us for? Not merely, one would hope, for an enlarged concept of personal satisfaction, so that, for example, those who prefer the experience of the Mac to that of a PC will be able to realize their preference. Rather, the result of a fully argued individualism expands the realm of the political, pointing toward an outcome that can only be measured in terms of social event rather than private satisfaction. (I discuss this question further in chapter 1.)

It is important to realize that Mill's assumptions in the passage I have quoted are also those of contemporary liberals. The consumerist character of individual choice as it appears in Mill may be rebuked, by liberals themselves, in order to assert a more firmly communal solidarity. But both these tendencies, the consumerist and the communal, dilute the actual risk and appeal of individual desire explored in writers like Nietzsche and Emerson—and Lacan.

John Rawls provides a good example of the oscillation between individual consumption and communal responsibility in liberalism. Though Rawls underlines the idiosyncratic character of each person's good, he also, in the interest of solidarity, optimistically emphasizes "the complementary nature of the good of individuals." But such complementarity in fact seems reluctant to appear, which makes Rawls's proposal on the subject appear utopian, even mildly Maoist: "There must be an agreed scheme of conduct in which the excellences and enjoyments of each are complementary to the good of all."[15] Richard Rorty, more pessimistically, celebrates the "private ironist" who makes his ideas safe by denying their relevance to the realm of public responsibility, mere fictions for solitary delectation. Yet, often, Rorty's examples of private irony turn out to have wholesome social relevance (so that Nabokov, for example, instructs us about the damages inflicted by cruelty).[16] Both Rawls and Rorty hesitate, as Mill does, between an insistence on the privacy of our preferences (their consumerist character) and an impulse to validate such preferences by suggesting that they contribute to social norms and to the education of the responsible individual.

This is no contradiction. The liberal thinker assumes that a wholesome society is a pacified one, in which the satisfied individual, by consuming ideas and experiences responsibly, provides an example for others. But the Nietzschean or Emersonian thinker argues that, in order to be responsible to the content of one's ideas, one must want to fight for them and against others, even to the extent of obliterating the line between private and public that liberalism cherishes.

Both Emerson and Nietzsche offer avenues to the combative individualism I describe. In a series of notes published posthumously in *The Will to Power* (*WP* #s 783–785), Nietzsche argues against the leveling pursuit of equal rights, associated with liberalism, in which the individual "instinctively posits himself as equal to all other individuals" (*WP* #784). Nietzsche argues for the recognition and retention of natural differences among humans, and—notoriously—even for an increased hierarchical consciousness of these differences. How can we, and why should we, follow Nietzsche in this direction, which insults our hard-won interest in human equality?

The liberal challenge to Nietzsche, as to Emerson, charges both with an unbecoming contempt for equality, and with a naturalizing of difference calculated to ensure privileges for the talented and to secure their quasi-aristocratic superiority. On this account, these two philosophers' supposed elitist disdain for liberalism's normative values implies a lack of care for impoverished or oppressed persons. This critique ought, I suggest, to look deeper into what kind of care might actually be needed, and wanted, by those we tend to treat with pitying, dehumanizing condescension. Emerson's and Nietzsche's resistance to charity has a useful counterintuitive impact, especially today. Alain Finkielkraut remarks that liberal solicitude, with its inclination toward pitying helpless victims, has today replaced ideology (which similarly substituted the masses for the individual) as the most common path of escape from what Arendt called "men in their infinite diversity":

With ideology it was the progress of man that put an end to human beings in the plural; with solicitude, it is the species man and the anonymous tribulations of his representatives. In the age of ideology, we believed we knew everything; in the age of doing good, we want to know nothing. . . . There is just as much political conspiracy at work when we compare conflicts between men to natural cataclysms as there is when we liken the hope for universal freedom to a total march forward.[17]

Emerson and Nietzsche make a strong case against this aspect of liberal values, against the solicitude for the faceless, unfortunate ones that Finkielkraut criticizes. Liberalism wills a vision of the human condition as commonness in order to argue for certain rights shared by all humans: nourishment, housing, freedom from violence. But the importance of these rights does not help us to define what matters about individuals, who need to rely on them in order to survive but who cannot be made identical to, reduced to, this need. Emerson and Nietzsche interrogate the motives of the liberal benefactor, asking why he wants to assert the equivalence of persons rather than their distinction. Liberalism must always be more interested in the anonymous ones, the neighbors or strangers who share a basic humanness with us, than in the privileged person who matters immensely, the friend or beloved. The fact that this person's specialness cannot be translated into the terms provided by relatively crude social criteria like superior talent, goodness, or intelligence shows not that our preferences are unjustifiable, but only that they cannot be justified by using society's heavy normative scales of respectability or usefulness. Emerson and Nietzsche challenge liberalism by calling our true interest in other persons, whether neighbor, friend or stranger, a form of privilege: a decision to give them our attention, to make them creatures to be recognized and judged. In doing so, Emerson and Nietzsche defend a way of responding to the other that, they argue, offers her more respect than the liberal's automatic declaration of rights to food, shelter, and freedom from oppression, a declaration that remains indifferent to the actual identity of its addressee.

The contrast between a weak liberal sense of the individual and the strong individualism shared by Emerson and Nietzsche animates this entire book. I am not suggesting that liberalism's concern with the individual as an abstraction, a simple bearer of rights, ought to or can be abandoned. Social justice often must rely on a shorthand that remains indifferent to the personal qualities of individuals. The liberal definition of citizenship raises such indifference to a near-absolute form, and for good reason: as a strong abstraction raised against the rival claims of ethnicity and gender, against the rites of all particular cultures. But in our era liberalism, by inflecting the common and human with the pathos of victimhood, has largely given up such salutary aloofness. The popularity of multiculturalism is another example of the loss of liberal aloofness.

In *Toward the Genealogy of Morals* Nietzsche hopes for a society that could apportion benefits and punishments while refraining from moral judgment, from solicitude as well as vengeance. Such a society would go the abstract liberal idea of citizenship one better by admitting that it cannot possibly know or possess the souls of its citizens. The troubling aspect of contemporary liberal thought is precisely that it does not refrain from such possessive moralizing. As Finkielkraut charges, the contemporary liberal seems determined to see the cases he attends to as pitiable, worthy of his superior concern. Such a defense of the dignity of the wretched remains deliberately blind to their real identity, and therefore actually robs them of dignity.

The alternative to pitying concern, the Pontius Pilate–like detachment Nietzsche advocates, may seem more than a touch too cold and incurious. It is important to remember, though, that Nietzsche inclines toward such detachment, not because he is indifferent to others, but because he needs an antidote to their too-strong presence within him. Nietzsche allows himself both to imagine other people with dangerously wholehearted interest and to aspire to the disinterest that separates and judges, and builds fairness.

In sum, the argument between liberalism and its polemical opponents remains both healthy and necessary. In an effort to show the full dimensions of the argument, I have chosen the two strongest antagonists to liberal pieties that I know, Emerson and Nietzsche.

EMERSON, NIETZSCHE, AND TRADITION

Nietzsche learned the risk and promise of transformation from Emerson, not from Schopenhauer, who is usually named as Nietzsche's major influence. Emerson and Schopenhauer are, in fact, Nietzsche's two crucial philosophical fathers, though students of Nietzsche have usually granted Schopenhauer priority. My study aims to redress this imbalance. Emerson's championing of creativity and the poetic, I suggest, allows Nietzsche to affirm life against Schopenhauer's pessimism.

Despite the obvious connection between Emerson and Nietzsche, there have been few studies of their relationship.[18] Over a series of years and a sequence of remarkable writings, Stanley Cavell and Harold Bloom have offered the most intriguing suggestions of a kinship between the two thinkers. Yet, though Bloom and Cavell are irreplaceable in a study like this one, and though I frequently rely on both these great critics, neither concerns himself with defining the pressing differences between Nietzsche and Emerson.

My goal is to understand how Nietzsche enlists Emerson in his development, yet also diverges from him. The difference is rooted in Emerson's ideal of human expressivity, in its contrast to Nietzsche's ideal of self-criticism. Nietzschean self-criticism, in works like *Untimely Meditations* and *The Gay Science*, adjoins his experience of asceticism, while yet refusing the ascetic's refined brutality and espousing, in place of ascetic over-intimacy, a distance and tact toward the suffering individual—especially when the individual in question is oneself.

For Emerson, expressivity is inherently critical. Our imaginations do not need to be reminded to stay properly suspicious, because we know all too well that worldly consequences will always spring an ironic trap on our imaginative overreaching. Nietzsche, by contrast, exposes a gap between imaginative enthusiasm and the energies of demystification. This difference stems from Nietzsche's consciousness of the vast pressure of history, a pressure that prompts our skeptical consciousness of how history continues to work through us, in contrast to Emerson's sense of the unpredictability, the potential newness, of both the situations we find ourselves in and the strategies we use to beat these situations. Emerson is no naive optimist; his skeptical side shows us that he senses the difficulties of practical, present-tense action. But only Nietzsche, with his focus on how the past grips the changed present, demonstrates a profound awareness of how this past can make us betray ourselves.

The divergence between Emerson and Nietzsche carries over into their heirs. In the American pragmatist line that derives from Emerson, Kenneth Burke is the great champion of revising and transforming situations. In Burke, as in Emerson, what obstructs transformation is an insistent conformist rigidity, the idolatry of common wisdom that blocks the recognition that cultural and personal crises should be occasions for improvisational renewal. In both Emerson and his descendant Burke, there is little sense of the characteristic Nietzschean melancholy, the inescapable pain of a history that lives on within the self, not as mere unthinking custom but as the self's deepest and hardest identity—a sense that we find often in Freud and Mann, two of Nietzsche's truest inheritors. Reading Nietzsche, we confront ourselves at the midnight hour, the "loneliest loneliness" (*GS*#341): a time when decisions are epochal and irrevocable, and when we bitterly fight the hold of the past.

This serious difference between Emerson and Nietzsche on the question of the past hints at the possibility of a debate between two rival ways of developing the individual's powers. Nietzsche helps us understand the element of necessity in what Bloom calls strong misreading, the way we (often unconsciously) distort the past to suit our own ends.[19] Emerson cannot account for this necessity as Nietzsche can. He lacks Nietzsche's interest in how repression works, in how we are mastered, despite ourselves, by influence. Yet there is a genuine hopefulness in Emerson that makes us rethink what we meant by necessity in the first place. Often, Emerson argues, our resignation to Ananke is a defensive inventing of only *supposedly* necessary limitation, a self-crippling that can be healed. Emerson's healing promise requires an embrace of necessity as rightness, a true part of us and our striving. Nietzsche similarly hopes for an *amor fati*, the capacity to see what is necessary as desirable. But Nietzsche recognizes much more clearly than Emerson the ascetic's desire to be elsewhere, which culminates in the nihilistic impression that the necessity of being here and now is an unbearable wound. *Amor fati*, a cherished possibility for both thinkers, is more accessible to Emerson than to Nietzsche.

Yet Nietzsche also remains akin to Emerson, gaining from him the advantage of the comic thinker.[20] As I have said, reading Emerson enabled Nietzsche to temper the influence of his other major precursor, Schopenhauer. Nietzsche overcame Schopenhauerian pessimism by diverging from Schopenhauer's sense of the ephemerality and real-world uselessness of the artistic perfection he treasured. On the effectiveness of art, Nietzsche follows Emerson rather than Schopenhauer; he affirms life by claiming the actual, realistic force of artistic imagination. Imagination, for both Emerson and Nietzsche, is visible in the form of a clever bias woven into the fabric of the world, and preceding the work of any individual author. Seen rightly, the world is made of metaphor; and its figurative character gives the human individual a chance of freedom unimaginable in Schopenhauer's brutally solid, literal-minded reality.

PLAY, ASCETICISM, CRITIQUE

Nietzsche's Emersonian gestures begin very early on. In his youthful essay, *Philosophy in the Tragic Age of the Greeks* (written between 1873 and 1876), Nietzsche explores, only to reject, the image of Heraclitus as a Schopenhauerian sage, the weeping philosopher for whom all existence is a vain effort to expiate guilt. "Is not the entire world process now an act of punishment for *hubris?* The many the result of evil doing?" Nietzsche's answer to these questions is a decisive *no:* in Heraclitus "not *hubris* but the ever self-renewing impulse to play calls new worlds into being" (*PTAG* 60–62). For Heraclitus, as for Nietzsche, the world is a child at play, capricious yet lawful, and thoroughly innocent in its artistry. Tragic hubris marks the individual who vengefully resists the direction of existence. In response, existence, an everlasting game, renders hubristic self-assertion insignificant, rather than avenging hubris or punishing it as a sin. Each move, memorable as it may be, will be forgotten as the game rearranges itself and continues, erasing the past moment by moment. Later, when he developed a more compromised and complicated sense of historical action, Nietzsche abandoned as overly optimistic any such definitive picture of the overcoming of vengefulness; but his attraction to the Heraclitean game persisted.

It is Emerson who inflects Nietzsche's Heraclitean image of play in *Philosophy in the Tragic Age of the Greeks.* Emerson draws from Heraclitus an emphasis on the creative, metamorphic aspect of the world, imaged as a vast game that both surpasses and guides the individual intentions of its players. But both Emerson and Nietzsche move beyond Heraclitus by introducing the human agent into the image of the game, as if agency could only truly be upheld in the context that most seems to defeat it, the cosmic roll of the dice and ever-shifting contest that no contestant can rule. "For though gamesters say, that the cards beat all the players," Emerson writes in "Nominalist and Realist," "though they were never so skilful, yet in the contest we are now considering, the players are also the game, and share the power of the cards" (*E* 583). You're not the player you think you are; instead, you're just a piece of

the game. But if you can get over the affront to your poor pride entailed by this revelation, you might find you have more power than before. Emerson finally makes this irony prove useful, which is to say that
he turns our knowledge that the universe accomplishes its aims *despite*
our paltry wills into our strong sense that the universe's aims are accomplished *through* us.[21]

Nietzsche stands with Emerson against Schopenhauer's insistence on the futility of human action. Both Emerson and Nietzsche
describe the game's meaning as the way it shows itself in the thoughtful, surprisingly resilient stances of its actors, in comic moments
rather than in monumental postures of tragic beauty, victory, and defeat. Yet the relentless Nietzschean drive toward truth does often take
on a tragic form, based in the self-punishing character of the quest.
For Schopenhauer, critical analysis plays a tragic role in a very different way: it proves, or produces, a tautology, capable of discovering
only its own beautiful protest against the universal reign of the will.

Nietzsche's turn away from Schopenhauer and toward Emerson
is, to be sure, not the whole story. As I have already noted, Nietzsche introduces a historical dimension into his thought that Emerson refuses.
Emerson wants to establish what he calls in *Nature* "an original relation
to the universe," a living present freed from the frozen, secondhand
ideas that surround us every day in society (*E* 7). The basic Emersonian
aim is conversion experience, liberation from the prison of conformity. But, because he remains more interested in momentary inspiration and the choice fragment of experience than in a deliberate
organization of one's life as truly personal and owned history, Emerson cannot measure the influence of the past, the conformity that has
lived within and through us, on our present lives.

Nietzsche, by contrast, develops a model of ascetic perfectionism
based on the individual's will to manage and transform his existence,
an effort that means recognizing the real force of the historical nature
that one already is, as well as the will to break through that nature into
newness. Nietzsche, in other words, recognizes the internal force of the
history that oppresses us, instead of suggesting, with Emerson, that historical constraints might melt away, overturned by the light of an original spirit. With his insistence on the need to violate conformity, an
insistence that sees conformity's true strength in the toll the revolutionary project takes on the individual, Nietzsche generates a forceful
criticism of social and historical practices. In formulating his model of

the critical stance, Nietzsche illuminates the cost of ascetic ideals—a cost that Emerson already suspected in shying away from them—as well as their promise. In Nietzsche, ascetic discipline must itself be disciplined. Nietzsche's architectonic ideal offers a way of achieving a solidity or balance, of preventing asceticism from tearing the self to pieces. His musical/theatrical ideal, by contrast, surrenders to such dispersion and triumphs by doing away with the ascetic's discipline of resistance.

Nietzsche gets from Emerson a powerful notion of the liberating possibilities of language and action. Yet his perspective, though leavened with its special forms of irony and comic surprise, continues to be shadowed by tragedy. The Nietzschean ascetic of *Toward the Genealogy of Morals* is a tragic hero. His intense pursuit of a critical stance, what Nietzsche calls the ascetic's "will to truth," dooms him to an exemplary, and sublimely impressive, overreaching. "This penchant and passion for what is true, real, non-apparent [Un-Scheinbaren], certain," as Nietzsche puts it in *The Gay Science,* will not let him rest (*GS* #309).

Nietzsche's dilemma, his simultaneous attraction to passionate certainty and to cold, demystifying doubt, speaks to a contemporary crisis. A pervasive academic "hermeneutics of suspicion" (to use Paul Ricoeur's phrase) suggests the dominion of the demystifiers, but also a disquiet with this dominion, a wish for "what is true, real, non-apparent, certain." Arnoldian and liberal claims for the power of critical awareness to rebuild what has been demystified, to correct our moral consciousness and our sense of cultural value, may no longer be plausible. Critical thought is now known to be not just an exposer of ideologies but also an agent of corrosive skepticism, a dangerous force that just might disillusion us about *all* ideals.

Academics often seem to take a grim satisfaction in just this disillusionment, the cynic's joy that (as Gianni Vattimo writes) "fac[es] up to the fact of the world as a totally administered system."[22] It is no surprise that Foucault is still the most influential figure for young and ambitious professors of humanities. Yet the contemporary academy remains attached to an ideal of human perfection and seems to be (somewhat covertly, to be sure) dissatisfied with its own habit of proving the power of disillusion, the constant triumphs of ideology and mere rhetorical force. Current academic perfectionism, of the sort perhaps best represented by Martha Nussbaum, recommends a discipline of virtue that is at once moral and political, a critical individualism that can indulge in self-invention and yet also remain reflective and responsible about social values. I sympathize with these goals, but I ask for a more searching and hard-edged understanding of the perfectionist impulse, with its peculiar attachment to what Freud calls "moral masochism." The severity of Nietzsche's asceticism makes his perfectionism, in contrast to Nussbaum's, a form of self-punishment rather than self-reward. The bitter, inquisitive eye Nietzsche turns on notions of social equality and fairness, I argue, is closely linked to his sense of the pervasiveness of moral masochism. Pervasive but not inescapable: the tragic view exemplified in Nietzsche's *Genealogy* (written after *The Gay Science,* but planned and meditated long before) must be answered by the comic mood of *The Gay Science,* which allows us to evade moral self-punishment through an architectonic building of selfhood. These two texts represent for me two halves of an argument essential to, but mostly overlooked in, contemporary debates about perfectionism and the self.

THE ARCHITECTONIC VS. THE MUSICAL SELF IN NIETZSCHE

Nietzsche, in the astonishing series of books he produced in the 1880s, engages the risk of moral masochism as contemporary criticism does not. In doing so, he shows current notions of perfectionism to be overly optimistic. Nietzsche finds himself at once allured and repelled by the tragic pathos of self-punishment. He survives as an exemplary thinker because he continues to strive for a path beyond the passion of self-ruin, a way to the fully mature comedy of his gay science: the perfect flowering of self-making, poised between shrewd self-suspicion and indulgent fantasizing. Specifically, Nietzsche's use of an architectonic model of the self in *The Gay Science* allows him to propose a way of individual self-trust that is conscious of its precarious, constructed character, yet strives to locate itself firmly on this earth.

There is a connection between the careful balancing act of Nietzsche's *Gay Science* and Emerson's notion of refinement in his late *Conduct of Life.* Yet Nietzsche, unlike Emerson, remains dissatisfied with the ideal of a sure, sophisticated self, however agile its grounding. As Vattimo has emphasized, Nietzsche wills, as well, the present-tense life of a musical, Dionysian existence, an utter identification of being, knowing, and doing. The reign of the Dionysian mask is instantly, instinctively effectual; its force lies in the mobility and subtlety of a playing that has transcended theater's fakery. The mask's music must finally prove more alluring to Nietzsche than the architectonic self, because it incarnates the self as difference, as Dionysus, instead of (as in the architectural model) esteeming the self for its will to discipline or master difference. In this respect *Ecce Homo* provides the inevitable explosion at the end of Nietzsche's development, the rule of the mask that overcomes any possibility of control.

Fragment 842 of Nietzsche's *Will to Power* (spring 1888) directly juxtaposes these two options, the architectonic and the musical. Nietzsche here identifies the grand style with an apotropaic architecture, a warding off of others:

> It repels; such men of force [i.e., those who display the grand style] are no longer loved—a desert spreads around them, a silence, a fear as in the presence of some great sacrilege—All the arts know such aspirants to the grand style: why are they lacking in music? No musician has yet built as that architect did who created the Palazzo Pitti—Here lies a problem. Does music perhaps belong to that culture in which the domain of men of force of all kinds has ceased? Does the concept grand style ultimately stand in contradiction to the soul of music—to the 'woman' in our music?[23]

The grand style of the conqueror is before all else defensive in Nietzsche, a repelling of the other (i.e., of the woman). But, in more relaxed versions of this ideal—in *The Gay Science's* portrait of the Genoese, for example (*GS*#291)—the grand style builds a home and a horizon for itself by striking a balance between a questing and an embattled posture. In *The Gay Science's* Genoa, what surrounds the architectonic self is not "a desert . . . a silence, a fear," as in the 1888 fragment, but a rich and tempting vista, a foreign land to be discovered (see chapter 4). Such grandeur, whether it takes on a poised and fragile character, as in *The Gay Science,* or a sublime extremism, as in the Second Essay of the *Genealogy,* with its proud establishing of conscience, is always, to Nietzsche, fundamentally masculine. It stands in contrast to the feminine soul of music, which requires a surrender, a dissolution of self-defense, in order to captivate. For Nietzsche, the feminine represents the impossible assurance that needs no grand fortress and no blunt force in order to conquer. "Woman" triumphs in her fluid, apparitional nature, which destroys the difference between yielding and holding back, between a solidly realized self and an elusive, playfully dishonest one.

Another passage from the *Nachlass* (*WP* #800) makes it clear that the grand style is for Nietzsche a form of masculine architecture. But in this note, from March-June 1888, unlike the one I quoted earlier, Nietzsche tries to reconcile a (feminine) musical intoxication, dispersed and Dionysian, with the erect, consolidated strength of the grand style:

> The feeling of intoxication, in fact corresponding to an increase in strength; strongest in the mating season: new organs, new accomplishments, colors, forms; "becoming more beautiful" is a consequence of *enhanced* strength [die "Verschönung" ist eine Folge der *erhöhten* Kraft]. Becoming more beautiful as the expression of a victorious will, of increased co-ordination, of a harmonizing of all the strong desires, of an infallibly perpendicular stress [eines unfehlbar perpendikulären Schwergewichts]. Logical and geometrical simplification is a consequence of enhancement of strength: conversely the apprehension of such a simplification again enhances the feeling of strength—High point of the development: the grand style.

Here the function of display, of exuberant and multicolored excitement, becomes an expression of "an infallibly perpendicular stress." In this passage, Nietzsche unites the desire for the mask (Dionysian play) with a high architectural economy (Apollonian structure).

Usually, though, there is a split between these two modes in Nietzsche. *Ecce Homo,* at the end of Nietzsche's career, portrays the transition from a severe architectonic isolation, a self who has built a refuge among ice and high mountains, to a musical self who, like both Dionysus and the Crucified, renders himself up to his admirers, who are also, in this all-too-real ritual theater, his tormenters. Nietzsche cannot recover from such perilous defenselessness. Here the feminine, again, woman in her difference from Nietzsche, threatens him. For Nietzsche the mystery of woman is that she can defend herself while surrendering herself; but Nietzsche himself cannot know this mystery, and therefore cannot make such a double movement. Nietzsche's striving after an architecturally unified, forbidding, and guarded self, then, finds itself overturned by a musical conception of the feminine entity that lives out difference, or plays with it, instead of mastering it.

The Nietzschean motif of a sublime, sacrificial self must, finally, be balanced against Emerson's skepticism. Emerson doubts the wish for the grandeur of transcendence as he doubts all great names and causes. In rough ease, he stands aloof from the committed, trying pursuit of an ideal, the quest that is basic to Nietzsche's demand for a higher, purer, more sacred possibility for our lives. Even in his many praises of focused, concentrated will, Emerson stops short of encouraging complete belief in one's central project. According to Emerson, we must see our aim for the nothing it is. By testing the notion of commitment that the world demands of us, Emerson illuminates a realm of thought and action more basic than, and prior to, Nietzsche's self-critical asceticism. The very ironies that compensation, the iron law, deploys against us also favor us in ways we could not have anticipated. And the only way to draw on this favor is to practice an Emersonian receptivity fundamentally alien to Nietzsche's architectonic style, which demands a censoring of outside voices, a living to oneself, that Emerson could never endorse. To be sure, Emerson prizes nomadic and stringently retired ways of existence, a life of "abandonment" and lonely self-support. But these disciplined strayings from the path of society are, for Emerson, ways of keeping the self open to the vagrant possibilities of the alien meanings that might meet us. For Nietzsche, by contrast, all meanings present artful, pointed foils to what we thought we knew, so that the truly alien never appears, never *can* appear, as it does in Emerson.[24]

The pragmatist insight Emerson sponsors in American thought attains an undeniable strength by dissolving a false sublimity, by insisting that what we actually do, and how we do it, precedes the glorified and heroic images of action to which we devote ourselves. But Nietzsche, unlike Emerson, can help us more truly estimate the pain, and the usefulness, of our heroic commitments.

Emerson and Nietzsche remain two rival options for contemporary thought, options whose respective appeal hinges largely on whether we embrace, at the basis of our efforts at self-making, Nietzsche's emphasis on the split between a guarded, architecturally founded self and an ecstatic, playful one, or Emerson's Gnostic unity, which champions a self that is at once assured and open, called into original being, as if inevitably, by situation. Nietzsche in his most Emersonian book, *The Gay*

Science, suggests more than once that comedy enfolds tragedy, just as the figure of woman surrounds the masculine quest of the philosopher; that the freedom of masks is a more pervasive or infectious truth than the building of self. But this victory of the mask proves to be a catastrophe in Nietzsche's own life and career, in which the drive to enactment finally wins out over cold judgment, even as Nietzsche fantasizes about uniting the two and making judgment instinctive. The unmoved judge, secure in his pathos of distance, remains an idealized figure for Nietzsche, a wished-for role that he cannot play. It is not for nothing that he named Pontius Pilate his favorite character in the Gospels, though he was most attracted to Jesus, that divine, Dostoyevskian idiot.

NIETZSCHE'S NEW JUSTICE

"Those who are evil or unhappy and the exceptional human being," Nietzsche writes in *The Gay Science,* "all these should also have their good right, their philosophy, their sunshine":

> What these people need is not confession, conjuring of souls, and forgiveness of sins; what is needful is a new justice! And a new watchword. And new philosophers. The moral earth, too, is round. The moral earth, too, has its antipodes. The antipodes, too, have the right to exist. There is yet another world to be discovered—and more than one. Embark, philosophers! (*GS* #289)

Characteristically, Nietzsche here places himself as the opponent of Christendom's practices of "confession, conjuring of souls, and forgiveness of sins"—the Christian attack on the individual which, he argues, is shared by liberal and socialist reformers. Instead of a redemption of humanity that would absolve it of its differences and convert it to a universal realm of freedom or goodness, Nietzsche calls for an exploration and acceptance of individuals as worlds unto themselves, however repugnant or miserable some of these worlds may seem to us. At first glance, then, Nietzsche seems at this moment in *The Gay Science* to forecast the generous pluralism of the contemporary academy, with its devotion to the self-constituting validity of local practices and (to invoke a contemporary shibboleth) cultures. (For Nietzsche in this passage, individuals in all their peculiarity would make up the defining units of culture.) Yet *The Gay Science* passage, by combining an image of voyage and discovery with the need for judgment, for a "new justice," passes beyond such pluralism. The moral earth's roundness means that it is not limited as we thought it was. We won't fall off the edge if we go too far, as we were afraid might happen. The earth will support us because its very radical differences prove to be integrated in an unexpected but entirely consistent way. It is in his quest for such consistency that Nietzsche's Zarathustra asks for a loyalty to the earth. As Leo Strauss points out, he wants to descend from his isolation, from his independence, unlike the Socrates of the *Republic*.[25] And this descent means his desire for a recovery of a truth to nature that will transcend the poetic uses of the mask, the mere force exploited by creative revision and experiment (which is visible in the contemporary academy's weak pluralism).

The new justice asks, among other things, for an acceptance of the subtleties of our acting as somehow implied in our deepest nature, an acceptance that may require unprecedented tact. Don't act like a saint, especially if you are one, says Nietzsche (as Strauss put it in his lectures on *Zarathustra*): an injunction that not only pushes urbanity to a new extreme, but asserts a divine reluctance that should and could become natural, and that looks mannered only to our currently weak eyesight.

Nietzsche's ambition to temper the destructiveness of the ascetic will to truth, the extreme rigor of the saint (whether religious or *wissenschaftlich*), makes him turn to the poet. Nietzsche wants to raise poetry beyond mere evasion of the ascetic's cold, hard truth, to show how it is, instead, a necessary mediation of that truth. Being poetic, in Nietzsche as in Emerson, means representing, giving words, to what both demands and resists representation.

It may seem, though, that the aim of the poetic is to soften this resistance, to manage desire by invoking its objects in safely mediated form, as representation rather than actuality. In *The Birth of Tragedy*, Nietzsche runs the risk of praising poetry for its therapeutic power, for being a compliant source of consolation. Freud's designation of us as creatures of wish, along with his descriptions of how our wishing may fail by remaining merely consolatory, helps to illuminate Nietzsche's early reliance on the power of the poetic to fulfill or complete our desires—and his later critical reflection on this fulfillment. In Freud, as in Emerson and Nietzsche, the human impulse to wish-fulfillment combines in odd ways with the urge to experiment, to newness, to remaining unsettled and stubbornly unsatisfied. In his book *Terrors and Experts*, the psychoanalyst Adam Phillips writes,

> In so far as psychoanalysis merely traffics in new proprieties, in fresh forms of respectability, it betrays something of its radical legacy as a conversation in which people cannot help but experiment with themselves. When psychoanalysis loses its unusual capacity to both comfort and unsettle — and its modern sense that you can't have one without the other — it becomes either a form of compulsory radicalism or a new way to learn an old obedience. It was, after all, to the subtleties of compliance that Freud addressed himself. If psychoanalysis is not the means to a personal style, it merely hypnotizes people with a vocabulary.[26]

Like Freud, Emerson and Nietzsche address themselves to the "subtleties of compliance," to the conformity that generates "fresh forms of respectability." The latter phrase is an adequate summary of much current ethical theory, which is, however, at times neither fresh nor subtle. Emerson and Nietzsche have something in common with psychoanalysis at its best, as Phillips describes it: they try to shake us free from the hypnotic vocabularies of propriety and responsibility that animate our thoughts on the self and its place in the world. But the vocabulary of self-making, of achieving "a personal style," as Phillips puts it, may also turn out to be a conformism, implying the narcissistic self-regard that sells better than anything else these days. Seeing the self as a work of art, as Rorty and Alexander Nehamas do, risks turning personal identity into a kind of consumer good.[27] The actual career of individualism in Emerson and Nietzsche is altogether more dangerous, and more interesting.

NIETZSCHE WITH (AND EMERSON WITHOUT) LACAN

Charles Altieri comes close to the true sense of Emersonian individualism when he writes of two Americans, Frank O'Hara and Robert Creeley, whose poetry "becomes actual habitation. . . . And its test of value becomes the mobility and intensity immediately made available to the poet, without relying on any of the abstract versions of those values or even on any of the formulated social ideals that establish the markets in which cultural capital is traded."[28] "Every touch should thrill," as Emerson writes in "The Poet" (*E* 448). In Altieri's eloquent anticonsumerist vision the poet, experimenter *par excellence,* becomes the apostle of a Gnostic light embodied in literary style and easily recovered against the fallen world of the commodity, a self-communion offered, with a touching immediacy, at once to reader and author.

For Nietzsche, no such communion is possible. *Ecce Homo* shows the final trajectory of *Maskenfreiheit* as a captivation by the mask or persona, and an imprisonment by the demands of cultural capital, of public, declared performance: demands that Emerson, like Altieri's Creeley and O'Hara, is able to evade. Nietzsche's self-alienation as he works through his images of personal identity in *Ecce Homo* proves the Burckhardtian "self as a work of art" to be a cold pastoral indeed.

Nietzsche's bondage is, I suggest in later chapters, tied to the dominion of the Lacanian object *a,* the secret ingredient in personal identity that makes all the difference, and must remain hidden. When publicly exposed the object *a* spoils one's identity altogether, revealing itself as a nothing, inexplicable and trivial. Yet Nietzsche remains compelled toward such exposure. Emerson's apparent freedom from Nietzsche's attraction to shameful or triumphant publicity, like his easy overcoming of the Nietzschean strife between foundation and play, bears witness to the superior performative strength of Emersonian practice. Yet that very strength may lead Emerson to underestimate the difficulty of being located in one's life, and in the life that surrounds one: a difficulty that Nietzsche attends to profoundly in his effort to formulate a critical project for the self (see my discussion of *Untimely Meditations* in chapter 3).

THE PLAN OF THIS BOOK

In the first chapter I offer a reading of Emerson's "Experience," with frequent reference to other Emerson essays, that ends in an invocation of Nietzsche's *Zarathustra.* I explore the ways in which Emerson makes his texts available to radically distinct inclinations, encouraging a breadth of interpretive choice that puts into action the Emersonian model of liberation. There is a critical tradition of charging Emerson with the visionary's self-involvement, with an imaginative narcissism that refuses social commitments. Indeed, Emersonian vision, at its ecstatic, impatient height, is avowedly solipsistic, the gospel of a divine child who devours all he sees. But by recognizing how the social world both resists and thrives on the individual's prophetic sight, Emerson urges his solipsistic sublime into conversation with the common-sense realism that mocks and deflates it.

Individualist interpretation takes on a radical form in Emerson, one that circumvents the tragic persistence of the past in favor of our present desires to reimagine the world. Nietzsche, by contrast, embraces tragedy. Chapters 2 and 3 examine Nietzsche's development in the 1870s of an individualist sense of history based on a tragic mode. In his early *Birth of Tragedy*, the subject of chapter 2, Nietzsche figures tragedy as a phenomenon of cosmic scale, the weaving and unweaving of life and death, generation and decay. By the time of *Untimely Meditations*, however, just three years later, Nietzsche reinterprets tragedy as an individualist genre centered on the effort to carry on in writing, but also to contest, the memory of particular persons and events. With this movement to the level of the individual, the tragic sense becomes a source of critical power. Nietzsche's thought that poetry's proper role is the defense of the particular shape of history, its memorable events and actors, has its roots in Plato's *Symposium*, as well as in Emerson. Chapter 3 concludes with a study of Nietzsche's early versions of the architectonic self: the image of the builder of thought as cosmic judge in Nietzsche's final *Untimely Meditation*, "Richard Wagner in Bayreuth," and in another work of the mid-1870s, *Philosophy in the Tragic Age of the Greeks*.

In chapter 4 I investigate two central Nietzschean works of the 1880s, *Daybreak* and *The Gay Science*, in terms of their use of theatricality, particularly in relation to themes of love and sexual relationship, and with reference to Emerson's reliance on the theatrical. *The Gay Science* avoids the disastrous consequences of the *Genealogy*'s masochistic asceticism by espousing a carefully composed self that thrives on acting out, as if on stage, its distance from moral ideals. But this distancing, and the theatrical model it entails, means that the self becomes disturbingly isolated from the world Nietzsche set out to explore—even to conquer—with the critical ideal he invoked in his "Use and Disadvantage of History for Life." (Nietzsche's self-alienation will culminate in *Ecce Homo*, in which theatrical distance becomes Dionysian uncontrol, in place of *The Gay Science*'s Apollonian composure.)

In *Daybreak*, Nietzsche meditates on the weakness of monumental history, already explored in "The Use and Disadvantage of History for Life." Monumental history founds a heroic grandeur that will inevitably devolve into blurry conformity, the vague fetishizing of greatness.

But the antidote offered in "History for Life" to the weakness of the monumental, the critical history that measures the present self against the influence of the past, is largely abandoned in *Daybreak* and its successor, *The Gay Science*. In these works, Nietzsche relies, in place of the critical, on a version of Emersonian refinement, though Nietzsche will confront a frustration foreign to Emerson: the encounter with the object *a*, a secretive core of identity that refinement both courts and stumbles over.

Chapter 5, after an excursus on Emerson's "Fate," studies *Toward the Genealogy of Morals*, focusing on how it concludes in a severe, self-frustrating irony. The attempt to liberate human possibility through a strenuous antagonism to priestly morality results in a new (but just as costly) morality, that of the ascetic philosopher Nietzsche. Chapter 5 goes on to encounter the destiny of the Nietzschean self that answers ascetic self-punishment with an outrageous playing out of roles, the musical, exploding self of *Ecce Homo* that presages Nietzsche's final madness.

EMERSON AND NIETZSCHE TODAY

Nietzsche resembles Emerson in that both have become, in today's academic climate, texts subject to judgment: are they acceptable or dangerous? (Lacan offers a more primitive version of such a shibboleth, dividing academics between those who see him as a demented charlatan with mystagogic habits and those who detect hints of highest truth in the slightest gesture of the master.) Is it risky even to think about Nietzsche? Are fervent readers of Nietzsche like myself guilty by association (of elitism, misogyny, proto-fascist worship of "honor" and heroism), and are we to respond to this imputation of guilt by describing a warm-hearted, quasi-liberal Nietzsche? On occasion I have encountered students who defend themselves against the reading of Nietzsche and Emerson by worrying that these texts might be "dangerous," all the while going to great lengths to make these writers say what they expressly do not say, so they then can be revealed as selfish idolaters of power. (A common impulse is to turn both Nietzsche and Emerson into members of the Carlylean hero-cult both despised; see *Daybreak* #298, and Emerson's "Self-Reliance" for their arguments against the worship of heroes.)

Such caricatures are not dangerous, of course, but rather the reverse: they enable the student to enjoy his politically correct symptom in undisturbed fashion by prohibiting access to the text itself. By insisting that Nietzsche is somehow responsible for European fascism and Emerson for imperial American self-aggrandizement, one keeps a sharp lookout only for those places in their writings where they take the risk of not defending themselves against readers who might devour and use them, not for new thinking, but for previously rehearsed ideological gestures.

We can police texts in this way only by refusing to think for ourselves, in our scared concern to think for—on behalf of, instead of—the texts we read. On the other hand, it is a mistake to make Emerson and Nietzsche acceptable to a tolerant liberalism, as Walter Kaufmann did in the case of Nietzsche, by downplaying their charged, inflammatory moments. Such a reading implicitly wishes that these thinkers had expressed themselves in a more measured, accessible way, one that would support us in what we already wanted to believe, whereas their actual effort is to outrage our security. Perhaps more than any other writers, Nietzsche and Emerson want to deny us the self-possession of being confirmed by the ego ideal, the big Other. To avoid their extreme, intransigent, or seemingly intolerable moments means, then, to fly to the protection of the big Other, to resort to non-thinking respectability.

THE QUESTION OF ASCETICISM

This book risks implying that, because Nietzsche is more twisted or pressured than Emerson, he is more worthy. But Emerson is not without his own twists, among them the idea that the Nietzschean wish for mastery leaves something out. Emerson suggests that, released from the forced, secretive inwardness of the ascetic impulse, we can yield to life's wildness in a way that conserves a healthier sort of inward "pudency" (*E* 483)—we can surrender without giving ourselves away. Finally, the difference between these two thinkers increases the strength of our understanding, even if, weighted ourselves by history and attitude, we cannot always choose freely between them.

CHAPTER ONE

Emerson's Individualism

"WE EAT AND DRINK AND WEAR perjury and fraud in a hundred commodities," Emerson announced in his 1841 lecture before the Me-
chanics' Apprentices' Library Association in Boston (*E* 137); the text
would reappear in 1847 as the essay "Man the Reformer." Emerson
here voices a mood familiar to the most suspicious of present-day readers: everything that surrounds us and constitutes our lives seems, in the
words of Milton's fallen Adam, "propagated curse" (*Paradise Lost*
10.729). In this miserable view, the world itself bears the fatal traces of
our weakness, urging our surrender to the worst conceivable impulses.
For literary critics at the turn of the millennium the sentiment is obvious; to Emerson it is less so—and therefore, to him, more pained and
real. And more fruitful: Emerson's moments of doubt point toward
hope. In this respect he parts company with our literary establish-
ment's professional skepticism, its frequent inclination to believe that
life is either meaningless or founded in sheer, brutal power relations.
By hinting at a recovery from such darkness, Emerson makes clear his
difference from our current emphasis on implacable institutional
forces. He serves the individual's hope for visionary fulfillment, while
acknowledging the corrosive doubt that necessarily attends this hope.

My intent here is to offer a defense of Emersonian hope against its
critics, and in particular against what seems to me the most common
suspicion of Emerson: that he cherishes the merely solitary self, isolated
from social engagement. From Carlyle, who warned his American
friend against "soaring away after Ideas, Beliefs, Revelations, and such
like,—into perilous altitudes," to Quentin Anderson, who accuses Emerson of "withdraw[ing] affect from the collective life," readers have
charged Emerson's vision with irresponsible egoism.[1] Cornel West, in
The American Evasion of Philosophy, offers probably the most influential

recent description of what this series of critics sees as Emerson's impe-rial selfishness.[2]

The constant possibility of authentic contact between souls signals, for Emerson, a univocal, though strictly speaking inexpressible, assur-ance. In this way, the risk of solipsism in Emerson is redeemed by its re-versal into commonness, into the communion hinted at by the secret conversational balance that gives Emersonian society its solidity. He re-mains uninterested in the play of dissimulation, the mysterious disrela-tion, between self and other, lover and beloved, that Nietzsche will explore. A Lacanian reading of Emerson, of the kind that I will attempt for Nietzsche, would be impossible because the Emersonian self is *both* Dionysian (or musical) *and* Apollonian (or architectonic), in a way that Nietzsche cannot manage. In Emerson, the self at once lives out an ec-static illumination and survives the exposure of this ecstasy to a some-times brutal skepticism. Emerson claims the possibility of a resurrected spirit, while simultaneously making this spirit vulnerable to the critical responses of its surrounding society. By doing so, Emer-son makes these antagonistic responses essential, part of our solidarity, a sharing of impulses both doubtful and illuminated.

Emerson is given to celebrating the sublime and solitary ego, cast-ing it against the conventionality that surrounds it, the conformities of the herd. But Emerson criticizes his flights of visionary egoism, even as he indulges in them. Instead of simply promoting an expansive Ameri-can selfhood in order to escape from thinking about American society, Emerson stays acutely aware that his dreams of prophetic grandeur re-main subject to the barbs, the deflating gestures, of his fellow citizens. Emerson, in other words, has the knowledge that West refuses to grant him. He recognizes, around and within him, the prickly to and fro of communal dispute. The recognition sustains Emerson's usefulness as a cultural critic determined to overcome pessimism by acknowledging its force, pessimism being the inevitable response to the degrading capitalist rapacity of Emerson's time, and our own.

The pessimism Emerson wants to overcome starts as a reaction against what "The American Scholar" calls "the vulgar prosperity that retrogrades always to barbarism" (*E* 63). And for Emerson the protest against the ever-expanding American marketplace becomes, like the disease it complains of, all-consuming and irresistible. Emerson's dark mood is skepticism as Stanley Cavell has defined it: a sneaking conviction that we lead not a real life but a poor substitute for one, shadowy and futile.[3] Emerson begins "Man the Reformer" by inciting us, mockingly granting our slide into skeptical convictions: "Let it be granted, that our life, as we lead it, is common and mean; that some of those offices and functions for which we were mainly created are grown so rare in society, that the memory of them is only kept alive in old books and in dim traditions; that prophets and poets, that beautiful and perfect men, we are not now, no, nor have even seen such" (*E* 135). Virtue has been reduced to hearsay; beauty and perfection are mere rumors from the antique world; originality, that fundamental Emersonian goal, seems unimaginable. Yet Emerson insists that, from our vice, virtue might arise. The basis for renewal is the sense of diminishment itself. The monumental inspiration of history has become a mirage of "old books" and "dim traditions." Our consciousness of our faded or secondary situation, and of the correspondingly faded character of the past, makes us want the spiritual immediacy, the "sources of human instruction," that we have been denied. Instead of complacent loyalty to consumerist narcissism, we feel a lack; we sense that we are merely partial, insignificant fractions or fragments of the universe. "That is the vice," he writes, "—that no one feels himself called to act for man, but only as a fraction of man" (*E* 138). As in "The American Scholar," with its persistent image of the desired whole, the integral and powerful body of national culture still belied by our fragmentary existences, Emerson celebrates in "Man the Reformer" our wish for wholeness, shown in the effort "to reattach the deeds of every day to the holy and mysterious recesses of life" (*E* 146). Emerson's envisioned wholeness implies the liveliness of the fully present: all our thoughts and actions will be endowed with the instantly convincing force of the truly original. "Nature . . . sleeps no moment on an old past"—therefore let man "put all his practices back on his first thoughts, and do nothing for which he has not the whole world for his reason" (*E* 146). Cast back on our "first thoughts," we will found ourselves, reattaining the sources of our strength.[4]

PRAGMATISM AND VISION

The recovery from skepticism that Emerson forecasts takes two divergent forms, pragmatic and visionary, and it is the presence of the visionary in the equation that makes Emerson's communitarian critics nervous. In "The American Scholar" Emerson argues the pragmatic line that the justification of new thinking *already* exists, since every good and innovative thought or action publishes itself, makes itself felt. What we don't yet know, in this reading, is the resource that we already possess without knowing it: the means to overcome the self-diminishing fears that render us partial, the anxiety that we are merely covert beings, not accountable to ourselves or to others.

But Emerson also turns toward the visionary. Still in "The American Scholar," he writes that the character of the times is astoundingly flimsy, a "house of cards" ready to be ruined by the first slight breath of genius. But exactly this apocalyptic hope, of a gesture that would "operate in a day the greatest of all revolutions" (*E* 147), speaks against Emerson's insight that revolution has always been occurring, on a scale too minute and integral for our eyes, focused as they are on the prospect of sublime enormity, to notice (*E* 148–49). In Emerson, the visionary impulse to overthrow all cohabits with a quiet pragmatism — a sense that "what works and is" lies all around us, ready for the taking — as it does in no other American thinker.

In the interest of developing a political argument for Emersonian individualism, I want to explore Cavell's understanding of Emerson as a pragmatic philosopher of the ordinary, of the social everyday, who at the same time acknowledges the extraordinary attraction of solitary, antisocial visions. Cavell sets himself the task of giving us the image of Emerson as a social thinker. In doing so, he replies to the critical tradition of disdaining Emerson as an irresponsible egoist, willfully isolated from the politics of his America.

For many of his readers, Emerson remains an ineffectual idealist intent on asserting that the true, divine existence of the self occurs in a higher realm than the merely earthly city. Cavell argues against such a reading of Emerson as imaginative escapist by pursuing the ways that his writing, even as it distinguishes individual acts and persons from their social surroundings, uncovers the hidden presence of an attunement between individuality and social forms. This attunement, in Cavell's reading, may look dangerously tenuous. Yet Cavell's focus on the fragility of communal norms, the way they may suddenly disappear in the face of individual whim or inclination, provides grounds for an optimism that looks beyond the frustration at our failure to reach a secure social consensus. Emerson traces our differences from one another to our differences from, or within, ourselves. Such precarious self-division can profit us if we abandon ourselves to the argument of contrary moods, instead of trying to end the argument by establishing a false coherence or conformity within the self.

EMERSON, THOREAU, AND CATS

Emerson's emphasis differs decisively from that of his inheritor Thoreau, who concerns himself not with an Emerson-like abandonment to the unforeseeable instances that revolutionize the self and its world, but rather with developing the self-surveying capacity necessary to pursue an accurately grounded education. Thoreau remarks that "our life is like a German confederacy, made up of petty states, with its boundary forever fluctuating, so that even a German cannot tell you how it is bounded at any moment."[5] If we trouble to take account of this manic contention within us, we can, in Thoreau's view, bring ourselves to a solid sense of where we are. Thoreau insists that we are not yet truly native to ourselves because we have not measured, with a naturalist's precision, our legitimate borders, our *actual* place in the world. This lack of exactitude leads to our continued dwelling in hasty, self-confirmed illusions, the fantasy life of what is called society. As Cavell shows in *The Senses of Walden,* Thoreau fights such unreality by trusting to his continual effort to attend to, and thus reform, our words and actions, weighing them with the care of a good psychoanalyst.[6] But Emerson, in contrast to his disciple, doubts that we can find Thoreau's "solid bottom everywhere." Instead of exhorting the reader to—in *Walden's* words—"be a Columbus to whole new continents and worlds within you,"[7] Emerson in "Experience" considers that such introspective discovery may turn out to be delusive, comparable to the neat, self-absorbed visions of a cat chasing its tail. This rich feline solipsism mocks the grave explorations of Columbus and Kepler:

> Do you see that kitten chasing so prettily her own tail? If you could look with her eyes, you might see her surrounded with hundreds of figures performing complex dramas, with tragic and comic issues, long conversations, many characters, many ups and downs of fate,—and meantime it is only puss and her tail. How long before our masquerade will end its noise of tambourines, laughter, and shouting, and we shall find it was a solitary performance? . . . What imports it whether it is Kepler and the

sphere; Columbus and America; a reader and his book; or puss with her tail? (*E* 232)

"When I play with my cat," Montaigne writes in his "Apology for Raymond Sebond," "who knows if I am not a pastime to her more than she is to me?"[8] A similar appreciation of perspective informs Emerson's passage. Emerson the essayist, like puss with her tail, relies not on the Thoreauvian prospect of settling or establishing a practically demonstrable sense of our native grounds, but on an extravagant and self-involved performance. This playful "masquerade," unaccountably strange and evanescent, Emerson both celebrates and mocks. He unsettles or disorients us, not just refusing to institute a secure sense of political and moral order, but even casting doubt on our (often conformist) motives for ordering self and society. Yet Emerson, precisely because of his disconcerting disdain for settlement, offers a more exacting and useful picture of our social relations than the meditative Thoreau's quest to find in the ordinary a hard basis or (as *Walden* puts it) "rocks in place." Emerson defines social concern in a way that removes it from the quest for foundations of any kind: for example, identifying and satisfying the interests of our fellow citizens, in order to (as "Self-Reliance" scornfully phrases it) "put all poor men in good situations" (*E* 262). Instead, Emerson shows his investment in society by depicting it as a skein of human interactions that evince a dawning unity. This unity displays itself in coincidences and telling frictions of meaning (not struggles of interest or intention), so that our true life in society stands unveiled as prior to the necessarily rigid, conformist ways we define our identities, as master or slave, husband or wife, child or adult.[9]

With the help of Cavell's reading, I will entertain Emerson's surprisingly ironic practice of shifting between indulgence in visionary sublimity and the exposing of his visions as self-involved illusions akin to his cat's "solitary performance." Emerson's characteristically American impulse to sublimity walks hand in hand with America's impatient, apocalyptic solipsism: the will to see in the landscape present here and now the overwhelming promise of a transfiguring newness addressed to the self alone. As Harold Bloom writes, "The poetic humanism of Emerson, finding itself upon a stonier ground" than Wordsworth's, "had not the patience to wait upon nature's revelation of herself."[10] In place of Wordsworth's patience, Emerson incites a pathos, eagerly remaking the universe in the exalted, breathless image of his own creative power. But he then undermines this sublimity with pragmatic doubts.

EMERSON AND THE SOCIAL AGON

Emerson's contemporaries delighted in criticizing the airy and sometimes ludicrous magic spun by Emerson's transcendentalist friends. In the early 1840s, after Emerson became editor of the *Dial*, Carlyle wrote to Emerson that "I love your 'Dial,' and yet it is with a kind of shudder. You seem to me in danger of dividing yourselves from the Fact of this present Universe, in which alone, ugly as it is, can I find any anchorage."[11] Carlyle here underestimates Emerson's appetite for reality. Emerson, who delighted in depicting himself in crude and sturdy attitude, surveyed with sympathetic amusement the angelic progressivism emanating from the world of New England reformers, at Brook Farm, in the *Dial*, and elsewhere. As Holmes writes, "He knew human nature too well to believe in a Noah's ark full of idealists."[12] But the transcendentalist associations stuck. Stephen Whicher succinctly phrases the disappointed realist's condemnation: "For human relations Emerson substitutes ideal relations."[13]

In the subtle and sharp polemic of *The Imperial Self,* Quentin Anderson attacks Emerson's individualism by describing it as a refusal of social commitments. Anderson charges Emerson with turning against social roles, in particular the role of heterosexual father, in order to insist that "only the activity uniquely mine can manifest the inclusive." The iridescent and extreme color of Emersonian claims to individual distinctiveness, his focus on *your* mood at *this* moment, means for Anderson a kind of genial and soft, but therefore all the more dangerous, anarchy. According to Anderson, this is an anarchy without an opening for meaningful action, since an illumination so utterly specific to individual soul and yet so all-encompassing leaves no room for struggle against historical obstacles and toward historical goals. In Anderson's reading, Emerson denies history, "the succession of the generations." Instead, he becomes "the divine child who eats up the world," preaching a perpetual newness.[14] By the 1830s, the generation of the American founders was gone, their place taken by a corrupt and bitter caricature: President Jackson and his cronies. Anderson sees Emerson as responding with too much facility to this decline, and advocating the replacement of political patriarchy by the inspired self.

(Why not simply incorporate in oneself the powers formerly, mistakenly, credited to paternal authority?)

But Emersonian illumination is not so easy. Even Anderson recognizes a difficulty in Emerson's "secular incarnation," the individual self's ambition to swallow and recreate the world. For Emerson, the self's overexalted expectations necessarily court disappointment. Emerson begins his career not, as Whicher claimed, by trying to overcome this disappointment through an escapist idealism, but rather by attending to its character and meaning, since the frustration of solitary hope must prove a part of our collective difficulty. Knowledge of this difficulty leads to a new aspiration that thrives on democratic argument. Emerson moves past the facile ecstasies of Bronson Alcott and Unitarian suggestions of the simple divinity of everyday existence. Instead, the world resists; and the others who surround the self in society become the agents of this resistance. The insolent boy-man of "Self-Reliance," to come into his own, needs a culture of conformity fighting against him. The self-reliant youth's "neutrality," his cool disengagement from the canons of accepted value, masks an intense ambition to transform, root and branch, the ways of society itself: "He would utter opinions on all passing affairs, which being seen to be not private, but necessary, would sink like darts into the ear of men, and put them in fear" (*E* 261). Here is the salutary political dimension that Anderson, Whicher, and West refuse to see in Emerson.

"New England Reformers," the final essay in *Essays: Second Series*, provides the fullest statement of Emerson's approach to his society. "This union," writes Emerson—the American polity itself—"must be ideal in actual individualism." "The union is only perfect, when all the uniters are isolated" (*E* 599). It is necessary, Emerson means, for each individual to be thrown back on him- or herself, to live through an inward argument that will prove the reality of our collective political engagement. The argument requires a form of high-minded self-distrust, a testing of one's favored impulses that can only happen through the antagonistic presence of comradelike "enemies": "We are not so wedded to our paltry performances of every kind, but that every man has at intervals the grace to scorn his performances . . . he puts himself on the side of his enemies, listening gladly to what they say of him, and accusing himself of the same things" (*E* 601). Emersonian "magnanimity," the noble mood of self-possessed honor that makes each one of us, at certain moments, representative of a fully human, fully persuasive glory, depends on the experience of being dispossessed by someone else's opinion. Being shown up before our fellow citizens turns the style of our convictions from a superficial to a thoroughly founded thing: "What is it we heartily wish of each other? Is it to be pleased and flattered? No, but to be convicted and exposed, to be shamed out of our nonsense of all kinds, and made men of, instead of ghosts and phantoms. . . . All that a man has, will he give for right relations with his mates. All that he has, will he give for an erect demeanor in every company and on each occasion" (*E* 603). No matter how erect one's demeanor, how implacably lustrous and dazzling one's style, one "still finds certain others, before whom he cannot possess himself, because they have somewhat fairer, somewhat grander, somewhat purer, which extorts homage of him" (*E* 603–4). Such extortion, graceful rather than warlike, makes up the mortifying yet enlivening truth of social relations in Emerson. The moment that robs you of your old confidence exposes proud claims to identity as merely wishful, and unmasks as well the judgment of ages as just a provisional experiment. As George Kateb asserts, such ceaseless renovation of the self participates in the tentative, testing character of American democracy. The American impulse to democratize all human relations, Kateb writes, means "a wish to ensure that all relations are characterized by the delicacies of constitutionalism, not only fairness but compunctions, hesitations, and avoidances." The energy of the provisional provides a sign of positive value in its "voluptuous uncertainty as to how to judge and what to think and what, even, to want."[15] The tentativeness that democratic powers afford ensures, for Emerson and for us, that an aggressively confident self-reliance will not descend into tyranny.

Democratic uncertainty or self-criticism relies, as Kateb remarks, on the twofold sense of independence as both a claim to autonomy and a resistance to inclusion.[16] In order to enter ably into the argument of democracy, we must first be born alone, as individuals, out of conformity and into self-reliance: we ought to bear the singularity of purpose that the argument deserves. "Society gains nothing," writes Emerson, "whilst a man, not himself renovated, attempts to renovate things around him" (*E* 596). Moreover, the self, as it finds its way to argument, learns to keep others at the admonitory, challenging distance that true union requires. But there *is* a place for others here; for an other, first of all, within the renovating self.

Emerson asks us to look beyond the representative man as embodi-

ment of a strident social myth, and toward what Cavell calls "the conditions for my recognizing my difference from others as a function of my
recognizing my difference from myself."[17] The struggle within the self
prepares for Emerson's sense of society itself as an agon of mutually resistant and mutually informing differences. "No sentence will hold the
whole truth," Emerson writes in the bewildering, Protean essay "Nominalist and Realist," "and the only way we can be just, is by giving ourselves
the lie. . . . All things are in contact; every atom has a sphere of repulsion" (E 585). "Just"ice and "whole"ness appear not in easy continuity
but rather in schismatic inward debate, "giving ourselves the lie":
"Strange alternation of attraction and repulsion! Character repudiates
intellect, yet excites it; and character passes into thought, is published
so, and then is ashamed before new flashes of moral worth" (E 503). In
"The Method of Nature," a lecture from 1841, social unity or "symmetry," like nature's harmonies, appears as the result of this argumenta-
tive friction: "Each effect strengthens every other. There is no revolt in
all the kingdoms from the commonweal: no detachment of an individual" (E 120).

For Emerson in 'The Method of Nature," representativeness
takes on a communal, discursive fluidity, since each individual "seen
by himself," even a heroic, "eminent soul," appears a "spotted and defective person" (E 121). As "Experience" puts it, "it needs the whole
society, to give the symmetry we seek" (E 477). Yet the self continues
in its partiality, its solitary, asymmetrical ambition. The very unsteadi-
ness of the relation between the self and its others makes for Emerson's lesson.

Emerson does split the self off from its social setting. He does so,
however, not so that he can shore up the self, but rather so that he can
disorient and divide it. The self-flattering heroic image of the subject
turns out, in Emerson's hands, to be as much a mirage as conformist
society itself. Here Cavell's definition of how skepticism emerges—
when the ostensibly solid realities of world and self suddenly appear to
be mere phantasms—proves centrally relevant.

Emerson's crisis, as Cavell defines it, begins in thought's permanent and unavoidable temptation: to surrender so far to the inward,
dreamlike character of imagination that imagination begins to look
alien, forbidding in its self-involvement. After such distraction, thought
needs to be rediscovered as a public, living form, rescued from mere
fantasy and vain wish-fulfillment, which remain partial, subjective, and

therefore unreal. In Cavell's work, putting skepticism in perspective, taming its isolationist impulse, means accepting a world by recognizing in others an echo of your own thoughts and actions—the first prerequisite for political community.

ALIENATED MAJESTIES: THE LESSON OF "EXPERIENCE"

Emerson's "Experience" starts from the imagination's shaken confidence in the world, and in the healing powers of reality: its tragedy is the skeptical loss of the real. Emerson, who noted in his *Journals* his obsessive esteem for the "Intimations Ode," presents a bleakly ironic reversal of Wordsworth by expressing grief for a world that has faded into inaccessibility and that, as a result, cannot even be properly mourned. Like the memory of his dead son, little Waldo, everyday experience seems to slip through Emerson's fingers, conveying only an anaesthetic numbness:

> An innavigable sea washes with silent waves between us and the things we aim at and converse with. Grief too will make us idealists. In the death of my son, now more than two years ago, I seem to have lost a beautiful estate,—no more. I cannot get it nearer to me . . . it does not touch me: some thing which I fancied was a part of me, which could not be torn away without tearing me, nor enlarged without enriching me, falls off from me, and leaves no scar. . . . I grieve that grief can teach me nothing, nor carry me one step into real nature. (*E* 473)

"I cannot get it nearer to me," Emerson writes, referring to the reality lost along with his son. "Ghostlike we glide through nature, and should not know our place again" (*E* 471, 473).

Emerson, like Wordsworth, tries to overcome the distance between thought and the world. He wants to heal the corrosive irony of skepticism, remedying our disconnection from reality by binding us to reality's everyday forms. But Emerson does not find Wordsworthian reconciliation at the end of "Experience." The compensations for loss that he proposes are too slippery, too evanescent, to form the basis of a renewed covenant with ordinary reality. This consciousness of failure marks Emerson's difference from Wordsworth, and from Thoreau, though he continues to proclaim his ambition to restore and renew the world.[18]

THE WORK OF WHIM

Cavell's description of the forms of life as idiosyncratic and unstable, because resistant to articulation, differs decisively from the rather more sober communitarian visions that are currently so popular. Emerson, like Wittgenstein, sees our unformalizable learning of the world's ways and means as a casual process, getting the hang of an example rather than memorizing a rule. This process generates intuitive, mostly tacit communal agreements about everyday realities. But as Cavell points out, becoming acquainted with the world also means uncovering the unfamiliar nature within us, knowing the inestimable privilege of our unknownness to ourselves in a way that separates us from all others.

In Emerson, the moment of skeptical isolation proves crucial in its exposing of a lack of grounds because such exposure opens the way for invention, an uncommon and perhaps unshareable moment. (Not, as in Wittgenstein, a discovery of the inevitable human grammar we must all partake in.) As Cavell writes, "Finding ourselves on a certain step we may feel the loss of foundation to be traumatic, to mean the ground of the world falling away, the bottom of things dropping out, ourselves foundered, sunk on a stair. But on another step we may feel this idea of (lack of) foundation to be impertinent, an old thought for an old world" (*This New Yet Unapproachable America*, 109).

Emerson calls this strange futurity *whim*, a genius that jumps unpredictably from one person to another. "Like a bird which alights nowhere, but hops perpetually from bough to bough, is the Power which abides in no man and in no woman, but for a moment speaks from this one, and for another moment from that one," he writes in "Experience" (*E* 477). Richard Poirier, more than any other reader, has illuminated for us the fleeting impersonality of Emersonian genius, its debt to whim.[19] Despite his occasional wish to give his poet and scholar the skills of heroic creators, Emerson much more often makes them mere receptors of cosmic influence like anyone, or anything, else. In the essay "The Poet," Emerson sees the poet as a kind of deep-dish antenna for the "rays or appulses" that nature supplies, or an empty canvas awaiting the universe's input (*E* 448). The poet, as Nietzsche describes him in *The Birth of Tragedy*, is the supremely intense and untroubled eye of the sun: untroubled, first of all, because divinely unmoved.[20] "As, in the sun, objects paint their images on the retina of the eye," Emerson writes, "so they, sharing the aspiration of the whole universe, tend to paint a far more delicate copy of their essence in his mind" (*E* 458). This receptive capacity enables the poet to transmit or "impart" poetry to others (*E* 448). The transitory, elusive nature of Emersonian genius, which remains proudly uninterested in any project for a consistent or self-explanatory ego, distinguishes it from Wordsworthian imagination, with its drive to develop the self's capacities through coherent narratives of its own and others' personal history.

This, to be sure, is not the whole story. As early as "The American Scholar," Emerson saw the scholar's project of envisioning, and even building, communal union as requiring a purgatorial journey, a project of descent and heroic reemergence, that far surpasses in its power the casual workings of what Emerson called nature or (later) genius. The "first in time and the first in importance" of the influences on the scholar, and on all our existence, Emerson writes, is "nature": "Ever the winds blow; ever the grass grows. Every day, men and women, beholding and beholden" (*E* 55). These sentences assimilate social life, the conversation of men and women, into the timeless and interminable network of physical life: "There is never a beginning, there is never an end, to the inexplicable continuity of this web of God, but always circular power returning into itself." The seamless indefinition of this cosmic marriage is not enough, however, for the scholar, "he of all men whom this spectacle most engages." As an "ambitious soul," Emerson asserts, "he must settle its value in his mind." The scholarly soul, busily classifying nature, finds itself "tyrannized over by its own unifying instinct" (*E* 55). Only when the scholar disengages himself from the entrancing and entranced ongoingness of nature, abandoning as well the effort to discipline and regulate its wildness, can he formulate the brave project of discovering an American culture, of redeeming America itself. In order to do so, he must turn inward, to self-discipline: in "periods of solitude, inquest, and self-recovery" the scholar's native rights are won (*E* 58).

> Long must he stammer in his speech; often forego the living for the dead. Worse yet, he must accept, — how often! poverty and solitude. . . . [H]e takes the cross of . . . the self-accusation, the faint heart, the frequent uncertainty and loss of time, which are the nettles and tangling vines in the way of the self-relying and self-directed. (E 63)

In place of the fluid interconnections of nature we find now a grating prison of self-irritation and internal rebellion, the harsh and tangled, half-articulate stumbling of the reflective spirit. "For all this loss and scorn, what offset?" Emerson asks (*E* 63). The compensation for the scholar's punishment turns out to be a boldly public office:

> The instinct is sure, that prompts him to tell his brother what he thinks. He then learns, that in going down into the secrets of his own mind, he has descended into the secrets of all minds. . . . [H]e is the complement of his hearers . . . they drink his words because he fulfills for them their own nature; the deeper he dives into his privatest, secretest presentiment, to his wonder he finds, this is the most acceptable, most public, and universally true. The people delight in it; the better part of every man feels, This is my music; this is myself. (*E* 65)

The scholar's lonely trial here finds itself translated into the prophetic cultural duty of inventing a true American union. Most wonderfully, the thoughts of "utter solitude" equal those of all who hear or read them; author and audience combine into a newly whole body (*E* 64). From the mutilated corpse of a society whose amputated members "strut about" boasting of their partial powers, "a good finger, a neck, a stomach, an elbow, but never a man," the scholar has put together a resurrected being. So Emerson reads the age-old fable of the body politic: "the individual, to possess himself, must sometimes return from his own labor to embrace all the other laborers" (*E* 54).[21] By the time of "Experience," Emerson has backed away from such fervent trust that the scholar will find his echo in a fit audience. But he retains the scholar's exalted, world-discovering mood, the insistent triumph that solitary heroism announces to itself.

Emerson's emphasis on the merely casual or momentary nature of genius, which he also calls reception, the modest inspiration that fitfully contacts or connects persons, marks his difference from the Romantic tradition's ambition for a concerted, fashioned consciousness. But Emerson, as we saw in "The American Scholar," is not entirely happy with his momentary genius. Though he often recommends the low-key, pragmatic acceptance of genius's transient character, such pragmatism also disillusions him. The common, impersonal character of genius can, at times in Emerson, descend too far; it can make the common seem too easily achieved, or even slightly trivial in its chanciness.

In "Experience," Emerson's response to this occasional disappointment with his own ease, with the availability of genius, has two phases. First, he reacts against the evanescence of genius, its status as what "Self-Reliance" calls a "moment of transition" (*E* 271), by proclaiming a visionary solipsism that would render the self's imaginative will a permanent, autonomous creation. This is a far more radical and risky descent into self than "The American Scholar" imagined, since it brings no promise of communal acclaim at its end. Celebrating the will's force in this solitary way does not lend it the desired autonomy; it will not stand and endure. The failure of the visionary imagination's efforts to make its solipsism viable leads to the ironic, perverse aura of doubt attached to Emerson's assertions of a transcendent self. Julie Ellison, an acute commentator on the interplay of irony and sublimity in Emerson, writes that

> At times, in Emerson's prose, irony and sublimity accomplish the same end and appear interchangeable. Frequently, however, irony follows sublimity, deflating its pretensions without relinquishing its pleasures. . . . Emerson intermittently becomes a transcendental buffoon. . . . Emerson's irony alternates with his yearning for transcendence and teleology, a tonal emblem of his fluctuation between self-consciousness and surprise.[22]

As Emerson writes in "Circles," his mood swinging wildly, "I am God in nature; I am a weed by the wall" (*E* 406). Such oscillation is itself an expression of the genius that works through us, our animating moods. Though Emerson weds himself to the creative possibilities of displacement and distraction that genius promises, he remains uncomfortable with its transient character.

THE SOLITARY SUBLIME IN EMERSON

To illustrate how the Emersonian quester's radical, solipsistic desire turns ironic, I offer the following well-known exultation from "Experience": "I clap my hands in infantine joy and amazement, before the first opening to me of this august magnificence . . . the sunbright Mecca of the desert. And what a future it opens! I feel a new heart beating with the love of the new beauty. I am ready to die out of nature, and be born again into this new yet unapproachable America I have found in the West" (*E* 485). With this prophetic image Emerson evokes the experience of gradually dawning "illumination," "when I converse with a profound mind, or if at any time being alone I have good thoughts"

(*E* 484). But as the passage's sun ascends, he withdraws from the model of conversation to be alone, to pursue his own soul's apotheosis. It is true that Emerson here partly belies his solitude with an implicit parallel between himself and his nation. The American sublime makes the august latecomer young again, and this is a public as well as a private fact. The tired, overexperienced Emerson becomes in this passage a baby bearing "infantine joy," a little Waldo, just as we as a nation are both the latest and the newest on the planet. The child is the man, not just the father of the man: thus the perpetual youthfulness of American aspiration. This seems unequivocally happy. But then why does the author label this marvelous find, that belatedness translates into fresh possibility, "unapproachable"?

At least part of the answer depends on Emerson's relation to his audience: that is, here, his withdrawal from them. With his shift from the "we" he used earlier on in "Experience" to his new solitary "I," Emerson becomes less approachable, abandoning us at the very moment of his grandest public pronouncement about the new America. Explaining this apparent forsaking of audience, Cavell writes: "If we consider that what we now know, know now, of this writer is this writing, that says we and that says I, then wherever he is we are—otherwise how can we hear him? Do we? Does his character make an impression on us? Has he achieved a new degree of culture? To have us consider this is a sensible reason for his saying 'I,' as it were abandoning us."[23] Cavell argues that Emerson leaves us behind in his sublime ascent so that we may estimate both his position and our own: even this shunning of audience points toward a renewal of our common conversation. But he also suggests Emerson's awareness that we may not hear or know him, that we may not take his measure. Emerson's turn from community, his saying "I" rather than "we," could be still more serious than Cavell indicates. What if, at this moment, Emerson really wants his own visionary America, antithetical to the one everyone else lives in—"the world I think," as he puts it elsewhere in "Experience," rather than "the world I converse with in the city and in the farms" (*E* 491)? In the lines envisioning his "new yet unapproachable America" Emerson's quest seems more extreme, more severe and solitary, than any responsible version of society can allow. Emerson in his vision of Mecca does, as Cavell claims, use visionary imagination as a sign for the establishing (or not) of community, a compass that will enable us to investigate, and maybe find, our bearings in this land of promise that is also a desert. But the vision's unapproachability runs deeper: it threatens the very possibility of a common life.

There is still another risk that Emerson must contend with in his visionary mood. What "History" calls the "unattained but attainable self" (*E* 239), the beautiful future we aspire to, may turn out to be, after all, a futile, unrealizable prospect, a mere fantasy image. The provisional, unfinished character of American optimism means that we can never wake up to it completely, never make it fully reliable and explicit for ourselves or for others. Perhaps America's sunbright newness, the gleam of the desert, will always repel our advances. Its Mecca may be a mirage out of one of the exotic travelers' tales so popular in Emerson's day, like John Lloyd Stephens's *Incidents of Travel in Egypt, Arabia Petraea, and the Holy Land* (1837). Seized by an enthusiasm strangely comparable to what Emerson feels when he envisions Mecca, Stephens writes:

> I stand upon the very peak of Sinai, where Moses stood when he talked with the Almighty. Can it be, or is it a mere dream? Can this naked rock have been the witness of that great interview between man and his Maker? . . . strange as the feeling may seem, my very soul cleaved to the scene around me. I too felt myself lifted above the world, and its petty cares and troubles, and almost hurried into the wild enthusiasm which had sent the tenants of these ruined convents to live and die among the mountains.

Stephens follows this rhapsody with a rude moment of deflation, a shift reminiscent of Emerson's juxtapositions of the sublime and the crude everyday: "Blame me not, reader, nor think me impious, that, on the top of the holy mountain of Sinai, half-unconscious what I did, I fired at a partridge."[24]

Emerson's America, like Stephens's Arabia, proves unapproachable, liable to be punctured by a low reality, precisely because he fantasizes about it with such grand arrogance.[25] The fantasy's sublime intensity seems meant for the self alone, and so he abandons the political "we" for the antipolitical, isolated "I." Emerson, at this point, does not want his audience to join him. Instead, he displays to his readers, in his magnificent, unreachable America, a radically private attempt to overcome the skeptical doubts he has voiced in "Experience." Prophetically and single-handedly, he makes a world for himself, not for his community. Yet he knows, all too well, that his gloriously high-minded solipsism will fade when touched by a reader's mundane doubts. What follows the sight of our "unapproachable America" suggests it is Emerson's own ephemeral property: a few pages later, Emerson refers sardonically to "our constitutional necessity of seeing things under private aspects, or saturated with our humors" (*E* 490).

Emerson's idea of unapproachability in the passage from "Experience" I have been discussing recalls a sentence from earlier in the essay. "Well, souls never touch their objects," Emerson writes (*E* 473). Never, even in the sharpest tragedies, does the soul provide us with the reality-assuring friction we seek (*E* 473). Emerson in "Experience" looks toward his newfound America as a presence momentous enough to be capable of meeting our souls, overcoming "the evanescence and lubricity of all objects, which lets them slip through our fingers then when we clutch hardest" (*E* 473). But this sublime apotheosis also slips through Emerson's hands, since it remains a dream vision rather than a hard fact.

We can characterize Emerson's egotistical sublime as what he calls, in "Experience," "unhandsome," a clutching conscious of its clumsiness as well as its grandeur. The unreachability inherent in any ideal suddenly appears to him as an aggravating, nagging imperfection of vision. Emerson craves more than reality: once again, his impatience contrasts with Thoreau's rock-solid courting of the real. In line with his customary practice of slyly deflating his own idealizing gestures even as he pursues the ideal, Emerson declares the promised land unreachable at the very moment that he most fervently desires to grasp it. The awkwardness of this grip derives from the irony of Emerson's effort to enjoy a world, imaged here as America, that he wants to exist for him in innocent immediacy, before the strivings of will, and even before language itself. "I do not make it; I arrive there, and behold what was there already," Emerson writes of his vision, concluding in babyish protest, "I make! O no!" (*E* 485). "Infantine joy," Emerson's reaction to his sight of the new America in the section quoted earlier, has its root in *in-fans*, literally unspeaking or prelinguistic: the phrase resonates with the impossible wishes that appear elsewhere in Emerson for a mode of description that would emanate from, and thus palpably incarnate, its object. "The Method of Nature" refers to genius speaking "like a river; it has no straining to describe, any more than there is straining in nature to exist. . . . Genius . . . is itself a mutation of the thing it describes" (*E* 129).

"Patience and patience," Emerson calmly repeats near the end of "Experience," "we shall win at the last"—but there is no "last" (*E* 492). The Emersonian text looks endless, incapable of producing any vision of impending success that is not, as in "Circles," also a term in a new, unforeseeable succession. Such endlessness generates Emerson's lightly knowing self-delusion—as we see in "Circles," which associates its own boasting with the self-aggrandizements of "dreams and drunkenness" (*E* 414).

The solipsistic instinct for success is only one of several Emersonian moods. Emerson also has a strange, contradictory desire to lose: specifically, to lose his ordinary self-possession, which may be the only way to be surprised out of his conformity into a poor but lively self-reliance. Loss becomes a playful way of acknowledging the receptivity of genius, Emerson's counter to visionary power. Often enough, Emerson, like Kierkegaard's Socrates in *The Concept of Irony*, simply enjoys playing with the "nothing" he has, his whim. Whim could be proof against the questing critic's melodramatic excesses. Here Emerson shows us a way out of the dire, belated fixation on successes we feel we must, but can't, have. He offers, at times, a flirting with failure, a surrender to poverty instead of a rough passage through and beyond it.

Losing and getting lost are related concerns for Emerson, but getting lost—that is, getting thrown off the balance provided by one's usual self—can also lead to unexpected success. What we seek, according to "Circles," is "to do something without knowing how or why" (*E* 414). In illustration of the curious blessings that await such rather oblivious readiness, "Self-Reliance" features the fable of a drunkard who wakes up in the bed of a prince and is treated like royalty as a result: a whim-inspired version of arriving in the promised land. "Man . . . is in the world a sort of sot, but now and then wakes up, exercises his reason, and finds himself a true prince" (*E* 268). Being mistaken for a prince here means being found to be one. With his sot-prince anecdote, Emerson recommends a wry gratitude that will not trouble itself about the authenticity of its sudden luck. Just relaxing into acceptance of a happy error becomes a stylish triumph of role-playing, like the aplomb of the woman who, at the beginning of Mitchell Leisen's and Preston Sturges's film *Easy Living*, finds precipitously descending upon her a mink coat ripped from the hands of a stranger, the wife struggling with her husband on a balcony above. So Emerson touts the genial forsaking of the old life: in Frost's words, he "only has at heart your getting lost." Disorientation is a crucial part of whatever awakening we receive from Emerson. Like the sot-prince, we ought to be thankful for such beneficent shocks.[26] The rewards of being astonished, being at a loss, make any quest for a more established, less surprising home look rather fainthearted.

Some decades before "Self-Reliance," Schopenhauer produced his own version of the sot-prince story. He writes in *The World as Will and Idea* that "for the knowledge that sees through the *principium individuationis*" — that is, for the universalizing perspective of the wise man — "a happy life in time, given by chance or won from it by shrewdness, amid the sufferings of innumerable others, is only a beggar's dream, in which he is a king, but from which he must awake" (*WWI* 1.353).[27] As always, Schopenhauer here warns that wish and fantasy are evanescent, not to be trusted. But Emerson, with his image of the sot-prince, allies himself with the delusion Schopenhauer fears. He suggests that dreaming is worthwhile because dreams realize themselves occasionally, or on occasion, quite apart from our intentions, and in a way that makes our customary distinctions between illusion and reality seem overly fastidious and defensive.

Richard Poirier has expertly brought out the side of Emerson that is most at ease with the work of genius, the pared-down poise ready to welcome any alien sensation or estranging energy. But Emerson is not always at ease. There is an imperial impulse in him that, impatient with the receptivity required of genius, generates a tension that has mostly been lost in the American poetic and philosophical traditions he began: the division between an urge to prophetic creation, and consumption, of the world and an acknowledgment of the world's indifferent alienness to us (which, in a certain mood, like Thoreau's in parts of *Walden*, might be synonymous with its interest for us). Thoreau, like Frost, and like American pragmatism in general, tones down the Emersonian need for visionary will.

BIRTH AND THE FUTURE IN EMERSON AND NIETZSCHE

Emerson's hope becomes more palpable and less visionary when he tempers his impulse to offer an image of the "sunbright Mecca" that beckons to us and instead lets the perhaps glorious, but perhaps dully faltering destiny of America remain unclear. Here I turn back to Cavell's reading of "Experience" in order to reveal a hidden connection between Emerson and Nietzsche, one that secures the kinship of these two thinkers as actors of their own ironies. Cavell proposes that Emerson's inability to mourn little Waldo implies the bearing of a future. Waldo's death is "caducous" — he "falls off from me, and leaves no scar," like a fragment liberated into freedom (*E* 473).

This death, then, is also a birth. Cavell argues that the death of Waldo figures a demise of Being, the withdrawal of the world from our touch: we are "the Para coats that shed every drop" (*E* 473). But Emerson's statement of this withdrawal, like his refusal to offer the unquestionable fulfillments a true prophetic vision would provide, is not a mere admission of lack. Emerson points to a greater and more unpredictable profit, the authentic future of his text. For Cavell, Emerson's essay declares itself to be pregnant, in its effort to "give birth to experience" through "the will of a listening, persisting reader." The temper of such a reader cannot be foreseen in advance, Cavell continues, since "an Emersonian essay is a finite object that yields an infinite response."[28] The posthumous birth of the Emersonian message cannot, then, be reliably envisioned by its author. Emerson welcomes the waning of authorial control, since it allows for the birth of a message that will be taken up by innumerable, separate readers, alien to themselves and each other, each in a different way forgetting and resurrecting this text's origin. (And will these partial readings come together? Again, Emerson hints at a positive answer, a Gnostic communion.)

This prospect of a centrifugal distribution of his text accounts, in part, for the seemingly fragmented character of Emerson's prose argument, whose interlacement remains a secret. Emerson's practice of writing, in other words, requires him to give over his child, his essay, into our necessarily diverse hands. Emerson, Cavell writes,

> can enact this practice [of separation of author from reader] if writing can, if his writing is his body in which he can bury Waldo, and the likes of you and me are accordingly, under certain conditions, given to discover him as if he were a new America, as if we are apprized of a new and excellent region, of a new being. Whatever this discovery takes is what reading Emerson takes. It may yield philosophy.[29]

The dead yet fruitful letter of Emerson's writing *may* yield philosophy. Will we have what this thinking takes, what it might exact from us in its exactness, its agility being so different from the vague rushes of eloquence Emerson is often charged with?

Cavell emphasizes Emerson's awareness of interpretive iffyness, the thrilling and chastening contingency of future audience. He does not know how he will be read, what or how much we will make of him, and accordingly he surrenders to us his power over his text's future: "Does one expect less of a writer whom we have never settled, who retains so much secrecy, who asks of us transcendence, transformation, aversion, the response to an infinite object, the drawing of a new circle, the rememberment of fragments torn from his work, from us? He cannot name his successor."[30] Cavell's remarks on Emerson bear a close affinity to Derrida's reading of Nietzsche's *Ecce Homo,* another text whose birth(s) will occur posthumously, and whose prophecy therefore remains as yet, and as ever, undecidable.[31] When he refers to the child of Emerson's writing, Cavell looks, implicitly but pointedly, to the end of Nietzsche's *Zarathustra.* Near the end of book 4 of *Zarathustra,* Nietzsche poses "all that suffers" [*alles, was leidet*] against "joy" [*Lust*]. In doing so, he renounces once more his early confidence in a Wagnerian rebirth of tragic art as a historically fated event. For the Nietzsche of *Zarathustra,* the tragic or suffering mood creates the future by reaching beyond such rebirth, beyond the enclosed, secure realms of self-understanding and self-possession:

> . . . all that suffers wants to live, that it may become ripe and joyous and longing—longing for what is farther, higher, brighter [sehnsüchtig nach Fernerem, Höherem, Hellerem]. "I want heirs"—thus speaks all that suffers; "I want children, I do not want myself."
>
> Joy, however, does not want heirs, or children—joy wants itself, wants eternity, wants recurrence, wants everything eternally the same [Lust will sich selber, will Ewigkeit, will Wiederkunft, will Alles-sich-ewig-gleich]. (*Z* 434)

I revert to my basic division between architectonic and musical impulses in Nietzsche, between his wish for the security of firm ground or fixed location, here identified with joy and eternity,[32] and his wish for the power of suffering, which produces dispersion, endless unpredictable change. Whereas (architectonic) joy wants self-continuation, (musical) suffering wants inheritors essentially other than itself. Suffering, *das Leiden,* looks toward a self-overcoming, the tragic breaking of the present that forces into being something strange and new. Neither mood, neither suffering nor joy, can eliminate the other.

Accordingly, Nietzsche remains divided between the feeling of a joyful, fated security—the serene comfort of egomania, assured even in its self-mockery, as it sometimes appears in *Ecce Homo*—and an equal will to surrender this security (also present in *Ecce Homo*). Such surrender of secure selfhood appears, in comic rather than tragically suffering style, when Nietzsche invokes, like Emerson, the centrality of unconscious whim, boasting that he cannot even master his current self-definition, much less the impression he will make on future readers: "That one becomes what one is presupposes that one does not have the remotest idea what one is," he writes in *Ecce Homo* (*EH* 64). (This sentence reads to me like a wishful evocation of Emerson's strength.)

At times in *Zarathustra*, Nietzsche aims at mastery through images of steady, happy self-generation—"Oh, my friends, that your self be in your deed as the mother is in her child" (*Z* 208). But elsewhere in the same book, he celebrates the fact that one cannot own one's deeds, that they cannot be proper to the self any more than one's children can. "The child is innocence and forgetting, a new beginning, a game, a self-propelled wheel, a first movement, a sacred 'Yes,'" not a continuation of its begetter's character or fate. "Thus I now love only my children's land," Zarathustra proclaims, "yet undiscovered, in the farthest sea" (*Z* 139).

Zarathustra's love for his children's land figures Nietzsche's hope for a future place that will metamorphose the concept of home in unknown and decisive ways. This land, then, represents "something higher than any reconciliation," superior to the Hegelian prospect of a future that would supply a secure conclusion to the past, a validation of where we already are and what we already know.

According to Nietzsche, good and evil want to break and transfigure, and so transvalue, themselves: an impulse he privileges over the wish to remain in a familiar, available world. The heroic, epochally ruinous character of Nietzsche's breaking of values, his lion spirit, stands in contrast to Emerson's focus on the ordinary yet at the same time wildly extraordinary fact of subtly transforming change. This difference entails Nietzsche's involvement in a maze of misrecognition from which Emerson, from the start, remains free. Emerson's picture of social being is transparent in a way unavailable to Nietzsche, who sees a realm of dissimulation and self-deceiving invention instead.

But there remains a profound likeness between the two thinkers in their desire for the unpredictable as the truth of futurity. Emerson, like

Nietzsche's Zarathustra, combats his impulse to claim proper owner-
ship of his deed of writing, to declare himself already at home and self-
possessed. He voices instead, as does Nietzsche, a wish to deliver this
writing wholly into our unpredictably transforming hands. When Emerson decides that his mourning for Waldo has failed, that an inheritance
has been lost, this discovery becomes a required moment in a new making of inheritance. The loss of Waldo resembles Nietzsche's necessary
"innocence and forgetting," the unclarity Zarathustra attaches to the
destiny of his message. What is born in or from Emerson must remain
nameless and obscure to him. As a result, the numbness or anaesthesia
that attends the birth, the strangely dissociated grief for the departure
of a beloved son, redeems itself as a solemn yet delighted care.

Emerson's prospective, as yet unimaginable birth remains too slippery and insubstantial to serve as an explicit motive for social action.
Yet precisely because of its exiguous character, Emerson's dedication
to a substantively different future conveys the creative antagonism of
the antiprogrammatic. Here Emerson's ornery and elusive nature, his
porcupine irascibility, may prove politically frustrating. Neither receptive patience with the fact of transient genius nor a prophetic and insistent remaking of the self and its world allows for familiar reformist
platforms. As "Experience" puts it, "Our relations to each other are oblique and casual" (*E* 473).

Emerson's casual receptiveness and his visionary will equally
refuse to shape themselves into modes of action aiming to reconstitute,
or even to describe, social relations in any lawful or definite way. Such
clarification of social bonds, the articulation of our casual contacts as
explicit forms of solidarity, appears only fitfully or accidentally in Emerson, despite the resolution of "The American Scholar" to shape us all
into equal members of one shining new body. As he writes in the Divinity School Address, "These laws refuse to be adequately stated. They
will not be written out on paper, or spoken by the tongue" (*E* 76). We
cannot, it seems, achieve a firm picture of our political order, because
it shares so much with chance and circumstance. Emerson shows us an
impersonal, evanescent social life, what Jean-Luc Nancy, troping
Heidegger's *Mitsein*, would call an "inoperative community," liberating in the very indefiniteness of its freedoms.[33]

"Experience" ends by making visible a contradiction between the
self's dreams and its real, public activities. Emerson both hopes for
the "transformation of genius into practical power" and notes the

inevitable frustration of this hope: "In the history of mankind, there is never a solitary example of success, — taking their own tests of success" (*E* 492). In an Emersonian mood, Charles Bernstein similarly describes the "gap between the world of our private phantasies & the possibilities of meaningful action." Bernstein argues, in direct opposition to a sociopolitical analysis like West's, that the gap between public and private constitutes a fundamental, and promising, condition of American imagination, instead of marking a failure imposed by political circumstances. (The gap is not, for example, a symptom of commodity capitalism and the passive consumer fantasies it encourages.)

The distance between first-person wish and third-person practice, Bernstein writes, "is the measure not so much of our desires or depression or impotence," or of feelings induced by the socioeconomic conditions a "Marxist analysis" uncovers, "but of ourselves. . . . It is at the root of our collectivity."[34] Digging beneath or behind socioeconomic divisions in order to seek a more genuine, and more genuinely divided, self is a longstanding trope of Emersonian individualism. In this way Emerson marks the limits of the idiom that would assign to ideology the true motives for our unions and disunions. A society whose cohesiveness could be assured by some wholesome ideological bias would in fact prove fatally uninviting. "There is a mystic separation between poetic vision and ordinary living," Susan Howe writes in an Emersonian vein. "The conditions for poetry rest outside each life at a miraculous reach indifferent to worldly chronology."[35] A latter-day Emersonian might ask: Could political change alter this indifference without erasing the division inherent in our lives as worldly and ordinary, yet also timeless, eccentric, and solitary creatures? Would we want it to?

Emerson, rather more than Nietzsche, seems to me a necessary commentator on the solitary imagination in and apart from social life. The lack of a commonly available American discourse, a communal *tertium quid* beyond both the self's visionary ambition and the impersonal genius that defeats the self, means that there is no plausible way for us to unite the self-articulating ego of "the world I think" with the haphazard encounters of "the world I converse with," to meld will and genius in the shape of the public sphere that contemporary social theory yearns after.

The lack of a place that would be at once imaginative, practical, and politically responsible remains a disconcerting fact of our current lives. But this distance between our formal or respectable expositions of community, on the one hand, and our solitary creativity and casual encounters, on the other, gives Emerson grounds for rejoicing rather than lament. With Emerson, I suggest that, in certain moods at least, such divergences between the public agenda of a culture and the private one of individual imagination might hold the promise of new, as yet unpicturable forms of collectivity. Since we cannot avoid the lack of harmony between first- and third-person commitments, we do well to watch for and exploit its antagonistic power. As Emerson warns in "Experience," "I observe that difference, and shall observe it" (*E* 491–92). In the face of our historical failures, wrongs, and repressions, and without letting its irony destroy its visionary hope, Emerson's individualism seeks out that which in America works and is.

CHAPTER TWO

The Birth of Tragedy

JUST AS EMERSON'S "FATE"—for the young Nietzsche the most important of Emerson's essays—divides the universe between two deities, Fate and Freedom, so Nietzsche in *The Birth of Tragedy* sees Greek culture as a battle between Apollo and Dionysus. Emerson, true to his capacity for synthesis, will "hazard the contradiction:—freedom is necessary" (*E* 953). But Nietzsche remains a dualist, poised between two poles: the Apollonian (architectonic) impulse to guard the image of the self-observing individual and to fortify such self-regard, and the Dionysian (musical) drive to assimilate the self to the cosmic play in which each phenomenon, including the individual, is merely a mask. As we have seen, Emerson preaches an abandonment to the hazards of our perspectives and a recognition of antagonism and self-division as the only places in which individuality can truly emerge. Nietzsche, by contrast, finds himself urged toward not the mere fact of antagonism, but instead the utter specificity that characterizes one's individuality as a secretive and vulnerable space: the object *a* (a term I define as fully as I can in the next section of this chapter). In other words, Nietzsche is a tragic thinker in a way that Emerson is not. For Nietzsche the individual's effort at mastery is, inevitably, overturned because individuality remains linked to the object *a*, the crucial element that cannot be mastered.

   The tragic character of Nietzsche's vision is bound up with the question of how and why past objects of desire persist within us, and what this persistence has to do with the permanence of desire itself as something that survives all loss. Desire in the course of Nietzsche's writing career shows itself as inescapably different from drive, the relentless quality displayed by eros (in Lacan's reading of Freud).[1] Drive, as a weirdly automatic or inexorable principle, seems to submerge individuality, and with it the particular shape of any individual love: just as language itself, in Nietzsche's "On Truth and Lie in the Extra-Moral Sense," covers over, in its ceaseless movement, any particular event or person. But the painful irony of this eclipsing of desire by drive, of individuality by process, is that it seems only to accentuate the significance of the thing that lies at the core of individuality, the object *a*.

Nietzsche in *The Birth of Tragedy* wants to erase the special character of the loved object in favor of an impersonal force or drive, which appears in the *Birth* as both healing and uncannily disruptive: it both enables us to rise above the pain of particular attachments, and at the same time makes clear that such attachments have a relentless serial quality, that they testify to drive as a process that seems forced on us, an automatism. In the books that immediately follow the *Birth* Nietzsche, by moving from drive to desire, asserts the individuality that this early glimpse of drive's automatic character conceals.

The exemplary individual of *Untimely Meditations,* the proud, discerning reader of himself, differs strikingly from the agonized personality who dominates Nietzsche's final works. But this final, ascetic self can be understood as the outcome of this earlier individualism, whose wish for mastery is based on the canny arrangement of one's life so that the past can be changed, even new created, to serve the future. The failure of this creative effort, the futility of its revolt against the permanent place of the object *a*, will lead to Nietzsche's asceticism in the *Genealogy of Morals* and *Ecce Homo,* which confronts and struggles with the object *a* more intensely, even desperately, than his earlier individualism did.

First, though, I want to outline this early individualism as a turn away from *The Birth of Tragedy*. Nietzsche moves from praising a tragic vision of universal injustice in *The Birth of Tragedy* to emphasizing, in *Untimely Meditations,* the necessity of particular unjust visions. Nietzsche develops from a recovery of origins to a reinvention of them, from the wish to offer a cosmic and timeless redemption *via* tragedy to the need to invent one's own present self under pressure from the past. With the *Untimely Meditations,* in other words, Nietzsche becomes a *historical* thinker. In its wish to transfigure the all and fix it in an eternal tableau, the *Birth* is preoccupied with visual metaphors for existence; the *Untimely Meditations,* by contrast, relies on temporal metaphors, images of history.[2]

In the *Birth* the tragic poet is the bringer of a collective integrity and freedom that supersedes the individual. The emblem of this liberation, for Nietzsche, is the archaic Greek polis. But Nietzsche in the

Birth remains (somewhat covertly, to be sure) fixated by the particular object of desire, the place of the Lacanian object *a*. (In the last of the *Untimely Meditations* the object *a* will be connected to the obsessive, elusive effects of Wagner's music.) Nietzsche's effort to free himself, or his text, from such fixation requires him to cast tragedy in the role of a redemptive, universal genre.

Tragedy in the *Birth* transcends the level of individuality, and therefore cures us of the peculiarity, the individual character, of our desire. In *The Birth of Tragedy*, Nietzsche writes that in Greek tragedy "the artist . . . has already been released [erlöst] from his individual will, and has become, as it were, the medium through which the one truly existent subject celebrates his release in appearance [seine Erlösung im Scheine]" (*BT* 52; *KSA* 1.47). In *Untimely Meditations* Nietzsche will abandon his search for such a redemptive solution, an *Erlösung*, and direct his attention instead to the individual, finding that our singular projects of self-creation do not need to be, and ought not to be, supplanted by a Dionysian world harmony that would dissolve our individuality. After *The Birth of Tragedy*, in other words, Nietzsche encounters the object *a* as cause of the individual's desire, in a way that the *Birth*'s interest in a superindividual and impersonal realm prevented him from doing.

THE OBJECT *A* DEFINED; EGO IDEAL AND OBJECT *A*; NIETZSCHE'S WAGNER

Lacan thinks of the object *a* as a permanent frustration for any self that wishes to assume its integrity, its satisfying wholeness. For Lacan, this wish, the satisfaction derived from the self picturing its own seamless unity, provides the origin of our humanness (in the famous mirror stage). The problem is that the unity is illusory. Malcolm Bowie comments that, for Lacan, the "permanent tendency of the individual" is "throughout life to seek and foster the imaginary wholeness of an 'ideal ego.' But this imaginary unity is an effort to find ways round certain inescapable factors of lack, absence and incompleteness in human living."[3] The object *a* can take the form of a momentary effect or impression that seduces, like Wagner's music as Nietzsche describes it, or it may be a glimpsed, alien presence, like the alluring figure of woman in *The Gay Science*. In either case, the object *a* presents itself as (in Joan Copjec's words) "a lost part of ourselves, whose absence prevents us from becoming whole." We can never possess this lost part—it remains "a disfiguring surplus" because we can never actually have it and have our own completeness with it.[4] The object *a*, then, as the self's crucial, secretive "missing piece," becomes a source of torment. The particularity of the object *a* and the fact that it cannot be readily possessed demonstrate that the self remains fundamentally wounded or incomplete. The object *a*, then, is a piece of the Real, which cannot be assimilated in Symbolic terms.

Renata Salecl describes the object *a* as a hole in reality demonstrating that reality's wholeness is an illusion:

> Our perception of reality is linked to the fact that something has to be precluded from it: the object as the point of the gaze. Every screen of reality includes a constitutive "stain," the trace of what had to be precluded from the field of reality in order that this field can [*sic*] acquire its consistency; this stain appears in the guise of a void Lacan names object *a*. It is the point that I, the subject, cannot see: it eludes me insofar as it is the point from which the screen itself "returns the gaze," or watches me, that is, the point where the gaze itself is inscribed into the visual field of reality.[5]

In Salecl's rendition of Lacan the object *a* is the stain or trace that mars (and is necessary to) the otherwise seamless screen of reality. This notion of the trace differs dramatically from Derrida's (which implies, through the endless mobility of iteration, a freedom to alter or rewrite the cause of things). For Lacan the object *a* is an indissoluble entity, one not subject to revision in the Derridean manner. It is unavoidably potent in its status as the one thing that has *necessarily* been left out of our otherwise consistent world. In Salecl's phrase, it, the object *a*, "watches me," in what looks like a daemonic parody of the confirmation of self the ego ideal provides (since the ego ideal observes me from the place from which I want to be seen, and thus constitutes me as a lovable or ideal subject).[6]

In Lacan's terms, the ego ideal is the big Other, assuring the subject of his place in the Symbolic order and protecting him against the object-cause of desire, the object *a*. (The ideal ego, by contrast, is an Imaginary entity, confirming the subject in his coherence and integrity by providing a perfect image of these qualities: the role of Apollonian art.)[7] In *The Birth of Tragedy*, it is Wagner who functions as ego ideal, the counter to and defense against the object *a*. Nietzsche begins his text by imagining Wagner's enjoyment as he sees his own image, the image of the master, reflected in Nietzsche's prose: "I picture the moment when you, my highly respected friend, will receive this essay. Perhaps after an evening walk in the winter snow, you will behold Prometheus unbound on the title page, read my name, and be convinced at once that . . . the author . . . as he hatched these ideas . . . was communicating with you as if you were present, and hence could write down only what was in keeping with that presence" (*BT* 31).

In Nietzsche's somewhat embarrassing, because too overt, expression of Wagner's meaning for him, the very thought of Wagner confirms and supports the young Nietzsche's mastery. Slavoj Zizek writes that "what characterizes the Master is a speech-act that wholly absorbs me, in which 'I am what I say,' in short, a fully realized, self-contained performative."[8] In consequence, the auditor, or disciple, becomes an author equivalent to the master. Nietzsche, in the passage I have quoted, finds himself reflected by the Master's gesture, by Wagner's perfect reading of him. The one who reads and what is read coincide completely, in the fully realized performative Zizek describes.

"To incarnate in the other the answer that is already there" is Lacan's fine description of the aim of the classical dialogue, and Nietzsche in the *Birth*'s invocations of Wagner aims at such incarnation.[9] Nietzsche, by his writing, brings to birth in Wagner the rebirth of tragedy itself. In Wagner's own work, such perfect coincidence of master and disciple tends to veer off into a tangled, loving, destructive fantasy that entails a desperate loss of mastery: for example, when Brünnhilde reads Wotan's thoughts and, in reckless loyalty to the father who has commanded her otherwise, saves Sieglinde in Act 2 of *Die Walküre*. In a Wagnerian instance like this one, desire steps in in answer to a failed performative (Wotan's command), a perceived gap between what is spoken and the person who speaks. The moment this gap appears, the sign of mastery's failure appears with it. Nietzsche's later acknowledgment of this sign, of Wagner's failed presence, or of a Wagner present in the form of his failure, marks the turn to the historical and individualist perspective that succeeds *The Birth of Tragedy* in Nietzsche's career.

Given Nietzsche's recognition of the richness of Wagner's reflection on the question of mastery, Nietzsche's relation to Wagner cannot possibly be as transparent, as perfectly coincident, as Nietzsche envisions it in the Preface to the *Birth*. Wagner's work, writes Nietzsche, implies that tragic ecstasy has returned; but Wagner's supposed wish for Nietzsche the disciple to announce this return is complicated by an obscurity. What does Wagner want from his audience, from his followers? In his final *Untimely Meditation*, "Wagner in Bayreuth," Nietzsche pictures a Wagner brooding, closed within himself, placing his disciples in doubt. Similarly, Wotan's wish in the *Ring* for the birth of the free hero, Sieglinde's child Siegfried, whose independence will allow him to know Wotan's will, is disrupted by his own darkness and ruinous doubt. The immaculate self-reflection the philosopher desires ("I, Plato, am the truth," as Nietzsche describes the first stage of philosophical assurance in *Twilight of the Idols*) is here made subject to an alluring and flawed relation between master and disciple. Authority is incarnated in a teacher (Socrates, Wagner) who guides his students by remaining, finally, inaccessible.[10]

In the Preface to *The Birth of Tragedy,* Nietzsche tries to place himself in the sight of the master, the ego ideal, to make himself lovable. But this attempt remains complicated by the object *a:* the real cause of desire, the thing in Wagner (and therefore in Nietzsche) that exceeds the confirmation of the ego ideal. Nietzsche, in a late work like *Ecce Homo,* will embrace the object *a* in the uncanny or otherworldly character of Wagner's music. The *Birth,* by contrast, tries to evade the object *a,* casting it as the aspect of the Dionysian that renders up not universal harmony but an especially fascinating or even gruesome point of dissonance.

THE SCREEN OF REALITY

"A personal influence is an *ignis fatuus,*" Emerson writes in "Nominalist and Realist," aptly conveying the delusive, elusive element that Nietzsche in his later works will feel as the Wagner effect, or affect (*E* 577). Emerson goes on to even out this bias. Great men (Washington and Franklin are Emerson's examples) "loom and fade before the eternal": "Wherever you go, a wit like your own has been before you, and has realized its thought. . . . I am very much struck in literature by the appearance that one person wrote all the books" (*E* 577–79). In Emerson, often, a proper grasp of universality seems to correct our lack of power when we are faced with the influences that intrigue and master us. The sense for the universal enables us to restate our fascination in broader terms. As Emerson's essay "Montaigne" puts it, for "a man of thought . . . the universe is saturated with deity and with law," and knowing this "he can behold with serenity" the shortcomings of his performance and the frustration of his desire, "the yawning gulf . . . between the supply and the demand of power" (*E* 708). And at the end of Nietzsche's Emerson-influenced school essay, "Fate and History," we are saved from being the mere "playthings of our own fantasies [wir selbst Spielbälle unsrer Phantasien]" by the hypothesis of an overruling, universal fate: "There must be higher principles, before which all differences flow together in a great unity."[11]

In the *Birth* as in Emerson, the thinker's artistry achieves its effects in part by evoking the universal: by underlining the way in which the screen of reality is a "great unity," a closed and perfect entity. Such wholeness provides proof of the strength of the aesthetic perspective, its success in justifying or completing (*Recht-fertigen*) the world. Nietzsche moves beyond Schopenhauer by claiming the efficacy of aesthetic participation as a means of freeing us from everyday obsessional practice, whereas Schopenhauer depicted humans as slipping back inevitably from the universal concerns of the contemplative aesthete to the tenacious and petty force of the will that is captivated by the object *a*.[12] Arguing against Schopenhauer, Nietzsche transfigures the will itself into a force that reaches toward artistry by means of the "art impulses of nature [Kunsttriebe der Natur]" (*BT* 38; *KSA* 1.31) and urges us to see beyond the individual.[13]

Tragedy is the necessary goal of Nietzsche's scheme precisely because it allows us to enter a realm in which individuality is superseded. According to Nietzsche, the lyric poet Archilochus falls short of the transformation from individual to collective that only tragedy can provide. Archilochus translates his private passions into the realm of art, freeing himself from the will by mirroring it in poetry: Archilochus is "completely released [losgelöst] from the greed of the will" (*BT* 55; *KSA* 1.51). But Archilochus does not go all the way with this redemptive possibility because, as a lyric rather than a tragic poet, he remains captive to an Apollonian *Bild* or construction of the self. He presents himself to the audience as an image turned shield-like against his own particular desire, and also against theirs; but he cannot invite the audience to enter into a freeing, impersonal art as the tragic poet can. Tragedy, writes Nietzsche, offers by contrast a participatory rite, "a new world of symbols" of an incarnational sort, allowing the audience to be born again into a clarity that individuation has denied them. This "ganze leibliche Symbolik" provides a language that has become wholly shared and embodied (*BT* 40; *KSA* 1.33).

In *The Birth of Tragedy,* Nietzsche attacks the shining edifice of the Apollonian in the interest of this collective incarnational vision. He will dismantle, "stone by stone," the "artistic structure [kunstvolle Gebäude] of Apollonian culture," in order to discern the Dionysian gulf it is founded upon (*BT* 41; *KSA* 1.34). The *Birth*'s continual battle between Apollo and Dionysus is also a kind of marriage, a procreative bond. This struggle bears witness to the triumph of the Dionysian, as the principle that reduces Apollonian individual identity to a fragile, transitory stay against the greater reality of cosmic union.

Despite the victory of the Dionysian that he depicts in the *Birth,* Nietzsche finds himself unable to assert the wholeness of Dionysus in any consistent manner. Instead, we learn, the Dionysian is really an abyss, already marked by the Real—a mark that appears as object *a,* the special thing that draws just me, but *is* always beyond me, more than me. The Dionysian is torn or wounded by individuation, precisely because it is the individual (Hamlet, Oedipus) who looks into it: forbidden to cross over into harmony because he remains lured by a singular question, the object-cause of his desire (the object *a*).

Dionysus, then, needs to be supplemented by Apollo so that Nietzsche can tame the disturbances of desire. The Apollonian principle is for Nietzsche a way to heal the injury at the core of personal identity. This injury, the primal wound or incompleteness associated with individuation, is referred to repeatedly in *The Birth of Tragedy.* But the character of the wound requires further explication. If Apollo is the god of art as therapy, "healing and helping in sleep and dreams," if aesthetic representation *as such* cures, what is the sickness that demands this cure? The Apollonian self's comfort or satisfaction seems to be a kind of self-admiration, the calling into being of a radiant fantasy, just as Faust calls Helen into being as the sign of his own power to idealize existence (*BT* 41, 113). But what is it that requires idealization? Not, I suggest, a monstrous reality swelling up behind the façade of idealized or falsely beautified existence, but rather the very gap that makes reality possible, the remainder that cannot be integrated: the object *a.*

For a more complete understanding of the *Birth*'s evasion of the object *a,* we must look behind Nietzsche's presentation to his Schopenhauerian source, and also to two other works of the 1870s, the essays "On Truth and Lie in the Extra-Moral Sense" and "On the Pathos of

Truth." In the *Birth* Nietzsche portrays individual existence trapped by the will as something necessarily imperfect or partial, an "incompletely intelligible everyday world [lückenhaft verständliche Tageswirklichkeit]" (*BT* 35; *KSA* 1.27) that is also, as in the case of Archilochus, the realm of "willing, longing, moaning, rejoicing" (*BT* 55). The Apollonian art of the dreamer, as Nietzsche depicts it in chapter 1 of the *Birth*, creates a seamless "world of fantasy" (*BT* 35) in place of this fragmented everydayness: "all forms speak to us; there is nothing unimportant or superfluous" (*BT* 34).

The discovery of our fragmentation is itself an interruption, rising with absurd abruptness in the course of our normal existence. In other words, we usually do assume the sensible continuity of ordinary life, and we are therefore shocked by our sudden discovery that the ordinary is broken, unhealed. Citing Schopenhauer, Nietzsche writes that this momentary lack of harmony in our usual worldly existence, the stumbling upon an exception to the "Satz vom Grund," the rule of sufficient reason that makes everyday life run smoothly and unexceptionally, causes a "tremendous *terror* [das ungeheuere *Grausen*]." This feeling of horror indicates our sense that the *principium individuationis* has for a moment broken down (*BT* 36; *KSA* 1.28). Nietzsche thus associates stark and ungovernable feeling both with the ground of individual personality, in his discussion of Archilochus's tormented desire, and with the perception that such individuality is really groundless, that the ego is an illusion. In both cases, such pathos of the abrupt, the interrupted, stands for an incompleteness that only art can remedy.

Nietzsche here alludes to chapter 63 of the first volume of Schopenhauer's *The World as Will and Idea*. Since he cites on the same page of the *Birth* Schopenhauer's image of the *principium individuationis* as a frail boat surrounded by a raging ocean, a passage that in Schopenhauer's chapter 63 directly precedes the discussion of the exception (*Ausnahme*) suffered by the principle of sufficient reason, we can safely assume that Nietzsche brooded over the logic of this Schopenhauerian argument. Schopenhauer writes:

> The eyes of the uncultured individual [den Blick des rohen Individuums] are clouded, as the Indians say, by the veil of Maya. To him is revealed not the thing-in-itself, but only the phenomenon in time and space, in the *principium individuationis*, and in the remaining forms of the principle of sufficient reason. . . .

[H]e sees not the inner nature of things, which is one, but its phenomena as separated, detached, innumerable . . . pleasure appears to him as one thing, and pain as quite another; one man as tormenter and murderer, another as martyr and victim. . . . He then asks where retribution is to be found [Dann fragt er: wo bleibt die Vergeltung?]. . . . He often tries to escape by wickedness, in other words, by causing another's suffering, from the evil, from the suffering of his own individuality, involved as he is in the *principium individuationis*, deluded by the veil of Maya. Just as the boatman sits in his small boat, trusting his frail craft in a stormy sea that is boundless in every direction, rising and falling with the howling, mountainous waves, so in the midst of a world full of suffering and misery the individual man calmly sits, supported by and trusting the *principium individuationis*. . . . The boundless world, everywhere full of suffering in the infinite past, in the infinite future, is strange to him. (*WWI* 1.352–53)[14]

The individual's fragile devotion to his self-interest is shaken when the principle of sufficient reason suffers an exception, an *Ausnahme* or *taking away* of the ground (we can compare Nietzsche's use in *The Birth of Tragedy* of *entsetzlich,* which means "terrible" but derives from *entsetzen,* to remove). Here Schopenhauer proclaims the appearance of an uncanny phase in which what is most immediate is not what is present, the individual's palpable objects of desire or hatred, but rather what invades presence from the past or future. The individual, Schopenhauer writes, experiences a "wholly obscure presentiment" [ganz dunkle Ahnung] that gives birth to a "dread [Grausen] common to all human beings," "which suddenly seizes them, when . . . the principle of sufficient reason in one or other of its forms seems to undergo an exception [Ausnahme]. For example, when it appears that some change has occurred without a cause, or a deceased person exists again [ein Gestorbener wieder da wäre]; or when in any other way the past or the future is present, or the distant is near" (*WWI* 1.353).[15] Schopenhauer quickly works through this uncanny phase in which death haunts life, and lays this uncanniness to rest in philosophy's realization that past, present, and future, pain and pleasure, life and death, are finally all one. "Eternal justice," Schopenhauer goes on to say, rests on the fleeting recognition that there is no fixed separation between the individual and the universal stream of life. The jarring of

the *principium individuationis,* the individual's realization that the time
is haunted or out of joint, as when a dead person suddenly appears before us and is "wieder da," or "when . . . the past or the future is present":
such disturbance submits to reconciliation, according to Schopenhauer, when we adopt a universal perspective, the perspective of the
will to live. No longer disrupted and disruptive, but rather eternally
just, life now appears a panorama of suffering that makes sense and
that is all of a piece, with no lingering division between wrong and
right, evil and good, murderer and victim.

Schopenhauer, then, tries to extricate his text from a repetition-
compulsion, an uncanny automatism that turns the foreign into the
immediate, the dead into the living. He wants to escape from the un-
easy moment "when it appears that . . . the distant is near," when a
spontaneous and oddly automatic intervention makes a hole in reality. In Salecl's words, the Lacanian Real as uncanny repetition, associated with the object *a,* is that which paradoxically cannot be included
in our narrative or picture of existence, that which cannot be effec-
tively remembered: it "cannot ever be forgotten in the first place,
since it repeats itself incessantly."[16] Nietzsche in *The Birth of Tragedy,*
like Schopenhauer, buries the uncanniness that testifies to the object
a, the exceptional character of the object of desire that endows it with
the power of haunting. But the corpse of the uncanny, the Real as object *a,* pops up repeatedly in Nietzsche. Dionysian universality as
Nietzsche depicts it is not merely harmonious and fluid but also torn
and terrible, the object of a gruesome fascination: "that horrible mix-
ture of sensuality and cruelty [abscheuliche Mischung von Wollust
und Grausamkeit] which has always seemed to me the real 'witch's
brew'" (*BT* 39; *KSA* 1.32). This magic requires a counterspell on the
part of Apollo, an aestheticizing defense against the odd, perhaps
even monstrous positions we occupy as creatures of desire.

The incompleteness that Nietzsche sees in us, the realm of the object *a,* he associates with the Dionysian—more specifically, with the Dionysian resistance to the Apollonian faculty of organization. Nietzsche's
ambivalence, his depiction of Dionysian ecstasy both as a realm of peace
and harmony and as a cruel witches' brew, reflects a division in his text.
On the one hand, he sees Apollonian art as a self-mirroring on the part
of the Dionysian impulse toward seamless universality, an impulse that
demands a marriage with the Apollonian because it wants to represent
and perceive itself. On the other hand, the Apollonian holds up an apo-

tropaic Gorgon shield, warding off the Dionysian (which now represents the frightening brokenness of existence) by means of a monstrous "Medusenhaupt" (*BT* 39; *KSA* 1,32).

When describing the Apollonian project in the *Birth*, Nietzsche repeatedly resorts to images of projection: the tragic hero, he writes in chapter 9, is "nothing but a bright image projected on a dark wall" (*BT* 67). Like the tragic Oedipus, the Socratic reasoner is also a sort of shadow on the cave's wall, peering into the "Unaufhellbare," the unrevealable, uncanny object that confronts him, and that by definition cannot be illuminated (*BT* chap. 15). In order to combat this object, Nietzsche in the *Birth* needs to argue for the fundamental fact of Dionysian universality: the transindividual will evoked by music and disclosed by the tragic chorus. The "most important insight of aesthetics," he writes, following Schopenhauer, is that music is different from the other arts, "not a copy of the phenomenon, but an immediate copy of the will itself" (*BT* 100).

The *Birth* needs a literalism of the will in order to establish superindividual, Dionysian nature as a consoling fact against the uncanny object *a*. This consolation is upheld by Nietzsche's fragmentary essay of the 1870s, "On the Pathos of Truth," but it is destroyed by the nearly contemporaneous (and better known) fragment, "On Truth and Lie in the Extra-Moral Sense." "On Truth and Lie" claims the irreplaceable status of metaphor. The essay stations poetic before literal meaning; by doing so, it unravels the *Birth*'s claim that music, as the natural or literal mirror of the will, has priority over other forms of expression.[17]

"On Truth and Lie," with its portrait of truth as "a mobile army of tropes, metaphors, and anthropomorphisms," famously asserts an aggressive sense of metaphoricity, or carrying-over itself, rather than what is carried over, as founding fact. "On the Pathos of Truth," by contrast, aims to disclose the object as such, the dreadful vista lurking beneath all our rhetoric. "On the Pathos of Truth" ends with a debate between the artist and the philosopher on what to do about our life of illusion. Life, for each individual, Nietzsche writes in an inflammatory fantasy, means hanging in dreams on the back of a tiger. (Both essays use the image of the tiger: presumably, the predatory drives which crystallize only in our dreams, and which we tame in those dreams, riding them as Plato rode the horses of madness.) The artist, predictably, calls for the dreamer to dream on—"Let him hang on!"—that is, to esteem the fabulous continuity of fantasy above all else. The philosopher, with his pathos of truth, wants the dreamer to awaken, but he fails to recognize that the waking world he calls for, or calls forth, is itself merely another dream, a fantasy about the ideas or the immortal soul (*KSA* 1.760). Because "*it* wants life," Nietzsche here gives art the advantage over the philosopher's knowledge. But the life that art desires is secured only by our trust in what fantasy provides, and is therefore only available if we turn away from the realm the *Birth* called the "real" Dionysian witches' brew.

The true contours of the tiger's back, Nietzsche writes in "On the Pathos of Truth," can be seen in the "greedy, insatiable, disgusting, pitiless, murderous" facts of life (*KSA* 1.760). Nietzsche here gives us one of his most remarkable fantasies, of life as a savage and relentless, but beautiful, predation. I am relying on Lacan's definition of fantasy as the primal support of reality, as the force that eclipses or smoothes over the Real. Fantasy makes "the world . . . symmetrical to the subject," Lacan says, and thus enables "the subject . . . [to] believe that the world kn[ows] as much about things as he d[oes]."[18] "A scene of passive suffering (subjection) is staged which simultaneously sustains and threatens the subject's being," Zizek comments on the fundamental fantasy described in Freud's "'A Child Is Being Beaten.'"[19]

In the case of Nietzsche's tiger, as in that of Freud's beaten child, the very thrilling violence of the fantasy is in the service of the subject's consistency of being: its intensity suffices to eclipse the hidden term in its structure. In Freud, the hidden term is the father who is beating me; in Nietzsche, it is the *Spalte* or gap beneath the tiger's daemonic strength. When we read "On the Pathos of Truth" through the lens of "On Truth and Lie," what we see is not the sublime or supernatural dominion of a glorious beast, the proverbial monster from the Id, but rather a glimpse of our own mean, ineradicable frustration. This frustration, the mark of the Real, of an excessive object that cannot be properly placed (the object *a*), impels us to construct a fantasy like that of the tiger's back. It spurs the "greedy, insatiable" rage that Nietzsche discerns underneath heroic strength.

This voice of Nietzschean melodrama, the roaring of its tiger, raises a Lacanian question about the place of fantasy as the basis for our sense of reality, in its triumph over the Real and the object *a*: over what doesn't make sense, but draws us nonetheless, the missing piece of our identity. In an effort to avoid confronting this missing piece, the individual's artistry dreams not just the saving fantasy, the boat in the midst of the storm, but the storm itself, the flagrant predator within us, the sublime, ravaging will. The hole torn in reality's fantasy-support may indeed be the effect of the Real, but when we look into, or through, that hole, we can see at all only by fashioning another fantasy: the tiger that carries us.[20] The thing itself, the object *a,* will continue to resist our sight.

In "On Truth and Lie" Nietzsche offers a classical demonstration of such fantasy construction by showing how any foundational image regresses behind the rhetoric that expresses it, leaving us with no ground to stand on (or no beast to ride). "What is a word?" Nietzsche asks. "The image of a nerve-stimulus [Nervenreiz] in sound. . . . A nerve stimulus carried over into an image [Bild]! first metaphor. The image stamped again [wieder nachgeformt] in a sound! second metaphor" (*KSA* 1.879). In Greek *metaphorein* means, famously, "to carry over." The first metaphor that Nietzsche refers to is, we surmise, not merely the carrying over (*Übertragen*) or, as it were, *metamorphorizing* of a nerve-stimulus into an image, but also, or rather, the metaphor of such a carrying-over. If the action of metaphor, of carrying, is itself a metaphor (why not an invasion, a seepage, a transubstantial sharing?), so also is the thing that is carried, the nerve-stimulus (what kind of stimulus? a tickling? a rubbing? If so, of what on what?).

The *Bild* depicts a nerve-stimulus but also, more boldly, pictures a *Bild* as the best image, or version (translation?), of a word. The second metaphor, *via* its word *Nachformen,* impresses or molds the visual onto the sonic much as the *Birth* gives an Apollonian form to the Dionysian. A word is neither a felt gesture (stimulus), nor a visible one (picture), nor a heard one (speech) . . . but we must give it forms like these in order to see/hear/feel it at all. Such metaphors are not just a gift-giving, but also an act of theft testifying to what Emerson in "Experience" calls the "evanescence and lubricity of all objects," and proving the faultiness of the handle, the "unhandsome"ness of what we rely on when we employ, as we must, metaphors to grasp life (*E* 473).[21] Nietzsche's passage sees (writes, hears) a spoken sound as a kind of picture, but to do so means to steal the realm of sound and recast it as vision. Owen Barfield writes, perhaps thinking of his own double profession of literary critic and barrister, that "one meaning is apprehended transpiring through another."[22] To catch such a thief would be like arresting the breath that expresses us.

When Nietzsche relies in the *Birth* on the image of the abyss beneath us, it is not usually the churning urn of a ravenous id and its monsters that he sees, despite his references to the Dionysian revel as a thrilling, unholy witch's brew. In place of this fantastic potboiler Nietzsche, as the *Birth* continues, gives us a more convincing image of the Real. The image is more convincing because more elusive, and lacking the contours of gothic fantasy: that which resists light or meaning, *das Unaufhellbare*.[23] Similarly, for the Emerson of "Experience" "the art of life has a pudency, which will not be exposed" (*E* 483): the obliqueness of our relations produces an opacity.

HAMLET AND OEDIPUS IN *THE BIRTH OF TRAGEDY*

Cavell remarks that Hamlet's nausea, as noticed by Nietzsche in chapter 7 of the *Birth*, carries "the sense of the unbearableness of human action—of its overdetermination and its overindebtedness, as of the unreachableness of justice."[24] The mention of Hamlet, as of Oedipus, alerts us that dreams, at least in tragic drama, do not take the form of a cocoon or safe illusion, despite Nietzsche's emphasis on the dreamer's heroic security in chapter 1 of the *Birth*. Instead, even when bounded in a nutshell, the dreamer experiences a violated, unbalanced world, one whose bearing toward us, like our implication in it, is almost intolerable. We are soiled in this world's working, wrong as well as wronged in it.

Yet because such wrongness, imbalance, or (to again use one of Cavell's words) *oddness* appears as a challenge, it tempts us to heroic transgression. Nietzsche, in his portrait of Oedipus, writes that "where prophetic and magical powers have broken the spell of present and future, the rigid law of individuation, and the real magic of nature, some enormously unnatural event [eine ungeheuere Naturwidrigkeit]— such as incest—must have occurred earlier, as a cause. How else could one compel nature to surrender her secrets if not by triumphantly resisting her, that is, by means of something unnatural?" (*BT* 68–69). Here Oedipus seduces nature, the mother, and forces her "to surrender her secrets." A Promethean conqueror, he trespasses into the forbidden world, the beyond, and survives, living on as a sacred monster. We can now begin to understand why *The Birth of Tragedy* so consistently connects the three figures of Prometheus, Oedipus, and Hamlet (as well as, a bit later on, Socrates). Nietzsche in his description of Oedipus reveals (i.e., gives fantasy-supported reality to) the undiscovered country that Hamlet evokes, the bourn from which no traveler returns: not merely death, but whatever morbid post-mortem animation death might veil, the realm of possibility that Hamlet in his most famous soliloquy pictures as undead survival plagued by bad dreams.

Nietzsche, commenting on Raphael's *Transfiguration* in chapter 4 of the *Birth,* argues that the "possessed," "confounded," and "terrified" sufferings of the figures on the ground generate a heavenly vision of a new, blissful "world of illusion [Scheinwelt]" (the upper half of the painting, centered on the floating Christ) (*BT* 25, translation modified).[25] In Nietzsche's description of it, the bifurcated vision of the *Transfiguration* shows how to extract a bright world of art out of the dark one of the will's pains. By contrast, Prometheus, Oedipus, and Hamlet make darkness visible by transfiguring the impossible object of desire into a forbidden one, cursed and therefore also cruelly blessed. What Hamlet and Oedipus have in common is their fixation, their violent devotion to unveiling an inaccessible secret. The secret occupies a place that is by definition impossible, and that therefore must be covered by fantasy. This impossibility derives from the fact that, as Oedipus learns, *you are whom you seek.*

This last point deserves elaboration. Zizek, citing Lacan's eleventh Seminar, *The Four Fundamental Concepts of Psychoanalysis,* writes that

> the essential feature of the scopic drive is "se faire voir" (making oneself seen). However . . . this "making oneself seen" . . . must not be confused with the narcissistic "looking at oneself through the other," i.e., through the eyes of the big Other, from the point of the Ego-Ideal in the Other, in the form in which I appear to myself to be worthy of love: what is lost when I "look at myself through the other" is the radical heterogeneity of the objet qua gaze to which I expose myself in "making oneself seen."[26]

Looking at oneself through the big Other—what Nietzsche did with the image of Wagner at the beginning of the *Birth,* as we have seen—is in fact a good description of the Apollonian ideal. In the Apollonian, as Lacan puts it in one of his rare references to a Nietzschean term, the gaze is pacified, laid down like a weapon.[27] Such secure self-observation, which would ground my identity as knowing subject, is disrupted by the scopic drive with its possibility of exposure, of being caught in the act of seeing ("the objet qua gaze to which I expose myself"). What is revealed in such a moment is the fact that I am not identical to my idea of myself as safe, because hidden, observer: I become the object as well as the subject of sight. (Zizek's example here is the great moment in Hitchcock's *Rear Window* when the murderer Raymond Burr confronts James Stewart's voyeuristic desire, asking, "What do you want from me? . . . Say something. Tell me what you want.")[28] This turning of the tables on the viewer forms a pivotal moment in tragedy: in the Oedipus story, when Oedipus is exposed as being himself the unbearable monster he seeks, blindness being a literalizing of this exposure, in *Hamlet*, to the degree that Hamlet's fascination with maternal sexuality makes him identify with Claudius, thus accounting for his delay;[29] and finally, in Euripides' *Bacchae*, whose hero Pentheus finds himself driven to transform himself into one of Dionysus's female celebrants, caught in the shameful posture of transvestism. In these tragic turnabouts or capsizings, the Apollonian calling forth of a godlike image of self finds itself suddenly reversed into the radical exposure of self. Fascinated and helpless, I am subject to the object *a* in the form of the gaze: that view of me that testifies to my incompleteness, the permanent insolubility of my desire.

The reversal finds decisive embodiment in the unexpectedness of Dionysus's arrival.[30] For the Euripides of the *Bacchae*, Dionysus himself can stand for the potency of the object *a*. In the *Bacchae*, Pentheus's architectonic solidity, the self-assurance of the ruler of Thebes, is upset by the lure of the mask, the object *a* that calls to him as a lost part of himself. Seeing this reversal of Apollonian security into Dionysian disruption, big Other into object *a*, allows us to understand why Nietzsche in the *Birth* moves on from epic and lyric poetry, with their ostensibly perfect achievement of self-reflection, to tragic catastrophe. But Nietzsche's picture of the Dionysian as the ground of the world, a maneuver allied to his claim for music as the basic metaphor of the will, is designed to conceal the traumatic character of the object *a*, which colors the Dionysian (as both Euripides and Nietzsche realize).

At moments, in the *Birth*, Nietzsche conceals the object *a* by portraying the Dionysian as monstrous. He points to the *unaufhellbar* abyss behind Apollonian form, a world of fearsome, half-glimpsed partial objects, like the dances that Pentheus sees and joins in the *Bacchae* and that tear him to pieces. Nietzsche recovers from this perception by remaking the Dionysian into a different sort of fantasy: turning it into an inchoate version of universal harmony, which requires only a marriage with Apollo to complete it. Both of these images are projections, however—the first as much as the second. The churning urn or witch's brew tames the object *a* of desire by transforming its crucial characteristic, its impossibility, into a hidden place, the forbidden. In a similar way, Zizek notes, the incest prohibition transforms the impossible into the forbidden. Contrary to the prohibition's claim, the incestuous object does not actually exist. Even if you "really" sleep with your mother, you do not gain access to a realm behind that of the Symbolic law, but instead possess a Symbolic object, one that exists only insofar as it is prohibited.[31] Promethean-heroic transgression remains an impossible endeavor. The disruption that troubles Nietzsche, then, does not arise from a primordial realm prior to civilized life (the enacting of incest), but instead serves as the originating impulse to transform life, to make a harmony that can overcome such disturbance.

I have mentioned that the Apollonian realm of dreaming, as Nietzsche describes it in chapter 1 of the *Birth*, seems to offer complete intelligibility, in contrast to the flawed and partial world of everyday existence. Apollo, god of dreams, overcomes the object *a*, the irritating and fascinating psychic fragment that suggests the fact that our identity cannot be parsed or made sense of, by means of the fantasy, the aesthetic work that supports our perception of reality. The object *a*, the phantasmic thing, is the piece of flesh or crystallized stuff that causes our desire and so exposes us to an image of the self as necessarily incomplete, since its identity resides in an inescapable flaw.

In the interest of overcoming the object *a*, Apollo builds the fantasy of the grounded, seamless, self-observant *I*, the perfectly staged ideal ego. The Apollonian dream world, Nietzsche notices, feels more authentic than our waking existence, because it offers the perfection of fantasy that constitutes what we call reality: a seamless, reliable screen for our projections. The Apollonian dreamer decides the dream's shape and continuity, announcing to himself, "I will dream on!" (*BT* 35). The Dionysian, by contrast, testifies to an unsubstitutable lack, "a yearning lamentation for an irreplaceable loss" ("einen unersetzlichen Verlust"— *BT* 40, translation modified; *KSA* 1.33). However much the Dionysian festival aims at an aestheticized repairing of bodily existence, "the intuition of a oneness produced once again" (*BT* 74, translation modified; *KSA* 1.73: "die Ahnung einer wiederhergestellten Einheit"), it still suggests the painful incompleteness that attends individuation.

Nietzsche's interest in the Apollonian in the early sections of *The Birth of Tragedy* implies a defense of poetry as a shield against the traumatic fragmentation associated with Dionysus. For Nietzsche, unlike Schopenhauer, the shield works. Nietzsche uses as his polemical target in the *Birth* a passage from *World as Will and Idea* in which Schopenhauer asserts that, for both the singer of lyric and its audience, "we follow" the artistic metamorphosis of personal misery into beauty, "but only for moments; willing, desire, the remembrance of our own personal ends, tears us anew from peaceful contemplation" (*BT* 51). In Schopenhauer the poet and his readers alike resemble the frustrated Orpheus who breaks faith with representation and turns around—with disastrous effect—to see his Eurydice, the beloved immediacy his art can only shadow. For Nietzsche, arguing against Schopenhauer in the *Birth*, art poses itself against reality not by offering a momentary escape but by presenting a permanently greater reality. Art's reality, Nietzsche writes, offers an unbroken solid state of perfected fantasy, the "unvarnished expression of the truth [der ungeschminkte Ausdruck der Wahrheit]" (*BT* 61; *KSA* 1.58).

In *The Birth of Tragedy*, then, Nietzsche expounds in some detail his anti-Schopenhauerian point about the efficacy of artistic representation. For Nietzsche, unlike Schopenhauer, art triumphs over the rawness of the world. Nietzsche cites approvingly Schiller's idea of tragic art as a weapon against crude, untransfigured reality, with its chorus, rather like Perseus's Gorgon shield, forming "a living wall that tragedy constructs around itself in order to close itself off from the world of reality [von der wirklichen Welt] and to *preserve* [bewahren] its ideal domain [Boden] and its poetic freedom" (*BT* 58, italics added; *KSA* 1.54). Here, Nietzsche's *bewahren* conjures up *Wahrheit*, truth, against the mere efficacy, or *wirken*, of reality (*die wirkliche Welt*).

PLATO AND NIETZSCHE ON POETRY

In addition to correcting Schopenhauer, Nietzsche argues against Plato in the *Birth*'s defense of poetry. Poetry's first crime, according to Plato, is its addiction to a closeted pathos. He writes in the *Republic* that poets want (in Edward Snow's words) to "keep loss fresh," to nurture it instead of putting it to rest within a larger, calmer perspective.[32] Thus the *Iliad* shows us an insomniac Achilles turning restlessly on the beach, stung by the death of Patroklos: hardly fit behavior for a hero, as Plato reminds us (*Republic* 388a). The other half of the poet's dangerous character, for Plato, shows itself in the way he devotes himself to mere images in preference to a solid, palpable everydayness. Book 10 of the *Republic* asserts that the poet offers a shadowy simulacrum in place of hard reality, substituting a gleaming castle of words for the actual city that surrounds us. Of course, Plato himself also describes a city of words, but *his* text, unlike the poet's, measures itself against the actual world instead of substituting itself for actuality as poetry does. Or so goes the accusation. The philosopher, in his combat with the poet, charges the poet with refusing to ascend to a higher perspective that would be metaphysically defensible, one that would look down on the world we know.

Let us deal with Plato's primary accusation first: that the poet exploits emotion for its own sake, futilely and emptily. In the *Republic* and elsewhere, Plato reacts with profound irritation to the poets' obsessive cultivation of passionate immediacy. To the philosopher, the poet seems interested not in resolving or understanding our desires, but in spurring them along through the force of mood. In Freud's terms, poets are not successful therapists because they take the side of melancholia rather than mourning, indulging unsatisfied desire and unconquerable grief as ends in themselves. It seems that the poets just don't want passion to end.

Plato himself knows that this is not the whole story. In the *Symposium* in particular, poetic pathos unveils itself as a generative force rather than a merely futile and endless desiring. As Nietzsche will do in *The Birth of Tragedy,* Plato in the *Symposium* defends poetry by transfiguring its restless eros into a luminous and concerted metaphysical vision. Plato calls the vision "philosophy," but philosophy here has enlisted poetry in its service. Specifically, Plato's philosophy draws on the poet's ability to transmit an image of desire. The philosopher's project does not stop with the praise of a beloved individual. In the calm, steady light at the end of the philosopher's quest, he sees a cosmos grander in its contours than any particular person, however bright his or her heroism might be. Plato moves beyond the memory of heroes, the concern of epic and tragic poetry, as he rises to the higher plane of philosophical justification. According to Socrates' report of Diotima's speech in the *Symposium,* she asks him to consider how men are in an

> awful state of love . . . wanting to become famous and "to lay up glory immortal forever," and how they're ready to brave any danger

for the sake of this. . . . Do you really think Alcestis would have
died for Admetus . . . or that Achilles would have died after Pa-
troclus . . . if they hadn't expected the memory of their virtue—
which we still hold in honor—to be immortal? . . . I believe that
anyone will do anything for the sake of immortal virtue and the
glorious fame that follows [*kai toiautēs doxēs eukleous*]; and the
better the people, the more they will do, for they are all in love
with immortality. (*Symposium* 208d-e)[33]

In this passage, Diotima's universalizing claim that "anyone will do anything for the sake of immortal virtue" (and for the *doxa* or good opinion attached to it) conflicts with her more discriminating praise for
those "better" individuals who are especially, sublimely, in love with immortality. The universal wins out: near the end of Diotima's speech,
the climactic passage of the *Symposium,* Plato delivers more sublimity
than he gives us in the earlier celebration of heroic deeds I have just
quoted. In accents that carry over into Emerson's essays as well as
Nietzsche's *Birth of Tragedy,* Diotima promises the philosopher a liberating detachment from the particularity of the heroic, in "beauty that
. . . exists in itself and for itself, simple and eternal, in which all beautiful things participate, so that neither birth nor death augments or
diminishes them . . . divine beauty in its unique form" (212a-b). But Diotima's dream of detachment clashes with her enshrining of Achilles, Alcestis, and the rest of the heroes celebrated by "Homer and Hesiod and
the other good poets" (209d). The beauty of heroes' deeds is only particular, after all, and their individual identities are there to be transcended in due time by the philosophical lover who has turned toward
the great ocean of the beautiful (210d).

The dream of philosophy Plato offers at the end of Diotima's
speech is the enfolding of the many in the one, the fantasy of a lover
who is finally able to transcend any particular beloved. If this dream
could be realized, the object *a* would be banished by Plato's philosophy; but the tragic hero, with his insistent, hubristic individuality, resists such transcendence. And Plato allows this resistance to appear
within Diotima's discourse itself.

Diotima reminds us that a perfect lover of the ideal, if he existed,
would be immortal, free from the bondage to mutability that afflicts
the rest of us (212a). Here transcendence is revealed as a gorgeous
dream, probably unattainable by mortals, who see the gleams of per-

fection only in the youths they love and in the heroes described by poets. For Plato, the problem with such attachment to heroic and beloved persons is their insubstantial yet illicitly compelling nature. The philosopher charges that poetry is a world of mere images, of shadowy unrealities. For Plato, one danger of the poetic image resides in its alliance with these shadows: with the subtlety of emotion, which excludes the consolation of philosophy, the sober comfort that would put pain and desire to rest. We find ourselves pursued by a remarkable poetic image as we do by the ghostly presence of the past, and this is a potentially unending occupation. For the logical sentence philosophy seeks in order to wrap up experience in thought, poetry substitutes an inconclusive, obsessive haunting. And philosophy, at least in the Symposium, cannot easily find an answer to poetry's obsessions.

But Plato's treatment of the poetic image also carries an opposite implication, which he develops not in the *Symposium,* but in the *Republic.* Instead of endlessly resonant and troubling, as in Diotima's speech, the poet's image of hero or beloved may be a shallow conjuror's device. From Plato's derogatory perspective in the *Republic,* the poet is a low magician, because he devotes himself to producing soothing, enticing effects. The poet's verbal image appeals in its convenience: it is more manipulable than reality, and therefore better suited to a therapeutic entertainment. According to Plato, poets use the same gimmicks as purveyors of "*trompe l'oeil* painting, conjuring, and other forms of trickery" (*Republic* 602d). The rhapsode of the *Ion* sets out to sway his audience in an artificial, too-easy discipline of showmanship. For Plato, then, we enjoy poetry as we enjoy a magic trick, an avowedly illusory freeing of reality from its usual prosaic constraints.

But poetry, in Plato's *Republic,* is not merely dazzling entertainment. In book 2 of the *Republic,* in the words of Socrates' interlocutor Adeimantus, Plato hints that poetry, as a kind of religious cult, promises a serious suspension of reality's rules:

> They present a noisy throng of books [*bibliôn de homadon parekhontai*] by Musaeus and Orpheus, offspring as they say of Selene and the Muses, in accordance with which they perform their rituals. And they persuade not only individuals but whole cities that the unjust deeds of the living or the dead can be absolved or purified through sacrifices and pleasant games [*dia thusiôn kai paidiâs hēdonôn*], whether those who have committed them are

still alive, or have died. These initiations [*teletas*], as they call them, free people from punishment hereafter, while a terrible fate awaits those who have not performed rituals. (364e)[34]

Plato here suggests that the religious mysteries (or, euphemistically, "pleasant games") poetry offers, like other Greek cult practices, express a deep interest in expiating crime and avoiding punishment. The poet and his audience collaborate in evading the more serious court of justice shadowed in the action of the *Republic* itself, the one based in a true evaluation of our deeds and responsibilities. The poet's consolatory rituals are inseparable, Plato goes on to argue, from his devotion to the image. Poetry invests in seeming, illusion, in order to help us escape from our actual behavior; it prefers, to real action in the world, the rituals of sacrificing to the gods that the poets praise so incessantly. "If the poets are right," Adeimantus remarks sardonically in the *Republic*, "we had best choose injustice and then sacrifice to the gods some of the profits gained by our wrongdoing" (365e).

Nietzsche in *The Birth of Tragedy* defends poetry against the first of Plato's worries: the harrowing, incessant character of its tragic images, which persist like grief itself. For Nietzsche, the (Apollonian) poetic image is consummate and contained, a defense against the unruliness of passion. But through this very defense Nietzsche seems to concede Plato's second charge, that the poet is an entrepreneur of religious mysteries who makes his images serve as means of self-manipulation, tools to absolve oneself of one's consciousness of injustice and sorrow, ways to buy off or quiet existential unease by representing it at a cool remove. For Nietzsche, the poetic image dwells apart, in pristine brilliance, precisely so that it may offer such an escape from life's incoherent tumult.

In *The Birth of Tragedy* Nietzsche presents Homer as the one purely Apollonian poet, who rejoices in the radiant clarity of his gods because they are so utterly separate from himself. Nietzsche writes that for Homer "even the image of the angry Achilles is only an image to him whose angry expression he enjoys with the dreamer's pleasure in illusion. . . . [B]y this mirror of illusion, he is protected against becoming one and fused with his figures" (*BT* 50). If you know the illusions you love, know that they *are* illusions, you will be immune to their traps, Nietzsche promises, and safe from disturbingly unmediated passions. Poetry in the *Birth* as in Plato remains a supplier of therapeutic removal, useful for appeasing the gods of human aggression, bitterness, and disappointment.

Nietzsche cites Hans Sachs, from Wagner's *Meistersinger,* on poetry as the wholesome "truthful delusion" ("wahrster Wahn") that cures the pervasive human craziness Sachs sees all around him ("überall Wahn"). *Wahn* as deliberate artistic construction becomes the antidote for *Wahn* as obsessive, destructive delusion, both collective and personal (*BT* 34). For most of the *Birth,* Nietzsche plays Walther, the ardent young disciple of art's curative powers in the *Meistersinger,* to Wagner's Hans Sachs, the aging, disappointed craftsman/poet who awaits such treatment. Poetry, Nietzsche implies, offers a private Wahnfried (Wagner's name for his estate near Bayreuth), a peace engineered through illusion.

Like Homer, the lyric poet Archilochus (according to Nietzsche) achieves an abstraction from personal emotion. Archilochus, in Nietzsche's *Birth of Tragedy,* differs from Homer only in that he takes "Archilochus, the passionately inflamed, loving, and hating man," rather than the passionate Achilles, as his subject. The poet Archilochus is no longer Archilochus the man. According to Nietzsche, Archilochus as poet is no more tempted to identification with his autobiographical protagonist than Homer is with Achilles or Odysseus. "The subjectively willing and desiring man, Archilochus, can never at any time be a poet" (*BT* 50).[35]

In a famous sentence, Nietzsche identifies the mastery lyric poetry offers: the power of separating oneself definitively from one's own restless desire. The lyric poet, like the epic poet Homer, is "completely released from the greed of the will"; he is "the pure, undimmed eye of the sun." Here, a fine literary alchemy turns the crude "unsatisfied feeling" of the day-to-day, inartistic self, the poet's "willing, longing, moaning, rejoicing," into a mere symbol, a mark of the way passion's strife animates any self, in the same way that it infuses the universe (*BT* 55). Insofar as we are artists of our lives, we can be redeemed through our casting of the Dionysian storm as an Apollonian image, a transformation that makes the turbulence that afflicts us into mere material for artistic work. The fierce pride of a guarded, architectonic self defends us against the Schopenhauerian will. Rather like Perseus bearing the Gorgon's head at arm's length, we must use poetry before it uses and possesses us, making us its hapless victims. *Contra* Schopenhauer, for whom the artist is always slipping back into the frustrated consciousness that he is a real, suffering person, Nietzsche insists that Archilochus the poet remains free from the torments of will he depicts in Archilochus the man. (I explain below why moving on from lyric to tragic poetry is necessary to complete this freedom.)

For Nietzsche in *The Birth of Tragedy*, lyric poetry, which takes the messy, passionate self as its material and transforms it into the brilliant permanence of art, appears to be a form of self-therapy. The image consoles, offering the distant, clear-edged profile of illusion in place of the shadowy, restless working of passions like anger, grief, and sexual desire. In Schopenhauer, too, the poet relies on an image to lift him above the chaotic stream of the will—but for Schopenhauer the effect is momentary. The cool, solar repose of the god Apollo offers merely a brief moment of pause, the shining tip of the iceberg. Accordingly, in Schopenhauer, the lyric poet's wish to rely on gemlike, utterly singular images of the self falls short. Knowing his failure, the Schopenhauerian artist gives himself over to desperation or, if he is wise, resignation. Nietzsche's argument against Schopenhauer in the *Birth* is that poetry is fully achieved in a way that prevents it from being tormented by the will. The poet qua poet does not slip back into the pain of the real world.

The idea that art produces a second nature, a supervisory power that frees us by letting us imagine freedom, is most memorably evoked in *The Birth of Tragedy* when Nietzsche states one of his characteristic insights, that man makes gods in his own image: a *motivated* making, as making is always motivated in Nietzsche. Instead of being degraded by their anthropomorphic status, their function as ideal ego, the Greek divinities find themselves ennobled by it. Lacan defines the ideal ego, in contrast to the ego ideal (the latter being an incarnation of the big Other), as the subject's "*Urbild* . . . through which he enters into the imaginary function and learns to recognize himself as a form."[36] The ideal ego is an Imaginary partner to the self whose form of validation is purely plastic or spatial, in contrast to the moral judgment dispensed by the ego ideal.

The Birth of Tragedy, then, moves from its initial dedicatory image of Wagner as master, big Other or ego ideal, to a freeing vision of the ideal ego (the gods man creates for himself). In "the Olympian world . . . the Hellenic 'will' held up a transfiguring mirror to itself. Thus the gods provide a justification for the life of man by living it themselves— the only satisfactory form of theodicy!" (*BT* 23). The gods, then, know as we their creators do that they are mere projections of human artistry; and in our godlike aspect we too become Burckhardtian selves-as-*Kunstwerk*. At this point in *The Birth of Tragedy*, Nietzsche relies on the metaphorical reversibility that sustains the Imaginary structure of his book: we are the gods' images as they are ours, and we have no way of finding the bottom of this representational swap. What is being mirrored, as "On Truth and Lie" makes clear, is an interruption, a gap in representation. Through this mirroring, the *Birth* tries to cover over the gap.

What Northrop Frye says of Shakespeare could also be said of Nietzsche in the *Birth*: he holds up not a mirror to nature, but a mirror up to another mirror.[37] In *The Birth of Tragedy*, we feel ourselves to be akin to gods not when we fancy ourselves Promethean creators, but when we see ourselves as the creator's product, as works of art. We then become our own spectators, like "the weird image [dem unheimlichen Bild] of the fairy tale which can turn its eyes around and behold itself" (*BT* 52, translation modified; *KSA* 1.48). In this passage Nietzsche adopts and transforms Schopenhauer's allegory of the will that matures and mirrors itself in the course of human history. "Only after the inner being of nature (the will to live in its objectification) has ascended," Schopenhauer writes, "vigorous and cheerful, through the two series of unconscious existences, and then through the long and broad series of animals, does it attain at last to reflection for the first time on the entrance of reason, thus in man. Thus it marvels at its own works, and asks itself what it itself is."[38] Like Milton's Adam in *Paradise Lost*, the Schopenhauerian will, suddenly all grown up, wonders who it is and how it came into the world (*PL* 8.275–82).

In chapter 3 of the *Birth* Nietzsche writes that "in the Greeks the 'will' wished to contemplate itself [sich . . . anschauen] in the transfiguration of genius and the world of art [in der Verklärung des Genius und der Kunstwelt]" (*BT* 44; *KSA* 1.37). But in Schopenhauer the will, instead of retaining its maturity as self-representation, continually slips back into its original state prior to representation and reason. Nietzsche in *The Birth of Tragedy* differs from Schopenhauer, first, by substituting art for reason as the mirroring force for the will's self-representation (that is, substituting the Imaginary ideal ego for Schopenhauer's choice, the Symbolic ego ideal); and second, by giving this Imaginary a completeness and sustainability Schopenhauer denies it.[39]

Nietzsche's insistence on the artist's detachment from any actual suffering life in the *Birth* signals his avoidance, in this early work, of any psychoanalysis of the artist, any study of motives of the kind he will furnish so expertly later in his career. Instead, Nietzsche here proclaims a cosmic perspective within which we *are* works of art, the sites of an impersonal, shimmering beauty. We are neither the ultimate authors nor the final spectators of this artistry. Instead, the real author and audience is the god of the world-process: "Insofar as the subject is the artist . . . he has already been released from his individual will and has become, as it were, the medium through which the one truly existent subject celebrates his release [Erlösung] in appearance" (*BT* 52; *KSA* 1.47).

Nietzsche's daring consists in the reversibility of his religious metaphor. "The one truly existent subject," presumably God, is the artist's creation, just as much as he is the artist's creator. Leo Strauss's remark that Nietzsche presents a vindication of God now perhaps begins to make sense.[40] In *The Birth of Tragedy*, at least, Nietzsche vindicates the human discovery of a godlike universal subject, an Imaginary ideal ego that uses us in the same way the artist uses his materials. What is most important to Nietzsche at this early stage of his work is that we are objects, figures in a setting: aesthetic phenomena, rather than the interested manipulators of aesthetic processes. Soon enough, in the *Untimely Meditations,* his focus will shift to the wiles we practice as subjective agents, as artists rather than artworks. Nietzsche in his later works argues that we need more than the merely formal, aesthetic validation of *The Birth of Tragedy;* we are no longer satisfied with being located by the ideal ego.

I have been arguing that Nietzsche in the *Birth* envisions the goal of art as the liberation from will and subjective personality, a blissful correcting of existence. But the idea of a humanity on passive display, designed for the enjoyment of an Olympian spectator, has an obvious shortcoming: the lack of a sufficiently substantial role for human agency. In the works he writes after *The Birth of Tragedy,* Nietzsche will try to develop a picture of masterful agency of the kind he omits from the *Birth,* while keeping in mind the danger that his defining appreciation of agency may become a praise of the mastery that deforms the world in order to remake it: a celebration of philosophy as the most spiritual will to power.[41] This will, which we can identify with the ascetic project to transform the human, argues in Nietzsche's work against the Emersonian notion of abandonment, Emerson's goal of a musical yielding to the forms of the world.

Pace Heidegger, Nietzsche's idea of eternal return is not the seal he sets on the strenuous imposition of the will to power; instead it can be seen as akin to the Emersonian gesture of abandonment. With the eternal return, Nietzsche tries to escape from the isolation or ascetic deformation that may result from an overly defended, too massively architectonic building of his stance.

I explore these matters further later in this volume, especially in chapters 4 and 5. But before I engage questions of agency and ascetic power, I wish to outline more definitely how, according to the Nietzsche of the *Birth*, tragic poets achieve the liberating clarity of the human-as-artwork. For the early, pre-ascetic Nietzsche, tragedy reveals our existence as epic and lyric cannot, precisely because both epic and lyric exercise an Apollonian detachment, establishing a firm boundary between art and life, even as they turn life into art. The epic or lyric poet, like the audience of these forms, stands apart from the image. He is not tempted to become his characters; and these characters, like Helen in the *Iliad,* speaking of her fame in future centuries, are therefore free to contemplate their afterlife as pure representation.

Tragedy, unlike epic and lyric, forces the spectator into a demanding identification, into a desire to cross over the boundaries between life and death, audience and work. As Cavell argues, *King Lear,* perhaps more than any other play, joins the aspect of tragedy that elicits the spectator's identification to the aspect that wishes for the resurrection of the dead, as Lear holds Cordelia in his arms and thinks she stirs. The stories of Alcestis and Eurydice, two tragic myths that have been important to poets' accounts of their work, engage fully this desire for resurrection through art.

The culminating tragic figure of the *Birth*, however, is not Alcestis, who is prominently mentioned at the end of chapter 8, nor even Oedipus or Hamlet, but rather Wagner's Isolde. In chapter 22 of *The Birth of Tragedy,* Nietzsche cites Isolde's consummation, her love-death. Imagining a resurrected Tristan who is smiling softly, surrounded by stars, and climbing to the heavens, Isolde sings,

> Gentle breathing
> Stirs his lips,
> Ah, how calmly
> Soft his breath: —
> See him, friends!

Feel and see you not?

[Wie den Lippen, wonnig mild,
süsser Atem sanft entweht—
Freunde! Seht!
Fühlt und seht ihr's nicht?][42]

This moment from the end of *Tristan and Isolde* has a specific relation to Lear's scene with the dead Cordelia. Lear's last living words, like Isolde's, invoke a barely perceptible breath: "Do you see this? Look on her. Look, her lips, / Look there, look there" (*King Lear* 5.3.312-13)—two lines that nearly break us by coming close to promising Cordelia's return to life, a return that Shakespeare's art, unlike Euripides' in *Alcestis,* refuses to perform.

But instead of Lear, Isolde is really closer to Shakespeare's Cleopatra talking with Dolabella, creating an Antony "past the size of dreaming": "His legs bestrid the ocean: his reared arm / Crested the world: his voice was propertied / As all the tunèd spheres" (*Antony and Cleopatra* 5.2.97, 82-84). Isolde remains beyond the others who surround and shadow her, who try to diminish her beloved, and beyond as well the attachment to phenomenal existence that constrains Lear. Like Cleopatra, Isolde *knows* that Tristan lives.

Isolde's rhapsody provides Nietzsche's crucial example in the *Birth* of "the world of phenomena . . . den[ying] itself and seek[ing] to flee back again into the womb of the true and only reality" (*BT* 131). This is no mere regression, but rather a bold embrace of the eternal dissonance invoked near the end of *The Birth of Tragedy.* By contrast, the Socratic investigator, according to Nietzsche, embraces not this womb or abyss, not the dissonance behind phenomena, but rather the less profound world of the phenomenal itself. His qualified "yes" to life, "I desire you; you are worth knowing" (*BT* 109), resembles the artist-dreamer's "I will dream on" in its attachment to particular forms. The alternative is that between Isolde, who revises the image of Tristan to express the cosmic "womb" that dissolves all individuality, and the spectator who judges life as "worth knowing" because of individual events and moments.

Perhaps thinking of Isolde, of Shelley's west wind ("Be thou me, impetuous one"), or of Wagner's Erda, Nietzsche speaks, in chapter 16 of the *Birth,* in the voice of Dionysian nature: "'Be as I am! Amid the ceaseless flux of phenomena I am the eternally creative primordial mother, eternally impelling to existence, eternally finding satisfaction in this change of phenomena!'" (*BT* 104). If *The Birth of Tragedy* begins with the uncanny disappearance of the ground, the sudden gap in the principle of sufficient reason that exposes a hole in the universe, it goes on to repair that hole, by means of the Dionysian song that transfigures lack or failure into an unending web of destructive/creative power. Along these lines, Nietzsche cites *Faust*'s *Erdgeist* in his chapter 8: "An eternal sea, an ever-changing weave, a glowing life [Ein ewiges Meer, ein wechselnd Weben, ein glühend Leben]" (*BT* 66; *KSA* 1.64). Nietzsche turns this undulating spirit, which eludes the grasp of the Faust who conjures it, into an origin. According to Nietzsche, the Greek chorus's welcoming of Dionysian force is the real beginning of tragedy, not the hole in reality that testifies to individual desire.

But the individual's desire cannot disappear completely within this new, harmonious destructive/creative order; it remains crucial to our experience of tragedy. We share with Lear a profound attachment to his youngest daughter, to a truth of gesture that belongs to her, or perhaps she to it, and that interrupts the world of the play. Along with her father, we will Cordelia's resurrection, the mere sight of her breath. If only she would stir. . . .

Such a case as Cordelia's threatens the harmony promised by *The Birth of Tragedy*. In the *Birth* Dionysus and Apollo join forces to insure that the tragic spectator remains shielded by the resilient powers of a synoptic, foreseeing artfulness, instead of being pushed toward the tantalizing realm of the object that contrives our desire. Nietzsche deflects the spectator's identification from this target, the protagonist's peculiar ground of self, to the chorus and its god, Dionysus. For Nietzsche, Dionysus founds and levels tragic mood: this divinity's pain is already cosmic rather than personal in its import. Nietzsche focuses on the identificatory sympathy "the satyr chorus of the dithyramb," the putative source of tragedy, feels for its god, Dionysus. The satyr is "an inspired reveller enraptured by the closeness of his god, a sympathetic companion in whom [the] god's suffering is repeated" (*BT* 40). And this response of the satyrs to the god finds itself repeated by the similar closeness of the audience, who become "the timeless worshippers of their god, beyond all social contingencies" (*BT* 43).

Clearly, the choral origins of tragedy represent for Nietzsche the presence of a Dionysian sympathy prior to the dramatic interaction of characters. Dionysus is the deep, dark ground out of which the shining form of the hero eventually emerges. But this emergence is not the birth of the individual as an oddity tethered to the object *a;* quite the contrary. The tragic hero comes onstage not as a lonely being, awkward in his contingency, but as a vehicle of the god's collected power, the Imaginary ideal ego. Nietzsche portrays this event in a memorable passage: "Now the dithyrambic chorus is assigned the task of exciting the mood of the audience to such a Dionysiac degree that when the tragic hero appears on the stage, they do not see the awkwardly masked human being, but rather a visionary figure, born as it were from their own rapture [Verzückung]" (*BT* 66, translation modified; *KSA* 1.63).

Nietzsche compares the chorus looking on at the sudden appearance of the tragic hero to the figure of Admetus met by his resurrected wife, Alcestis, the woman Hercules leads back to him at the end of Euripides' *Alcestis.*[43] Describing the return of Alcestis in *The Birth of Tragedy,* Nietzsche brings forward the figure and blurs the ground, using an effect similar to the work of a "focus-puller" in moviemaking. In the *Birth,* the unreal (a wish born out of the audience's own rapture) becomes the wished-for phenomenon, a living Alcestis, who functions as tangible proof of poetry's efficacy. Art, usually the figure to be measured against the ground of our experience, *becomes* the ground when life itself, in the *Birth's* most famous declaration, is revealed as an aesthetic phenomenon. This unveiling covers the sudden gap in reality that Schopenhauer describes, the uncanny interrupting of the *principium individuationis.*

In the *Birth,* tragedy bears the weight of the cosmos. Man is eternal, and eternally fading; tragedy meets the disappearance of the mortal individual by restating this oldest of all truths. By contrast, Nietzsche in his next major work, *Untimely Meditations,* enshrines individuality, our imaginings of particular, actual persons and events. Nietzsche addresses this difference between the *Birth* and his subsequent work in his belated "Attempt at a Self-Criticism [Versuch einer Selbstkritik]," appended to *The Birth of Tragedy* in its 1886 reissue.

Like Goethe's Faust, Nietzsche had written in the 1872 text of the *Birth,* the tragic poet wants an "art of metaphysical comfort . . . as his own proper Helen" (*BT* 113). The poet conjures "woman" as idea, imagining that his "longing" can embody itself and, by so doing, ground itself. Responding to the poet's longing, the audience of tragedy fantasizes along with him about stepping over the line that separates reality from sublime, redeeming illusion (*BT* 66). Like the poet, we stretch out our hands for a dreamlike beauty that promises to free us from the real world of pain and loss. This is Nietzsche's youthful vision as originally expressed in *The Birth of Tragedy,* and later criticized by him in 1886: born alike from the artist's and the spectator's will, the beloved image lures with its promise of a world beyond the everyday.

In the "Attempt at a Self-Criticism," Nietzsche cites one of the *Birth*'s rhapsodic exclamations and adds his own later repudiation of his youthful romanticism:

> Would it not be *necessary* for the tragic man . . . in view of his self-education for seriousness and terror, to desire a new art, the *art of metaphysical comfort,* to desire tragedy as his own proper Helen, and to exclaim with Faust:
>
>> Should not my longing overleap the distance
>> And draw the fairest form into existence?
>> [Und sollt' ich nicht, sehnsüchtigster Gewalt,
>> In's Leben ziehn die einzigste Gestalt?]
>
> "Would it not be *necessary?*" No, thrice no! O you young romantics: it would *not* be necessary! But it is highly probable that it will *end* that way, that *you* will end that way, namely, "comforted," as it is written, in spite of all self-education for seriousness and terror, "comforted metaphysically"—in sum, as romantics end, as *Christians.*
>
>> No! You ought first to learn the art of *this-worldly* comfort [*diesseitigen* Trostes]. . . . (*BT* 26)

Faust's Helen, whom Nietzsche invoked in the 1872 passage, stands for the possibility of a world redeemed through the beauty of artistic creation. In his career after the *Birth,* Nietzsche turns away from this romantic ideal to the study of "*this-worldly* comfort," to the ways illusion and artistry characterize our day-to-day existence. This Emersonian emphasis becomes the basis for Nietzsche's *Daybreak* and *The Gay Science.*

The later Nietzsche is concerned less with a figure like Helen, emblem of the masculine poetic power that evokes her, and more with the figure of woman as creator of her own illusion. In the mature Nietzsche, the myth of woman depends on a certain dynamic, the alternative of resistance or yielding to the male philosopher/seducer. But unlike the Helen of *Faust,* Nietzsche's woman is not the mere result of masculine wish-fulfillment. Instead, in her elusiveness she testifies to both the inescapability and the undiscovered nature of the object *a,* the locus of desire that Nietzsche in *The Birth of Tragedy* did his best to overcome.

CHAPTER THREE

The *Untimely Meditations*

> *Not to discriminate every moment some passionate attitude in those about us, and in the very brilliancy of their gifts some tragic dividing of forces on their ways, is, on this short day of frost and sun, to sleep before evening.*
>
> —Walter Pater, *The Renaissance*[1]

THE BIRTH OF TRAGEDY ARGUES AGAINST Schopenhauer by claiming the pervasiveness and efficacy of art. For Nietzsche, as for Emerson, art is not an antidote to life but a transformation of it. But Nietzsche in the *Birth* still speaks, at times, in Schopenhauerian tones, praising entry into the realm of art as a way of securing relief from the burden and pain of an untransformed, unaestheticized existence.[2] In the *Untimely Meditations,* and especially in its second essay, "On the Use and Disadvantage of History for Life," Nietzsche depicts the burden in a different way, as our consciousness that we have not yet achieved what we ought. Nietzsche, like Emerson, tells us that we ought to have a life that (in Emerson's words) enables us to "become Man Thinking," man animated by the chief virtue of "self-trust" (*E* 63). In this chapter I explore the connection between such Emersonian self-realization and the attaining of a critical, self-trusting stance: an attainment which for Nietzsche in the *Untimely Meditations* marks the truth of individualism. I also examine a work roughly contemporaneous with the *Untimely Meditations, Philosophy in the Tragic Age of the Greeks.* By imagining the philosopher as judge of existence, a type that will later be central to Nietzsche's *Zarathustra,* the *Tragic Age* represents the height of Nietzsche's aspiration toward an architectonic, founded individuality. On the way to this conclusion, I will consider Emerson's thoughts on fate and history, Derrida's criticism of the "philosophy of life" that appears in Emerson and Nietzsche, and the philosophy of the ordinary presented by Cavell.

Whereas Cavell decides in favor of life, seeking a palpable difference between the ghostly, mechanical, or dead on the one side and the living on the other, for Derrida this difference is undecidable, continually subject to revision. Derrida's critique of the philosophy of life, and of the individualist discrimination of worth allied to it, stands against both Emerson and Nietzsche. But Derrida himself must depend, somewhat covertly, on a philosophy similar to Emerson's and Nietzsche's individualism: on an enshrining of the decisive moment that frees the future from the past and separates the living from the dead. Nietzsche's posthumous revenge on Derrida is that Derrida also becomes, despite himself, a Nietzschean philosopher of life—and is a stronger thinker for this.

In the *Untimely Meditations* we witness the disappearance of a heroic character type that haunted the *Birth,* the tragic seeker moved by a transgressive will to know: Oedipus, Hamlet, Faust, Socrates. In place of these figures, all of whom were prominent in the *Birth,* a more prudent or quietly daring type appears, animated by what Nietzsche will call critical consciousness. The critical personality dedicates himself to a form of creation that, by measuring itself against the past and aiming toward the future, assures the self of its founded, substantial character, its architectonic stability. Such a solid self requires an openness to the involuntary and inspirational, to the (Dionysian) element of music that, sometimes covertly, sustains (Apollonian) structure. In the fourth *Untimely Meditation,* "Richard Wagner in Bayreuth," this involuntary or secretive factor is revealed as the place of the Lacanian object *a,* that fascinating thing "in me more than myself." Wagner, as the cause of Nietzsche's imagination in "Richard Wagner in Bayreuth," cannot be subject to the continual hermeneutic readjustment, the strong, self-serving practice of revision, that Nietzsche envisions with his ideal of the critical in "History for Life." Instead, Wagner (or Wagner's music) returns as the hidden center of Nietzsche's existence, the thing that precedes critical perspective and, precisely because it enables or supports that perspective, must remain outside of and untouched by it. The *Untimely Meditations,* then, when taken as a whole, make a claim for the critical consciousness (in "History for Life") but also show the limits of that consciousness (in "Wagner in Bayreuth").

NIETZSCHE ON ARTIST, PHILOSOPHER, AND SAINT

Sheridan Hough, in her book on Nietzsche's idea of the self, reflects on the Nietzschean vision in *Untimely Meditations* of "human potential being supremely realized." She begins with the second of the *Untimely Meditations*, "On the Use and Disadvantage of History for Life," a text that will also occupy my attention here. "History for Life," Hough notes, cites as its models of self-realization the saint, the artist, and the philosopher:

> All three share a particular kind of experience, which we might call the eclipse of the will, the will in the grip of a vision, an idea, a beautiful form that demands to be realized. All three are necessarily receptive to forces beyond their immediate reckoning, and this makes them in a sense inscrutable: they can communicate their embryonic sensibility only through a productive act, by bringing forth a treatise, a painting, a holy deed. In many cases, the results of their creative labors are unexpected—perhaps not even immediately recognizable.

The Nietzschean artist, saint, or philosopher, Hough concludes, "will recognize that the best form of 'yea-saying' is not an articulation at all, but a moment of joy."[3]

Hough does not mention that Nietzsche derives his association of these three creative types from Emerson. Emerson's "History" offers the examples of poet, philosopher, and saint as the triad to whom "all things are friendly and sacred, all events profitable, all days holy, all men divine" (*E* 242), and Nietzsche's *Gay Science* will draw on this passage for its epigraph (omitting the saint, *der Heilige*). For Nietzsche in 1882, the year of *The Gay Science*, both poet and philosopher are Emersonian aesthetes. Earlier, in 1874's "History for Life," the saint joined them as a figure whose *métier* is an ecstatic appreciation indistinguishable from creation.

If we accept Hough's beautiful description of the Nietzschean project for an affirmative self that realizes its work by adopting a receptive, somewhat passive posture, a stance of readiness for what it hopes will happen—the ecstasy of instinctive creation—we must go on to ask two questions. First, how is ecstasy, with its implication of Dionysian surrender to outside influence, related to Nietzsche's interest in a fully articulated critical consciousness, an interest that implies a more active role for the self? And second, why does consciousness so often, in Nietzsche, take a tragic form, in which the receptive, ready self becomes, like Dionysus or Jesus, a victimized and suffering one?

The first question bears on the eternal quarrel between philosophy and poetry. Philosophy relies on the Apollonian or (to use my term) architectonic: the persuasive force of an analytic clarification that assures the self of its position. Poetry, by contrast, exploits the lyric intensity that opens the self to a decisive influx (the Dionysian or musical). The second question confronts the strange bond between the individual's realization of self and his experience of tragic suffering. For Nietzsche, the tragic sense provides the means to a critical individualism, which in turn enables the overcoming of Schopenhauer's fatalism. In Schopenhauer, tragedy forms the common and unavoidable atmosphere of human existence. For Nietzsche, by contrast, tragedy represents, strangely, human success: the heroic flourishing that survives in singular and perceptive gestures of perception, the signs of a suffering acutely wrought, unmistakable. Tragedy shows acts of discernment shadowed, and also made possible, by the hardest human limits: death and mutability. Like Walter Pater, Nietzsche urges us to "discriminate every moment . . . some tragic dividing of these forces on their ways."

In Nietzsche, the tragic sense locates the determining kernel of the self and of its fate in a way that Emerson and Schopenhauer, Nietzsche's philosophical fathers, did not achieve. Nietzsche defines critical response as the discovery of what is closest to the self. The Oedipal and Promethean will to look through, or tear, the veil of universal nature, so prominent in *The Birth of Tragedy*, is nowhere evident in the *Untimely Meditations*. The *Birth*'s ambition for a redemptive transfiguration of the whole through the tragic hero's transgression and sacrifice is replaced, in the *Meditations*, by a much more selective—an individualist—process of self-knowing and self-formation.

INDIVIDUALISM, POETRY, PHILOSOPHY

Individualism, perhaps now more than usual, has a bad reputation. For many, it is synonymous with an aloof snobbery, an unquestioning preference for elite and esoteric positions, or a refusal to recognize the true value or interest of collective social life. Both Emerson and Nietzsche have been charged with such standoffish elitism, with a refusal to know the pull of common pieties, and with a resistance to the sympathetic instincts that make human solidarity possible.[4] In order to defend these thinkers, we must see in their aloofness a demand that we test the worth of our usual commitments to the *doxa* of the social world—and even, in Emerson's case, the worth of commitment itself.[5]

Without such trial, and the individuation it requires, the solidarity with unknown victims and anonymous masses so consistently celebrated these days as morality itself offers a mere flight into conformist death-in-life: a surrender to the easiest piety, one that spares itself any confrontation with conflicting ideas or contentious persons, with anything that might truly challenge us. Emerson and Nietzsche defend individualism by proposing as its result a new, higher—because more selective—solidarity, based on love for the friend, who does by definition contend with and challenge me. They find an alliance between aloofness and the recognition of the private ways we affirm our oddly separate worlds even within friendship, ways routinely obscured and obstructed by the demands of conformity, shaped as it is by the anonymous depths of social life. Both of them were to varying degrees disappointed, troubled allies of social and cultural causes: for Emerson, the Brook Farm reformers; for Nietzsche, Wagnerism. Together, they suggest an elusive test of a cause's worth: how it matters to oneself, a "how" that may not be defensible in ready, public terms. What matters cannot be predicted in advance, and perhaps cannot be explained to others.

There is a bond between this sort of individualist eccentricity and poetic enthusiasm. Emerson's and Nietzsche's interest in individual commitments and impulses, it is often said, seems to take a passionate rather than an analytic form. These two thinkers still appear too lyrical or rhapsodic and therefore not philosophical enough, at least for most Anglo-American philosophers. The worry philosophers sometimes express about the "poetic" thinker's enthusiasm for the strange and singular stems from philosophy's historical mission of evaluating and judging commitment. From Plato on, philosophy has presented itself as the discourse that is truly interested in testing our commitments by explaining them, by giving or (mostly) denying them the backing of hallowed public terms: truth, justice, the good. *The Birth of Tragedy* shockingly reverses the usual thought that imagination must finally secure or justify itself by an appeal to reflective moral standards, since Nietzsche tells the story of classical Greece as a decline from imagination into moral reflection, a fall out of poetic consciousness and into Socratic philosophizing. Only tragedy, in Nietzsche's view, can truly make the case for Greece as the origin of a modernity that has returned to archaic sources. Tragedy's concern with the unexplainability of affect, chance, and mortality makes the poetic the only truly answerable mode of perceiving our lives, prior to any merely wishful moral explanation.[6]

Given its interest in the unexplainable, can poetry know itself as philosophy hopes to? Socrates' interlocutors face a characteristic dilemma imposed on them by the philosopher: who can I be, and how can I be it, if I can't explain myself, my values and my beliefs, to others? To Plato, at times, poetry seems to provide mere consolation, a way to shore up the self in its ease. At other times, Plato sees poetry as producing a force of pathos that breaks or divides the self at a level more immanent, and therefore more dangerously uncontrollable, than that of practical action.

Nietzsche, like Emerson, seeks to integrate poetic and philosophical modes; for example, by insisting in *The Birth of Tragedy* that tragedy is itself philosophical, and is so in a deeper way than could be present in the explicitly philosophical discourse that begins with Plato's Socrates. The continuing development of Nietzsche's thought bears witness to this integration, as in *Daybreak* and *The Gay Science* the self's knowing philosophical estimation of its experience takes a poetic form: that is, one preoccupied with mood, the emotional coloring of existence, and with the image of the stage actor, with masking and disguise. As I argue in chapter 4, in *Daybreak* and *The Gay Science* Nietzsche moves past the critical ideal he praised in the *Untimely Meditations,* as the architectonic control necessary to the critical yields to a more fluid receptivity to mood. In these works, Nietzsche makes us welcome the unpredictable newness of mood in a way that leaves us (somewhat) undefended, even though we continue to observe, criticize, and manage our lives. In these works of the early 1880s, a lack of self-protection in the face of human impulse troubles Nietzsche's project, even as it makes for the real interest of that project. At this point, in *The Gay Science,* the object *a* becomes a threat; by the time of *Ecce Homo,* it has overcome Nietzsche's philosophical enterprise.

James Conant's persuasive reading of "Schopenhauer as Educator," the third essay of the *Untimely Meditations,* suggests that in this text Nietzsche submits the self to a perfectionist hermeneutic discipline.[7] Conant emphasizes the central injunction to the reader that Nietzsche makes in "Schopenhauer as Educator": line up the objects, the persons and texts, that you have been devoted to, and by studying this sequence, discover the law of your nature (*UM* 129).

But this hermeneutic vision of continual self-discovery, and hence self-construction, cannot be definitive in the *Untimely Meditations* because it leaves no place for the traumatic element, the one thing that affects the self more than, and in a different way than, any other object of devotion. For Nietzsche this thing, the object *a,* is Wagner's music insofar as this music suggests an elusive, inescapable, secret fact about the self that cannot be translated into critical argument. Music and the feminine are deeply linked in Nietzsche's work, as we have seen in the *Will to Power* passages discussed in my Introduction. Accordingly, the object *a* will be revealed in *Ecce Homo* as woman, she who reminds Nietzsche of a wound, a lack that haunts and interrupts all perfectionism, all projects to order and transform one's existence. The perfectionist series, the objects of our intellectual devotion enshrined in "Schopenhauer as Educator," will, by the time of *Ecce Homo,* fall victim to what must remain excluded from the series: Nietzsche's feminine origins.

SELF-RELIANCE, MOOD, AND EXCLUSIVITY

In Emerson and Nietzsche, mood sometimes stands for individualism itself. On occasion, a person's mood takes the form of irrational aversion to public causes, resulting in the philosophical isolation that one must undergo in order to reach the truer, more distant society of the friend. In perhaps his most notorious set-piece, Emerson writes (in "Self-Reliance"), "Expect me not to show cause why I seek or why I exclude company. Then, again, do not tell me, as a good man did to-day, of my obligation to put all poor men in good situations. Are they my poor? I tell thee, thou foolish philanthropist, that I grudge the dollar, the dime, the cent, I give to such men as do not belong to me and to whom I do not belong" (*E* 262).

Who is the man who *does* "belong to me"? Emerson, like Nietzsche, will name this creature the friend, the chosen one who arrives without notice, bearing, like these authors themselves, unreasonable demands. Emerson in "Self-Reliance" makes a case for the indefinite or unpredictable nature of commitments, for the way they block our hope to locate ourselves in a realm of custom and approved thought, or in a set tradition, the historical continuity that identifies designated heirs or disciples. As Nietzsche writes in *Zarathustra*'s book I ("On the Love of the Neighbor"), "Higher than love for the neighbor is love for the most distant and future person [zum Fernsten und Künftigen]. . . . I teach you, not the neighbor, but rather the friend" (*Z* 87, translation modified).

The esteem for the friend's select character that Emerson voices in "Self-Reliance" can be redeemed for democratic purposes. Emerson knows that the other's claim on us shifts from situation to situation, from moment to moment. Absolutely *anyone* might turn out to be the chosen, the favored comrade.

Emerson runs a greater risk when he depicts a democracy so microscopic in its manifestations that it sinks below the level of the representative instance on which practical political and historical inquiries rely. "What does Rome know of rat and lizard?" Emerson asks at the end of "History." "Broader and deeper we must write our annals" (*E* 256). (In a perhaps related passage from *The Gay Science*, Nietzsche speaks of the qualities of human beings, those near-invisible traits never yet truly discerned by commentators, as akin to the "subtle sculptures on the scales of reptiles" [*GS* #8]: unlike our familiar moral cartoons, virtue and vice, actual human qualities hide themselves from our sight.)

But—we may reply to Emerson, with a parody of the Annales school in mind—a history so deep as to encompass rat and lizard is not recognizable history. Its sacrifices, its victories and disasters, remain invisible to us. Somewhat paradoxically, here Emerson the great individualist makes the individual, even the human itself, vanish. In the sure, infinite scope of cosmic time, no gains or losses can be seen. At times Emerson, like Nietzsche in "On Truth and Lie in an Extramoral Sense," flirts with such cold distances: "As the light on my book is yielded by a star a hundred millions of miles distant . . . so the hours should be instructed by the ages, and the ages explained by the hours," he writes in "History" (*E* 237). Pretending that we live on an alien planet, we can make all pressing and fateful events disappear into the perspective of light-years.

Such science-fictional transformation can be liberating, to be sure. In chapter 7 of *Philosophy in the Tragic Age of the Greeks* Nietzsche remarks on the alienated cheerfulness of Heraclitus: "And so, just as the child and the artist plays, so plays the ever-living fire. It constructs and destroys, all in innocence. Such is the game that the aeon plays with itself" (*PTAG* 62, translation modified). But there is a hard-hearted calculus lurking behind Nietzsche's *Heiterkeit*, one that applies to the things we think of as cultural necessities. In a similar mood, Emerson, reflecting on the supposedly irreplaceable Great Literature we treasure, insists that our need for it dissolves under such long-distance scrutiny. You can live on text as on shoe-leather. "We all know," Emerson writes in "The American Scholar," that "as the human body can be nourished on any food, though it were boiled grass and the broth of shoes, so the human mind can be fed by any knowledge" (*E* 59). In the same essay, he remarks that "the books which once we valued more than the apple of the eye, we have quite exhausted. . . . The man has never lived that can feed us ever" (*E* 67).

Emerson's lesson is the benefit we gain from alienation, and from the loss of that known world made up by our familiar cultural monuments. We learn that (as the "American Scholar" passage concludes) "it is one light which beams out of a thousand stars. It is one soul which animates all men" (*E* 67). The solidarity promised here, the glimpse of the Emersonian Gnostic fire, requires a sense of the exhaustibility of other persons, their expendable place in our universe: a realization that can only alienate us from them, even as it connects us all together.

One indication of Emersonian alienation is the fact that he embraces his world more gingerly than Whitman, with what Santayana saw as strange delicacy, the sign of a basic unfamiliarity with other people. William James, in contrast, remembered Emerson in 1903 as a "fastidious lover of significance and distinction," of "individuals and particulars."[8] James's defense of Emerson as a cherisher of the particular has proven to be a necessary one. Emerson's critics have sometimes accused him of capricious or escapist abstraction: a will to live in his ideal, and a cold disregard for the fellow humans who might interfere with this ideal. Already in 1898, John Jay Chapman in the course of a wonderfully appreciative portrait of Emerson balked at what he depicted as the master's superlunary ecstasies, even blaming such flights for the death of his beloved disciple Margaret Fuller.[9]

Emerson himself, in the essay "Love," initiates the charge of aloofness when he names himself one of the cold philosophers who have wronged eros: "I have been told, that in some public discourses of mine my reverence for the intellect has made me unjustly cold to the personal relations. But now I almost shrink at the remembrance of such disparaging words. For persons are love's world" (*E* 329). "I *almost* shrink," Emerson writes with canny self-incriminating qualification, not quite disavowing his coldness. Love, he adds, attends to the person, to the "melancholy details" of individual situation. But the individual, Emerson argues in "Love," withdraws or disappears from our view. Our devotion to persons, then, is necessarily a melancholy one, because in love we attach ourselves to that which leads us on by pushing us away.[10]

In fact, "Love" goes on to suggest, the personal attachments of the lover will be surveyed with nostalgic condescension by the mature Emersonian philosopher. To illustrate the youthful genesis of love, Emerson composes a scene of picturesque, almost infantile charm: "The rude village boy teases the girls about the school-house door;—but today he comes running into the entry, and meets one fair child disposing her satchel; he holds her books to help her, and instantly it seems to him as if she removed herself from him infinitely, and was a sacred precinct" (E 329). When the girl becomes the beloved, her allure comes into its own as an evasiveness that approaches the sacred, a coyness practiced, it seems, not by her, but by the universe itself. Rather surprisingly, Emerson's homespun plot ends not by bringing the happy couple together, but by detaching them permanently and "infinitely." The telos of love, here as in Diotima's central speech in the *Symposium*, is such detachment. The difference from the *Symposium*, though, lies in Emerson's stance, his claim of healthy superiority to any object of desire. He is careful to defend the soul's aspiration by stating its payoff, by justifying vision as pragmatic gain:

> we are often made to feel that our affections are but tents of a night. Though slowly and with pain, the objects of the affections change, as the objects of thought do. There are moments when the affections rule and absorb the man, and make his happiness dependent on a person or persons. But in health the mind is presently seen again,—its overarching vault, bright with galaxies of immutable lights, and the warm loves and fears that swept over us as clouds, must lose their finite character and blend with God, to attain their own perfection. But we need not fear that we can lose any thing by the progress of the soul. (E 337)

In "Love" as in "Friendship," Emerson writes a principle of coincidence, the consolations of cosmic harmony: "the progress of the soul." It can seem a rather cold reward. The Gnostic spark reflected from and to all persons is not, for Emerson, a communion, but rather a coherence that at once distances us from, and draws out our similarity to, one another. This shared illumination also characterizes Emerson's essay "History." In all these Emersonian instances, we are allowed to rise above our attachment to particular objects: our "warm loves and fears" "lose their finite character."

THE PHILOSOPHY OF LIFE: CAVELL, DERRIDA, EMERSON

In Emerson, then, the soul's progress means the realizing of an illumination, one that lets us overcome our melancholy, grasping attachment to the mortal and particular by redefining the particular as the common, what we share even in our divisions and distances from one another. For Schopenhauer, unlike Emerson, such progress cannot occur. In *The World as Will and Idea* all life is finally consigned to oblivion by the will, and philosophy's task is to remind us that the will's exertions are mere transience. Schopenhauer takes sides against the common character of existence. With heroic gestures he protests the disappointment of our survival, the survival of our desire as repeated, futile striving. Emerson, by contrast, devotes himself to the remembering or bearing of human transience, and, therefore, the redemption of it as new, and newly common, meaning.

Cavell suggests a comparison between the Emerson who maintains and bears witness to our commonness, instead of taking sides against it, and the Freud who values remembering over repeating.[11] Unlike Emerson and Freud, and unlike Nietzsche, Schopenhauer devalues memory. In Schopenhauer, human history appears as a fallen world of sheer repetition. We are the servants, or prisoners, of time. But Emerson detects a crescive power traced in history that matches human energies to the fluctuating course of time, and the times. In "Fate" he suggests that, however fierce our resistance to this course, and however determinedly we mourn the real costs of historical events, this resistance itself, when brought out into the open, testifies to our involvement with what it protests. "If there be omnipotence in the stroke," he writes in "Fate," "there is omnipotence in the recoil" (*E* 954). Cavell glosses this sentence as follows: "Every word is a word spoken *again,* or against again [i.e., for memory and against repetition]; there would be no words otherwise." So Emerson gives power to the "breathers of words, mortals," whose "strokes may be given now, and may gather together now—in a recoiling—all the power of word-creating words."[12]

What Emerson's strokes (of the word, of the pen) remind us of is their, and our, exemplary nature, our unexceptionable position here and now, which responds to, and takes the impression of, all the punishment history places on us. Suffering the universe's "savage accidents," as "Fate" puts it, means voicing that suffering, and bearing it, *as necessity:* the necessity not of a force that drives us, like Schopenhauer's will, but of the words that draw us, our words, and what these words invoke. We have no real choice but to affirm such suffering as freedom, to acknowledge the living wishes that join us, in conversation, to the dead. Emerson's writing proves the point by not merely describing, but also enacting this choice. Emerson claims, Cavell writes, that "human freedom, as the opposition to fate, is not merely called for by philosophical writing but is instanced or enacted by that writing . . . as though human thinking is not so much to be expressed by language as resurrected with it."[13]

Instead of trying to call for freedom, to call freedom into being, as Nietzsche will do (with some interesting hesitations) in the *Untimely Meditations,*[14] Emerson *presents* such freedom, exemplifying it in his writing. The manner of this presentation elicits suspicion from those who, like Derrida, insist that the calling forth of presence, the conjuring away of unreal and fantasized existence—a common gesture in Emerson, as in Nietzsche and Marx—must also, simultaneously, conjure up such unreality. Derrida draws our attention to the blurring of the line these thinkers want to draw between the unreal and the real, the dead and the living.

Nothing could be further from the spirit of Emerson's work, with its trust in the resurrection of voice and presence, than Derrida's dwelling on absence: for example, his suggestion that "the work of mourning is not one form of work among others. It is work itself, work in general."[15] In his *Politics of Friendship,* Derrida describes the individual as a survivor whose interlocutors, even if they are literally speaking still alive, figure as dead and gone: passed over by time, yet apt to return in memory.[16] For Derrida, we are always speaking with the dead, with the history that inhabits us. And working through history, whether history takes the form of the past's texts or of its persons, is labor that is never done. (These past texts and people, telling absences, are never done with us.) As a result, the urge Emerson and Nietzsche share, to pass from past to future, from the dead to the living, must appear to Derrida to be a wish to avoid encountering the ghosts that haunt us.

Derrida accuses Marx of a similar avoidance, since, like Emerson and Nietzsche, Marx attempts to call freedom into being, to create it by invoking it, at the expense of the dead past. In *Specters of Marx,* glossing Marx's statement that history weighs like a nightmare on the brains of the living, Derrida writes,

> The specter weighs [*pèse*], it thinks [*pense*], it intensifies and condenses itself within the very inside of life, within the most living life, the most singular (or, if one prefers, most individual) life. The latter therefore no longer has and must no longer have, insofar as it is living, a pure identity to itself or any assured inside: this is what all philosophies of life, or even philosophies of the living and real individual, would have to weigh carefully.[17]

Specters of Marx focuses on Marx but alludes to the spectral presence of "a certain Nietzsche" as well,[18] presumably the same philosopher I have been considering: the advocate of singularity, of individual self-realization, of becoming what one is. Derrida implies that his philosophical antagonist, or other, can be found in both Marx and Nietzsche. In the passage I have quoted, he makes a somewhat tentative, sidelong approach to this other, which he identifies as vitalism and individualism of a rather unspecified sort ("all philosophies of life, or even philosophies of the living and real individual"), but which I identify specifically with Emerson and Nietzsche.[19] Derrida's caution to such philosophy is that it must "weigh carefully" the pressure of the dead within the living. Given Derrida's terms, though, this seems an impossible bit of advice: impossible because this very pressure or weight would seem to preclude, according to Derrida himself, the kind of studied decision, the careful weighing, that he calls for.

The decision that Derrida points toward appears to be the kind that Nietzsche invokes in "History for Life": to what extent can I afford to deny the past, to claim to be other than it, to revise its presence within me? But these central questions in Nietzsche's essay are rendered unaskable by Derrida, because his concept of the dead's presence inside the living prevents the separation from the past that Nietzsche aims at.[20] For Derrida, then, it seems the decisions Nietzsche demands from us are impossible, because Nietzsche's impulse toward a searching and specific measuring of the difference between past and future is blocked by Derrida's insistence on the indefinite, indeterminate hold of the past on us.[21]

I now must digress to his account of Marx in order to illuminate

Derrida's sense of history, and to show why he needs to protest against a philosophy of "the real and living individual" of the kind that Nietzsche and Emerson, like Marx, offer us. According to Derrida, Marx's project of dispelling the phantoms of ideological fantasy and idealized belief and replacing them with the real conditions of "labor, production and exchange" fails partly because the commodity form, which is at the very center of these real conditions, is itself a spectral presence, illustrating as nothing else can the fact that capitalist value is based on nothing.

A signal example of the ghostly nature of capitalism was provided by the anxious mood on Wall Street in the final years of the twentieth century. Investors feared that the U.S. dollar was too strong, that too much money was being made on the basis of too little. Stocks held in internet-based companies like Priceline and EBay reached a value that was felt to be absurdly high, causing worried allusions to the fact that these companies possessed practically nothing in the way of "real" assets: no factories, no airplanes, etc. This nostalgia for a value that would be grounded in reality is telling, and goes much deeper than mere anxiety over the virtual character of the cyber-marketplace as opposed to, say, piles of hay, pork bellies, or pharmaceuticals. In fact, the capitalist market, whatever it ostensibly trades in, *is* based on exactly nothing; this was especially, but not uniquely, clear in 1998–99 (and in the ensuing crash that began the new millennium).

The strength or weakness of the market depends on investors reading other investors' fears about whether the groundlessness of the entire system is sufficiently pressing, or close enough to the surface of consciousness, to cause a small cataclysm or collective lapse of faith— a crash. Marx exposes the nothingness that drives capitalism's Symbolic system, which is based solely on the confidence ascribed to others, but he then defends us against this nothingness by substituting for it the realities of work and the means of production. In Marx as in life, however (despite Marx's intentions) nothingness wins out: the brute realities of mechanical production will always be less real to us than the allure of the commodity and the specter of our own fear, prompted by our knowledge of the commodity's genuine worthlessness.

In a fascinating passage from *Specters of Marx,* Derrida writes that Marx's "pre-deconstructive . . . ontology of presence as actual reality and as objectivity" is a "relatively stabilized knowledge" that nevertheless "calls for questions more radical than the critique itself and than the ontology that grounds the critique." These questions, he continues, are "seismic events" that "come from the future . . . [and are] given from out of the unstable, chaotic, and dis-located ground of the times."[22]

One might ask: (how) does Marx's "pre-deconstructive" reduction of the world to its material conditions call for questions, or call for events? Perhaps in the way that revolutionaries call for revolution—an event that, Derrida implies, is bound to overturn the readiness of those who call for it, as well as those who are called. The upsetting event, the thing that could not be predicted or planned for, demands to be recognized. As Zizek suggests, politics is the art of the impossible, and therefore not an art at all; in a truly political moment, predictability, strategy, and rhetoric all fail.[23] Virtually every revolution Marx describes, from 1789 to the Paris Commune, was (like the fall of the Marxist, or "Marxist," regimes of eastern Europe in 1989 and after) essentially premature, too much too soon, an annoyance to Marx's emphasis on proper historical conditions. But such annoyance, in its rebuke to propriety, is the actual shape of the political. In Derrida's words, it "come[s] from the future" rather than the past, a "seismic event."

Here a gap seems to appear in Derrida's writing, through which the Real appears as a presence not spectral (i.e., not, or not yet, subject to citation, not yet past), not elusive in the manner of a ghost, but rather all too soon and too abruptly *occurring*. We may be tempted to think that Derrida here lacks a concept: perhaps, that he must lack it. He inclines toward a Hamlet-like desire to interrogate the specter and looks for shapes that are always already past, insubstantial and shadowy— but now something appears from the future.

Derrida, like Marx, senses the approach of a radically new future, but he does not quite know how to address it, to make it "stand and unfold [it]self." I have suggested that the lacking concept that would permit such address might be the Lacanian Real (through which I have read Nietzsche), but it might also be the Cavellian ordinary (through which I have read Emerson).

Cavell, speaking of Derrida's critique of Austin, describes Derrida as "already in flight from the specter of the ordinary."[24] The flight is apparent in the way Derrida emphasizes how the persistence of citation and of iterability could, or should, dissolve our common assurance that meaning remains reliably present to us. But Derrida nevertheless concedes a realm of the ordinary in which such reliability is indeed commonly assumed. A bit unexpectedly, he construes this realm as the habitual reduction to empirical fact. Describing the world of habit, Derrida starts looking like the Humean skeptic who banishes his speculations when he plays billiards at his club, and also like Marx with his "pre-deconstructive" ontology. You can't cross the street without being able to count on the meaning of red and green lights: this is the level at which Derrida at times pitches his observation in his extended answer to John Searle, *Limited INC*. He defines the ground rules of customary existence as the basis of our reality.[25]

Here Cavell's challenge to Derrida is *apropos*. Cavell charges Derrida with not taking the ordinary seriously enough, with assuming (at least in *Limited INC*) that everyday interaction can be understood, as skepticism traditionally claims, on an analogy with the consistency or reliability of the physical world. Instead of seeing our conventional practices as analogous to the assumed stability of places and things, Cavell, following Emerson, reads the ordinary as a challenge, one that forces us to reckon with the import of our words, as they escape us *and* as they return to us. (What impels this reckoning are the situations that join us to, and separate us from, the other breathers of words.)

Derrida, then, when he construes Austin's ordinary as a palpable consistency and accepts this consistency as the desired target of, and partner to, deconstruction, shares an impulse toward the "relatively stabilized knowledge" he charges Marx with. Derrida's reductive idea of the ordinary becomes a necessary counter to his own thought of melancholy persistence: a way of finding reality's comforting limits, so that he can then lose them (in theory, reverie, or fever).

For Emerson the ordinary, in Cavell's reading and mine, looks far more interesting than it does to Derrida; it means being exposed to the fact of one's own thoughts and deeds in a way that supports rather than diminishes us. The past that precedes us, too, is ordinary, and extraordinary, as our lives are; therefore, it does not really precede us. Emerson calls for a present-tense valuing of our history, personal and collective, for measuring the past by means of the still living Gnostic light, or "lustres," that gleam within it. "I read for the lustres," Emerson famously writes in "Nominalist and Realist": "It is a greater joy to see the author's author, than himself" (*E* 579).

There is a relation between this Emersonian mood and Nietzsche's way of exploring history for the possibility of new creation, although Nietzsche goes beyond Emerson by developing the idea of the critical stance. In order to move toward Nietzsche's argument in "History for Life," I must first examine Emerson's essay "History," which is both deeply related to and deeply divergent from Nietzsche's.

EMERSON ON HISTORY

In "History," from *Essays: First Series* (1841), Emerson definitively aligns history with the potential for birth into creative power. Emerson here writes that "the power of poetry to unfix, and, as it were, to clap wings to solid nature, interprets the riddle of Orpheus" (*E* 251). In the course of the essay, Emerson takes flight: "Upborne and surrounded as we are by this all-creating nature, soft and fluid as a cloud or the air, why should we be such hard pedants, and magnify a few forms?" (*E* 242). For Emerson, poetry makes mobile what to our prosaic, dull sight looked like stiff reality.

In keeping with his liberatory promise, Emerson's approach to the Orphic "riddle" in "History" equips us with an easy capacity for resurrection, as Emerson ameliorates the hard riddle of the Sphinx with which he began his essay ("the Sphinx must solve her own riddle" [*E* 237]). Rewriting the Sphinx's famous enigma about the three stages of life, he asks, "What else am I who laughed or wept yesterday, who slept last night like a corpse, and this morning stood and ran?" (*E* 251). The awakening from conformity provides the drama of "History." The conversion of death into sleep, resurrection into happy awakening, a mellowing of terms impossible for the doomed Oedipus confronting the Sphinx, gives the Orphic poet a consummate freedom with respect to reality: "Who cares what the fact was, when we have made a constellation of it to hang in heaven as an immortal sign?" (*E* 240). A characteristic Emersonian move here: he has the cheek, as he well knows, to write an essay on history animated by a profoundly antihistorical mood, just as he concludes his essay on friendship by transforming the friend into an impersonal collection of "lustres," a newly alien image of world (*E* 354). In the sentence I have quoted Emerson lightly mocks his own arrogance: "Who cares what the fact was?" (Does Emerson mock this mood in order to give way to it?)

The ordinary individual, Emerson writes in "History," shares Orpheus's power to "unfix" the normally unyielding world of death and hard fact. In giving us such imaginative power, "History" begins by domesticating the past, overthrowing the barriers that (we normally assume) stand between it and us. This overthrowing happens in the name of a Gnostic commonality, a striking kinship among the illuminating "thoughts" that occur in us, whatever our historical time and place:

> Every revolution was first a thought in one man's mind, and when the same thought occurs to another man, it is the key to that era. Every reform was once a private opinion, and when it shall be a private opinion again, it will solve the problem of the age. The fact narrated must correspond to something in me to be credible or intelligible. We as we read must become Greeks, Romans, Turks, priest and king, martyr and executioner, must fasten these images to some reality in our secret experience, or we shall learn nothing rightly. . . . Each new law and political movement has meaning for you. Stand before each of its tablets and say, "Under this mask did my Proteus nature hide itself." This remedies the defect of our too great nearness to ourselves. This throws our actions into perspective: and as crabs, goats, scorpions, the balance, and the waterpot lose their meanness when hung as signs in the zodiac, so I can see my own vices without heat in the distant persons of Solomon, Alcibiades, and Catiline. (*E* 238)

Here Emerson simultaneously attacks the gap that separates political from private life, and the one that divides past from present. He proposes an elementary hermeneutic principle in order to dissolve both these gaps, the idea that there is a necessary coincidence between the self and the public-historical realm: "The fact narrated must correspond to something in me to be credible or intelligible." When the thought of revolution occurs to two persons rather than one, it becomes a common and public fact; when we see the past in our own lives, it becomes ours. "In their grandest strokes we feel most at home," writes Emerson, speaking of "universal history, the poets, the romancers" (*E* 238). And such identification provides a judicious balance: "I can see my own vices without heat."

If we find such judiciousness too easily attained, we will eventually, and somewhat to our surprise, realize that Emerson himself, in an essay like "Fate," is similarly discontent with his own ease (as I will show in a few pages). We might well question the remedy proposed in "History" for "our too great nearness to ourselves" (*E* 238): locating ourselves even more firmly in history, as the place in which "we feel most at home." This solution seems only to underline the overfamiliarity it seeks to correct. How can the comfort of finding our home everywhere in history "throw our actions into perspective" by giving us a critical awareness of our "vices"? Rather, in such a mood our vices seem glorified by heroic comparison: they "lose their meanness," their commonness, but perhaps as well their capacity to provide a mean, to measure our lack. We fit ourselves to—Emerson's examples—Catiline, Alcibiades, or Solomon, ennobling our failings by comparing them to these heroes' grand faults. Like Nietzsche in *Ecce Homo* inventing his glorious fictive parentage—he might have been the descendent of Caesar or Alexander, he writes (*EH* 12)—Emerson gives free rein to fantasies of power. Some perspective, indeed!

The opening pages of "History," then, argue that we can and should rule the past, fashioning it to suit our needs. The hermeneutic principle Emerson begins with in "History," which matches writing to reading ("the human mind wrote history, and this must read it" [*E* 237]), develops as the essay goes on into the belated reader's dominion over the heroic past: "The student is . . . to esteem his own life the text, and books the commentary" (*E* 239). The true, classic face we share with the past, the "incorrupt, sharply defined, and symmetrical features" of the Greek countenance, will make this past ours, rescuing us from the "confused blur" of modernity (*E* 248).

Our free use of the past on behalf of the present is what Nietzsche will call, in "History for Life," monumental history. Does Emerson recognize, as Nietzsche will, the risk of self-flattery entailed by such freedom? Emerson's alarmingly overt egotistical sublime makes us wonder. "Thus compelled" by our superior ways, "the Muse of history will utter oracles" (*E* 239), Emerson writes: but we know how dangerously tricky oracles can be to those who, like Oedipus, feel themselves to be strong readers. "The Sphinx must solve her own riddle" (*E* 237) suggests an attractive turning of the tables, or tablets, on the riddling monster, the belated seeker's challenge to the ancestral text he confronts.

Nature, interpret thyself! By uttering this command, the Emersonian seeker avoids the monster's power. The mortal danger of this encounter, a danger Emerson intends to bury, is resurrected by Nietzsche near the beginning of *Beyond Good and Evil* when he asks, "Who is Oedipus here? who the Sphinx?" (These two Nietzschean parties being,

perhaps, feminine speaker of mysterious truth and masculine en-
quirer, destined to tangle fatally.)

The "tablets of the law" that daunt us, and that Emerson in the long
passage I quoted urges us to wear as masks for our own "Proteus nature," bear witness to a divorce between political measures and "private opinion." We try to overcome this divorce by matching the public
fact to our "secret experience." Our impulse, however, is not merely to
see ourselves in the past and thereby to make it our own, but beyond
this, to fence ourselves off, with a forbidding legality, in order to enjoy
our new possession: "We hedge [human life] round with penalties and
laws" (E 238). "Property also holds of the soul, covers great spiritual
facts, and instinctively we at first hold to it with swords and laws, and
wide and complex combinations" (E 238). The "swords and laws" that
we use to establish our hold on the soul (or on the soul's propriety, its
properness to itself?) retaliate by establishing their hold on us, since
"property also holds of the soul."

"History" passes beyond its opening demand for us to "read as superior beings," to match the past to ourselves. As the essay continues, it
shows a way for history to challenge our assumptions of superiority, to
turn aside our swords and laws, the weapons we use to guard our understanding. History for Emerson, in other words, does not merely provide
an opportunity for us to transfigure the world of the past to suit our current desire. It also shows us the presence of an antagonistic, unreachable heroism that cannot be "easily domesticated" or "reconcile[d]"
with our current aspirations, but that instead serves our truer, better
selves by challenging or outfacing us. "Jesus overpowers and astonishes
sensual people," Emerson writes. "They cannot unite him to history, or
reconcile him to themselves" (E 249). In this passage, the unity or consistency Emerson so often champions, the project to "live holily" and
wholly (E 249), reveals its origin in a missing sign, a historical figure
who, in his very integrity, his wholeness, overturns our wish for wholeness and consistency. This exemplary figure, Jesus, who admonishes us
for our lack, cannot be "unite[d] . . . to history," or to ourselves. Not
peace but a sword: Jesus shows us a dissonance between the higher, "unattained but attainable self" and the lower, "sensual" one (E 239).

"History" relies in part on archaeology as an image for the relation between us and the past we investigate, or dig into. By means of
this archaeological model, Emerson tries to let us own the history we
find and sift through, making it a thing coincident with the self, and

therefore programmed to assure the self. But at the same time he implies that this inquiry might disorient or dislodge our complacency, so that history will confront us with our own fundamental otherness, our strangeness to ourselves.

We are, perhaps, not the legitimate masters of history, but rather its monsters, with our oddness bearing the portents, or *monstra,* of hope. We must not only "go over the whole ground" of history (*E* 240), but excavate it, Emerson adds: "Belzoni digs and measures in the mummy-pits and pyramids of Thebes, until he can see the end of the difference between the monstrous work and himself" (*E* 241). Emerson of course intends such burrowing as a reduction of the monstrous, in its "desire to do away this wild, savage, and preposterous There or Then, and introduce in its place the Here and the Now" (*E* 241). But seeing the end of the difference between the monstrous and oneself only carries power if it also carries a threat, implying the risk that the self might also be a kind of monster, the Sphinx facing its own riddle. This confrontation turns man into a many-legged, Protean beast, one not at home everywhere but rather lost in space.

The possibility of a monstrous, baffled self remains hidden, I admit, in "History," but it is there. In the later essay "Fate," from *The Conduct of Life,* it comes into its own. The possibility of facing the monster in the self, of (in Nietzsche's words) confronting the abyss that stares back into us, emerges in "Fate," which is in several ways a riposte to "History." In "Fate" Emerson depicts history as an irreversible turning of pages. Here, in contrast to "History," the legibility that occurs serves the cosmic writer's insistence, not the individual reader's. Nature or Fate is in charge, not us:

> The book of Nature is the book of Fate. She turns the gigantic pages, — leaf after leaf, — never re-turning one. One leaf she lays down, a floor of granite; then a thousand ages, and a bed of slate; a thousand ages, and a measure of coal; a thousand ages, and a layer of marl and mud; vegetable forms appear; her first misshapen animals, zoophyte, trilobium, fish; then, saurians, — rude forms, in which she has only blocked her future statue, concealing under these unwieldy monsters the fine type of her coming king. The face of the planet cools and dries, the races meliorate, and man is born. But when a race has lived its term, it comes no more again. (*E* 949)

In this passage of "Fate," Emerson gives us an echo of Job's statement, "our place knows us no more" (Job 7:10). He reminds us that we humans, lords of creation, will die out and "come no more again" — offering a premonition of Nietzsche's shocking parable of mankind as a briefly flourishing race of mosquito-like ephemera, at the beginning of "On Truth and Lie in the Extra-Moral Sense." Emerson's "Fate," as if in direct argument with his own "History," lays down the law of no "re-turning," no paging back to a past that we might draw to our use. As he depicts nature's sly concealment of "the fine type of her coming king" under "rude forms," Emerson conceals his grim conclusion: instead of nature's sovereigns, we human beings represent a mere cooling or leveling off of natural process. Emerson leaves no space between our birth and our extinction: "The face of the planet cools and dries, the races meliorate, and man is born. But when a race has lived its term, it comes no more again." ("Fate" will later, in a surprising turn, recover from this mood of decline by antagonizing it: "Man is not order of nature, sack and sack, belly and members, link in a chain, nor any ignominious baggage, but a stupendous antagonism, a dragging together of the poles of the Universe" [E 953].)

On the next page of "Fate" Emerson goes even further, reducing the careers of different races and nationalities to the material base of a furiously energetic capitalism presided over by nature: "See the shades of the picture. The German and Irish millions, like the Negro, have a great deal of guano in their destiny. They are ferried over the Atlantic, and carted over America, to ditch and to drudge, to make corn cheap, and then to lie down prematurely to make a spot of green grass on the prairie" (E 950). Emerson's rhetorical picture here is anything but shaded; it revolts against the chiaroscuro subtlety that will be his goal later on in The Conduct of Life. In other writers, the "prematurely" dead often appear as shades, as unfulfilled and ghostly presences, like the history Derrida invokes in Specters of Marx. But Emerson sees the dead as mere matter, races that will live their term (or, rather, barely survive it, "carted" and "drudg[ing]") and then disappear into the earth. No Derridean haunting, but rather abrupt termination, constitutes the plot of "Fate." The reigning image of "History" — individuals sharing a coincident thought of liberation, in Gnostic solidarity — is here replaced by a scene of empty, desperate mirroring among drowning men. In a tableau reminiscent of Cowper's "The Castaway," Emerson shows us the "men struggling overboard in the waves," who "glanced intelligently at each other, but 'twas little they could do for one another." "Well," he concludes, "they had a right to their eye-beams, and all the rest was Fate" (*E* 952). Emerson now reduces the proper, that to which one has a right, to a fatal act of seeing, a look that signals intelligence but, it seems, nothing specifically intelligible. Emerson's drowning men simply reflect to one another their separate lack of resource.

Yet elsewhere in "Fate" Emerson sounds a different note, one that will be taken up in Nietzsche's *Untimely Meditations*. Now the past, instead of being rendered as waste or dead ground, persists in and inhabits our present experience, shining through us in prismatic fashion:

> We sometimes see a change of expression in our companion, and say, his father, or his mother, comes to the windows of his eyes, and sometimes a remote relative. In different hours, a man represents each of several of his ancestors, as if there were seven or eight of us rolled up in each man's skin,—seven or eight ancestors at least,—and they constitute the variety of notes for that new piece of music which his life is. At the corner of the street, you read the possibility of each passenger, in the facial angle, in the complexion, in the depth of his eye. (*E* 947)

We are compelled to stick to the notes written for, or before, us, but the music itself is "new." It offers "variety," featuring now one motif and now, unpredictably, another. Here Emerson gives us not the telescopic economy of "History," its conflation of past and present, but instead a shifting constellation of influences that the shrewd street-corner observer can calculate. (Near the passage I have quoted, Emerson, invoking phrenology, speaks of the cabman who "looks in your face to see if his shilling is sure" [*E* 946].)

The form of sizing up others mentioned in "Fate," by detecting one ancestor or another coming to the fore in the individual face, seems at once subtle and hardheaded. "You read the possibility of each passenger . . . in the depth of his eye," in the gaze that looked so helpless and illegible in the case of the drowning men. Emerson, by equating the case of "our companion" with that of the "passenger," the street-side passerby, attributes a similar depth to both. The distance that characterizes the casual glance in the street also permeates the closest personal relations: a gap potentially infinite, but also telling, and available to canny observation.

EMERSON IN THE *UNTIMELY MEDITATIONS*

Emerson's reflections on history and fate are present in Nietzsche's *Untimely Meditations*, his series of essays from the mid-1870s, when he was still teaching in Basel. The place of Emerson in the *Untimely Meditations* becomes most overt when Nietzsche offers, near the end of "Schopenhauer as Educator," the third of the *Meditations'* four essays, a quotation from "Circles" (from Emerson's *Essays: Second Series* [1844]): *"A new degree of culture would instantly revolutionize the entire system of human pursuits"* (*UM* 193). Here Nietzsche harks back to the image of overturning the universe that he derived from, and turned against, Emerson in his school essay "Fate and History [Fatum und Geschichte]" (for further discussion of "Fate and History," see chapter 5). The sentence from "Circles" Nietzsche cites, in addition to giving Emerson the last word in an essay ostensibly devoted to Schopenhauer, draws our attention to the restless assurance of Emersonian *Bildung*, which will be important for Emerson. In Emerson the increasing movement toward an as yet unattained ideal, though truly speaking it is steady, carries volatile power: an incessant renovation or mobility, exposing the provisional character of all desire and knowledge.

Emerson's revolution of thought, as he describes it in "Circles," promises not merely an "out flank[ing]" of the old by the new, but a wider circumference that will incorporate and encompass the old, producing an Archimedean *Aufhebung* or shifting of the present by the future. "Literature," Emerson writes, "is a point outside of our hodiernal circle. . . . The use of literature is to afford us a platform whence we may command a view of our present life, a purchase by which we may move it" (*E* 408). As in "History," Emerson in "Circles" cherishes the hope of gaining a perspective on one's perspective. But despite this authorial wish, "Circles," at some crucial moments, generates discontinuity rather than continuity. As I explained in chapter 1, the revolutionizing power Emerson invokes often makes for imbalance and shock. In perhaps the essay's most memorable line, Emerson captures its formal strategy as well as its most disconcerting surprise: "People wish to be settled; only as far as they are unsettled is there any hope for them" (*E* 413). At the end of "Circles," Emerson reveals the only motive deeper than the wish for foundation, settlement, and continuity: "The one thing which we seek with insatiable desire is to forget ourselves, to be surprised out of our propriety" (*E* 414).

The desire to "forget ourselves" is insatiable because, as Emerson knew as thoroughly as Nietzsche, we cannot ever do so fully or successfully. When Nietzsche cites "Circles" in "Schopenhauer as Educator," he reflects on the limits of our wish to overthrow our current consciousness. The drive to abolish what Emerson calls our "propriety," our historical being in its blind loyalty to the present, is the source not just of originality but of the only true historical consciousness, the only consciousness that does not deprive itself of a future.

There is a major difference between Emerson's "Circles" and Nietzsche's "Schopenhauer as Educator," which cites Emerson yet significantly diverges from him. Emerson shares Nietzsche's exhilaration over the lack of a ground, but he is not, like Nietzsche, a genealogist intent on burrowing beneath the surface of custom and habit, on "tunnel[ing] into oneself," as Nietzsche will put it in his Schopenhauer essay. Commenting on the Delphic command *gnôthi seauton* (know thyself), Nietzsche in "Schopenhauer as Educator" asks,

> How can man know himself? He is a thing dark and veiled; and if the hare has seven skins, man can slough off seventy times seven and still not be able to say: "this is really you, this is no longer outer shell." Moreover, it is a painful and dangerous undertaking thus to tunnel into oneself and to force one's way down into the shaft of one's being by the nearest path. A man who does it can easily so hurt himself that no physician can cure him. (*UM* 129)

In images given to him by Emerson's "History" and "Fate" (two essays that picture life as a site for excavation and archaeological searching), Nietzsche sees *Bildung* not as construction, but rather as a "tunnel[ing]." In Nietzsche, unlike Emerson, such digging down means the harrowing or undermining of self, a quest for underlying foundations that, because it leads one to interrogate the self's motives more and more deeply, may leave one permanently injured rather than firmly grounded.

Education in "Schopenhauer as Educator" is not the easy thing it sometimes seems to be in Emerson, a mere sloughing of skin, a finding of the true under the obscuring layers of ephemeral social conventions. Rather, Nietzsche writes, the quest for self-education confronts two contrasting dangers: that it may prove endless and futile, and that it may turn out to be a profoundly self-wounding excavation. An inquiry into our true motives and interests threatens to expose, on the one hand, a lack of ground, a Peer Gynt–like infinity of selves; or on the other, an incurable mutilation, the result of a too-direct and forcible penetration into "the shaft of one's being." If we do reach the goal and succeed in tunneling to the core of our identity, that core might turn out to be a place that could be painful to lay open. The paragraph I have quoted, it is important to know, directly follows a quotation from Cromwell also taken from Emerson's "Circles": "A man never rises higher than when he does not know whither his path can still lead him" (*UM* 129; cf. *E* 414: "'A man,' said Oliver Cromwell, 'never rises so high as when he knows not whither he is going'"). In "Schopenhauer as Educator," Nietzsche the philosophical mole develops his subterranean project as an at least implicit reversal of Emerson's typical praise for the unknowing but confident impulse that takes an upward path, which he alludes to with his Cromwell reference.[26] Nietzsche changes the direction of the journey: it now descends into the self.

Nietzsche seems conscious of his difference from Emerson in "Schopenhauer as Educator," and, by the essay's end, he has healed that difference, bringing himself closer to Emerson. In one crucial passage, Nietzsche contrasts his underground work with the Emersonian mode of reflection on self and society (though he does not here name Emerson, the reference is clear). Speaking of the ascetic work of *Untergehen*, of self-undermining and self-study, Nietzsche writes, "What need should there be for it, since everything bears witness to what we are, our friendships and enmities, our glance and the clasp of our hand, our memory and that which we do not remember, our books and our handwriting?" (*UM* 129).

Nietzsche goes on to concede, in effect, the Emersonian objection to his painful tunneling. For Emerson, the casual external indications of our being, whether large or small, bear sufficient witness to who we are. In Emerson, knowledge is available without self-torture. The most significant of the witnesses to, or indications of, our being is the encounter with (to use Allen Grossman's term) the "hermeneutic friend."[27] In "Schopenhauer as Educator," this encounter is Nietzsche's meeting with Schopenhauer's texts, which he honors from the moment he comes across them. Instead of continuing on his descent into the self's truth, Nietzsche now moves upward and outward, envisioning a study of the "revered objects" that have "drawn [his] soul aloft," the things that have "mastered it and at the same time blessed it" (*UM* 129).

Nietzsche, at this point in "Schopenhauer as Educator," relies on Emerson to alleviate the ascetic impulse that produced his earlier image of excavation.

Nietzsche shares with Schopenhauer, as with Emerson, a polemic against the narrow, conformist self. The prime lesson of Schopenhauerian pessimism, Nietzsche writes in "Schopenhauer as Educator," is that "we *hate* ourselves as we usually are." This pessimism is "the root, not the flower" of all culture, its beginning, not its goal (*UM* 161).

But Nietzsche's argument in "Schopenhauer as Educator" is about to take a turn away from Schopenhauer. Having risen above conformity, Nietzsche writes, "in that elevated condition . . . we shall also love something else, something we are now unable to love" (*UM* 161). Nietzsche now dreams of a release from Schopenhauer's asceticism, from the self-hatred of being. He envisions a transformation of existence, based in love for a future that has not yet appeared. This hope is deeply Emersonian, and not at all Schopenhauerian. And the hope requires an anti-Schopenhauerian definition of how and why we might discover that we still lead a guilty or inadequate existence: not a realization of universally shared human weakness, but a confrontation with one's own answerable nature, its promises and avoidances.

James Conant, writing eloquently on "Schopenhauer as Educator," summarizes the ethical project in Nietzsche's essay: "If you press on yourself this question 'What have you loved up to now?' and then contemplate the answers you give, then a discovery will ensue: 'Set up these revered objects before you and perhaps their nature and their sequence will give you a law, the fundamental law of your own true self.'"[28] The sentence Conant cites from Nietzsche promises the discovery of "the fundamental law of your own true self," the perfected self that lies "immeasurably high above you," as Nietzsche puts it on the same page of "Schopenhauer as Educator" (*UM* 129). The discovery occurs through a careful examination of personal history: ask yourself what objects, what persons and texts, you have been devoted to up to now.

Perhaps the determination of one's influences and loves is not so simple, though, at least not for a skeptical Bloomian reader. Nietzsche will end his writing career in *Ecce Homo* with an account, or inventory, of his devotions, but he will take care to note that for Schopenhauer in "Schopenhauer as Educator" we should read Nietzsche, and for Wagner in *The Birth of Tragedy* we should also read Nietzsche (*EH* 58, 52).

In *Ecce Homo,* Nietzsche raises the Emersonian question of how we claim another's words as our own, and how this other's words claim us.[29] But in this, his last book, he answers the question with a rather megalomaniacal insistence that overwhelms his earlier interest in discriminating the self by carefully tracing the place of others in our lives.

The *Untimely Meditations,* like Emerson's essays, confront the question of realization more openly and flexibly, in contrast to *Ecce Homo's* dominating claim that Nietzsche has always been what he is, self-raised by his own power. Nietzsche in the *Untimely Meditations* senses that the crisis of modernity entails a sense of a spectral or unreal existence, a feeling that our lives are not yet achieved reality. Nietzsche becomes a genealogist out of his desire for a realizing of the individual. Individual realization, in the *Untimely Meditations,* differs decisively from the universalizing picture of life as art in *The Birth of Tragedy,* as it does from monumental self-praise of the individual "Nietzsche" in *Ecce Homo.*

There was little room in *The Birth of Tragedy* for the consideration of the individual Nietzsche begins in the *Untimely Meditations.* This shift is connected to the fact that, for the Nietzsche of the *Meditations,* aesthetic beauty is not a metaphysical comfort as it was in the *Birth,* the casting of a universal perspective that enables our escape from the particular. Instead it is tied to the particularity of a person's history, and with it to the role of the individual as artist of his life. Nietzsche, like Emerson, now praises a delusory and rewarding process of invention in which both lover and beloved, both knower and object of knowledge, participate.

To put the matter another way: after *The Birth of Tragedy,* Nietzsche moves away from the goal of consolation and toward that of critique. He scrutinizes the myriad ways we employ illusions, against ourselves as well as against others, and tries to estimate how we suffer and thrive in their service. In the *Untimely Meditations,* Nietzsche champions individual attachments as the site of a critical and creative power: the injustice of great love, which is the ground of all justice. Instead of the *Birth's* insistence that the spectator or worshipper "repeat" or share a hero's or god's sufferings (*BT* 40), Nietzsche's later work describes the elaborate human uses of pathos, whose artfulness prevents it, even in love, from being ecstatically shared as we may want it to be. The *Birth's* picture of communion, its evocation of the collective Dionysian festival, now yields to a new individualism.

NIETZSCHE'S "HISTORY FOR LIFE"

The Birth of Tragedy hoped for a redemption *from* history, a hope that Nietzsche inherited from Schopenhauer. By contrast, the second essay in the *Untimely Meditations,* "On the Use and Disadvantage of History for Life," aims at a cherishing of history in the name of life—an Emersonian hope. Here Nietzsche shifts from a universalist to an individualist notion of tragedy, and by doing so shows how the tragic sense proves essential to the making of the individual's critical stance toward culture.

In "History for Life" Nietzsche identifies three forms of historical consciousness: monumental, antiquarian, and critical. The modes of monumental and antiquarian history are designed to support an easy communal loyalty, Nietzsche argues in an Emersonian vein, and they therefore decline into the weakness that characterizes all conformity. But the third historical mode, the critical, serves creation by recognizing the task of the individual faced with a particular history and specific possibilities of self-making.

First, we need to define the three modes. In his essay, Nietzsche supplies these definitions by portraying representative characters who embody our characteristic ways of reading the world, just as Emerson frequently does, for example in "The Conservative" or "Nominalist and Realist." "History pertains to the living man in three respects," Nietzsche writes. "It pertains to him as a being who acts and strives [als dem Thätigen und Strebenden], as a being who preserves and reveres [als dem Bewahrenden und Verehrenden], as a being who suffers and seeks deliverance [als dem Leidenden und der Befreiung Bedürftigen]" (*UM* 67; *KSA* 1.258). The actor and striver, the heroic "man of deeds and power," requires monumental history (*UM* 67); the scholar whose piety makes him "as it were give thanks for his existence," who preserves and reveres the past, requires the antiquarian mode (*UM* 72); and finally, the sufferer who asks after deliverance from the past needs *critical* history, the summit of Nietzsche's ambition in his essay.

Why *deliverance* from the past? As Nietzsche famously writes in "History for Life," from the standpoint of the historical sense every past is worthy of condemnation. Yet such judgment cannot stand: there is a past for each of us that must be prized and praised, rather than condemned, because it is essential to our identity. From this fact Nietzsche derives his emphasis on the importance of selectivity. Justice begins in the injustice of selective love, Nietzsche powerfully writes. The focus of one's love, whether it be a person or a deed, is an island of light surrounded by "a dead sea of darkness and oblivion" (*UM* 64). Heroic individualization brings a figure in the foreground into sharp focus by blurring all that surrounds him (the focus-puller effect I mentioned in my discussion of *The Birth of Tragedy* in chapter 2). In this way, the hero who "loves his deed infinitely more than it deserves to be loved" serves life (*UM* 64).

Yet by shading all else with oblivion, the hero's selective love proves unable to attain the critical. Its affinity, instead, is to the monumental. The monumental is sublimely creative; but because it idolizes instead of analyzing, it remains utterly uninterested in discovering the dynamic relation between one event and another, one person and another, one value and another. The author or reader of monumental history cherishes a particular heroic example by seeing it in glamorous isolation.[30]

Nietzsche's second type, the antiquarian, resists such reduction since he wants a truer, because deeper and more thorough, embrace of the past. He replaces the isolation of the monumental with a context enriched by his solemn care, a thick description that, unlike the monumentalist's myth, fully deserves to be called scholarly. But the antiquarian courts a new danger: lack of selectivity. The supervisory neutrality of antiquarian appreciation, the idea that the entire history of the culture or community we belong to deserves to be cherished, leads to the antiquarian's repression of the healthy impulse to attack certain parts of the past.

The antiquarian fails to acknowledge the foreign, adversarial sting of the past; like the monumentalist, he claims history as proper to us, and therefore cannot see the threat it poses to the present. Only Nietzsche's third and final type, the critical historian, aims at explaining past deeds and persons while also furthering the creative force that rebels against the past.

This past must not merely be nourished in the antiquarian manner. It must also be resisted, if we are to achieve the power of the critical. Therefore, a proper thoughtfulness about who we are must seek its basis in genealogical reflection on the historical origins of our values. Such reflection forms, in "History for Life," the most crucial and dangerous territory of all, because it begins in a wholesale rejection of the past as unjust *tout court*. Describing his ideal of critical history, Nietzsche begins by associating the critical, in its first rough phase, with the desire to destroy:

[Sometimes life] wants to be clear as to how unjust the existence of anything — a privilege, a caste, a dynasty, for example — is, and how greatly this thing deserves to perish [den Untergang verdient]. Then its past is regarded critically, then one takes the knife to its roots, then one cruelly tramples over every kind of piety [dann schreitet man grausam über alle Pietäten hinweg]. (*UM* 76; *KSA* 1.270)

But Nietzsche then turns from the rampant destructive impulse that "cruelly tramples over every kind of piety" to a more selective urge, educated by a consciousness of one's share in the past one wants to destroy. We rebel against the past, Nietzsche writes, *because* we know it is part of us:

For since we are the outcome of earlier generations, we are also the outcome of their aberrations, passions and errors, and indeed of their crimes [ihrer Verirrungen, Leidenschaften und Irrthümer, ja Verbrechen]; it is not possible wholly to free oneself from this chain. If we condemn these aberrations and regard ourselves as free of them, this does not alter the fact that we originate in them. The best we can do is to confront our inherited and hereditary nature with our knowledge of it, and through a new, stern discipline combat our inborn heritage and implant in ourselves a new habit, a new instinct, a second nature, so that our first nature withers away. It is an attempt to give oneself, as it were *a posteriori*, a past in which one would like to originate in opposition to that in which one did originate: — always a dangerous attempt because it is so hard to know the limit to denial of the past and because second natures are usually weaker than first. What happens all too often is that we know the good but do not do it, because we also know the better but cannot do it. But here and there a victory is nonetheless achieved, and for the combatants, for those who employ critical history for the sake of life, there is even a noteworthy consolation: that of knowing that this first nature was once a second nature and that every victorious second nature will become a first. (*UM* 76–77; *KSA* 1.270)

In this magisterial passage Nietzsche, like Emerson in *Nature,* "Experience," and other works, acknowledges our feeling of secondariness or unoriginality, along with our striving to overcome this feeling.

Nietzsche's sense of the hard ghostly grip of the past contrasts with Emerson's easy statement in "History" that "the oppressor of [a man's] youth is himself a child tyrannized over by those names and words and forms, of whose influence he was merely the organ to the youth" (*E* 250). More closely, Nietzsche here echoes Emerson's knowledge, expressed in "The Poet," that the idolized first nature is actually a "second nature," owing its origin to the poet's brilliant naming of it. For Emerson, though, the poet's words represent not a strenuous cultural victory, as they would for Nietzsche, but rather proof of nature's own art: "This expression, or naming, is not art, but a second nature, grown out of the first, as a leaf out of a tree" (*E* 457). Emerson praises the continuity that turns art and nature, precursor and inheritor, into fair copies or versions of each other. In Nietzsche, by contrast, a strong individuality proves itself by proving unjust in Bloomian fashion: by displacing other individuals, rendering them diluted imitations, mere second natures, and by promising itself that it will turn its own second nature into a first.

Yet Emerson also forecasts Nietzsche's displacing of the past. In "The Poet" he conveys the power of new poetry by describing its tendency to obscure the old gods, to render them mere hearsay. Listening to a young poet, we find that the whole past fades away before us: "Rome,—what was Rome? Plutarch and Shakespeare . . . [are] in the yellow leaf, and Homer no more should be heard of" (*E* 451).

GHOSTS, GUILT, AND SELF-REALIZATION IN NIETZSCHE

The Nietzsche of *Untimely Meditations* takes up Emerson's concern in "Experience" and elsewhere with the ghostliness of existence and our desire to make it, to make ourselves, actual. Through a ruthless discipline of self-advancement, in "History for Life" the unreal becomes real. In a key example of the architectonic motif in Nietzsche, the self finds its place by constructing that place, building a monument of victory over what it has inherited.

This project requires an anti-Schopenhauerian definition of our guilt. For Nietzsche, as for Emerson, the characteristic human affliction is the pang of what remains unrealized. This is not a guilt derived from crimes of the flesh, the Pauline "law of the members" (Romans 7) that still possesses Schopenhauer; it stems instead from the insubstantiality of our yet-unachieved existence. In Nietzsche as in Emerson, when we start worrying about our unrealized nature, we also start cultivating the heroic wish to realize it.

This is a new turn against Schopenhauer in Nietzsche's thought. *The Birth of Tragedy* transformed a futile, blind will tormented by the object-cause of desire (the object *a*) into a tragic and just, because universal, striving. In doing so, the *Birth* made the will beautiful; but it was still Schopenhauer's will that Nietzsche transfigured. By contrast, the two central essays of the *Untimely Meditations,* "History for Life" and "Schopenhauer as Educator," share the crucial Emersonian hope for release into a newly substantiated existence committed to, and finding its substance in, the individual's desire (in contrast to Schopenhauer's wish to be freed from desire).

One of the means to such release into true existence, Nietzsche speculates in "Schopenhauer as Educator," would be the emotion of being "ashamed of oneself without any accompanying feeling of distress [Selbstbeschämung ohne Verdrossenheit]" (*UM* 163; *KSA* 1.385), a sense of being upbraided in one's imperfection without the self-contempt, the contempt for his own being, and for being itself, that the ascetic indulges in. Our imperfection, Nietzsche remarks in a tone that may remind us of Emerson's "American Scholar," is merely a sign that we are not yet whole, rather than a sign of nature's irremediable fallenness. In Schopenhauer, nature is guilty of original sin; not so in Nietzsche.

In a brilliant essay, Werner Hamacher describes the partial or incomplete character of the Nietzschean individuality that strives for greater integrity: "The individual is nothing other than the unreined, voluptuous self-outliving of life, the ongoing passing away of an excessive being no longer susceptible of being seized in the unity of a historical, social, or logical form. Individuality 'is' outliving [überleben]."[31] As Hamacher points out, whatever integrity the Nietzschean individual can approach must exceed the limits of normative definition, of "historical, social, or logical form." Individuality is a ghostly survival, an *Überleben.* Because of this ghostliness, the example of Hamlet is significant in "Schopenhauer as Educator," as it was in *The Birth of Tragedy,* and in Emerson's "Self-Reliance." Schopenhauer, Nietzsche writes, pursues "a clear view of the picture of life and existence as a whole" just "as Hamlet pursues the ghost" (and, we might add, just as young Nietzsche tracks the ghost of Schopenhauer) (*UM* 141). Hamlet interrogates his father's ghost, seeking to discover its truth; but a ghost by its nature traffics in unclarity. This obscure task, discerning the tracks of a paternal spirit, spurs the ephebe's quest for a "clear view," an integrity of action and being. Hamlet's father demands from his son a pure striving, a clear and simple revenge. As he conceives his project of vengeance, however, young Hamlet also avenges himself on his own existence, disintegrating the wholeness of purpose that vengeance promised to give him.

Yet this wished for wholeness was, from the beginning, troubled — and even called into being — by its opposite, an interruption or strange hole in reality. As Lacan says in his discussion of *Hamlet,* "The ghost arises from an inexpiable offense," inexpiable because Hamlet's father was betrayed, "taken by surprise in his sleep, in a way that is utterly foreign to the current of his waking thoughts."[32] Cut off in this way, unexpectedly, in the blossoming of his sins, old Hamlet epitomizes the very out-of-jointness that prevents Hamlet from killing Claudius when he has the chance. "What stays Hamlet's arm?" Lacan asks. "It's not fear . . . it's because he knows he must strike something other than what's there."[33] The phallus, the Symbolic importance of the father, cannot be located in Claudius. The phallus is not with the body, and therefore the ghost is with Hamlet: phallic authority remains unsure. There is no "Other of the Other," no support for the paternal big Other whose mastery has been shaken: old Hamlet's lack is handed down to his son. The deed that accomplishes wholeness is forbidden to Hamlet until the very end of the play, when he is no longer teased by the ghost's demand but acts in the name of a providence that solves such enigmas as Hamlet's by displaying them from a particularly remote and reassuring perspective, the providence shown in the fall of a sparrow.[34] Wholeness, then, requires a distance that cures.

Hamlet's disgust with the terms of existence, like Schopenhauer's, shows a partiality. The significance of such rejectionism for Nietzsche lies in the way it suggests that, even as a full picture of reality depends on integration or wholeness, moving toward this realization requires the partial, a fiercely antithetical stance toward others and even toward oneself. In "Schopenhauer as Educator," Nietzsche says of the "Schopenhauerian man" that "however much he may strive after justice," strive after a clear, just view of the whole, "he is bound, according to the human limitations of his insight, to be unjust," to remain tendentious and partial (*UM* 153). Schopenhauer's own stance, in its life-denying pessimism, is undeniably unjust, as Nietzsche recognized even before

The Birth of Tragedy.[35] And "History for Life" theorizes the necessity of injustice on the most general scale, in its famous statement, already cited, that every past is worthy of being condemned. The move toward realization, then, requires both an unbalanced or partial view of existence, an attack on the past and the self, and an ambition for wholeness that would embrace both past and present, the individual and his ancestry.

REALIZING THE WHOLE IN NIETZSCHE

Nietzsche seeks a route out of an oppressive sense of inescapable and universal injustice through an ideal of individual heroism that relies on a practice of dramatic artistry. In "Schopenhauer as Educator" Nietzsche recapitulates, but also significantly alters, his assertion in *The Birth of Tragedy* that the world is justified only as an aesthetic phenomenon. In the Schopenhauer essay, Nietzsche cites Goethe to the effect that "'the *causa finalis* of the activities of men and the world is dramatic poetry. For the stuff is of absolutely no other use'" (*UM* 160). The conclusion Nietzsche draws from Goethe's championing of dramatic form as the self-justification of existence occurs here not on the grand scale occupied by the *Birth,* in which the individual was diminished by his placement in a vast cosmic canvas produced for the universal creator's benefit alone, but on the level of the single man. "Why and for what purpose 'man' exists should be of absolutely no concern to us," wrote Nietzsche in a *Nachlass* fragment from summer-fall 1873, in Emersonian tones, "but why *you* exist, ask yourself that" (in "History for Life": "Ask yourself why you, the individual, exist" [*UM* 112]).[36]

Yet this individual may also turn back to the whole and attempt to identify with the cosmos (to "eat the world," as Emerson says). In "Schopenhauer as Educator," Nietzsche writes that "nature at last needs the saint, in whom the ego is completely melted away and whose life of suffering is no longer felt as his own life—or is hardly so felt—but as a profound feeling of oneness and identity with all living things" (*UM* 160-61). This is Nietzsche's transfiguration of Schopenhauer's hope for freedom from the will. Nietzsche consecrates the exemplary life of the saint, who becomes a vessel of universal sympathy in a way reminiscent of the sacrificial hero of *The Birth of Tragedy.* The focused revisionary stance described in "History for Life"'s picture of the critical historian yields, in "Schopenhauer as Educator," to an ideal of identificatory union: the saint becomes a true exemplum of Dionysian, universal harmony.

The messianic aspect of Nietzsche's vision of the saint in "Schopen-hauer as Educator," a figure who takes on and transforms all of exist-ence, will achieve final form in a sublime passage of *The Gay Science*. As the vision develops, it becomes capable of carrying the heft and variety of a whole dramatic world. In *The Gay Science* Nietzsche's hero lives through a multiplicity of perspectives, of divergent human characters, as the saint of "Schopenhauer as Educator" did not. An ecstatic bal-ance, Nietzsche claims in *The Gay Science*, might be achieved by one per-son. All these possible identities might be held in solution at once, in a single *Gefühl*, a feeling or mood:

> Anyone who manages to experience the history of humanity as *his own* history will feel in an enormously generalized way all the grief of an invalid who thinks of health, of an old man who thinks of the dreams of his youth, of a lover deprived of his be-loved, of the martyr whose ideal is perishing, of the hero on the evening after a battle that has decided nothing but brought him wounds and the loss of his friend. . . . [I]f one could finally con-tain all this in one soul and crowd it into [zusammendrängen] a single feeling—this would surely have to result in a happiness [ein Glück] that humanity has not known so far: the happiness of a god full of power and love, full of tears and laughter, a hap-piness that, like the sun in the evening, continually bestows its in-exhaustible riches, pouring them into the sea, feeling richest, as the sun does, only when even the poorest fisherman is still row-ing with golden oars! This godlike feeling would then be called—humaneness [Menschlichkeit]. (*GS* #337; *KSA* 3.565)

Nietzsche here fantasizes the compressing of an unimaginable multi-tude of *ethoi* or characters, representatives of the entire spectrum of human experience, into a single pathos, "one single feeling."[37]

Such comprehensive, salvational historical consciousness as Nietzsche envisions in *The Gay Science*'s "god full of power and love" must begin from an Emersonian impulse to overcome the insubstanti-ality of the conformist present. Almost a decade before *The Gay Science*, in "History for Life," Nietzsche wrote:

> Fragmented and in pieces, dissociated almost mechanically into an inner and an outer, sown with concepts as with dragon's teeth, bringing forth conceptual dragons, suffering from the

malady of words and mistrusting any feeling of our own which
has not yet been stamped with words: being such an unliving and
yet uncannily active [unheimlich regsame] concept- and word-
factory, perhaps I still have the right to say of myself *cogito, ergo
sum,* but not *vivo, ergo cogito.* Empty "being" [Das leere "Sein"] is
granted me, but not full and green "life"; the feeling that tells
me I exist warrants to me only that I am a thinking creature, not
that I am a living one, not that I am an *animal* but at most a *cogi-
tal.* Only give me life, then I will create a culture for you out of
it! — Thus cries each individual of this generation and all those
individuals will recognize one another from this cry. Who is to
give them this life?

"No god and no man," Nietzsche concludes, answering his own question, "only their own *youth*" (*UM* 119–20). But, as we have seen in the
case of Hamlet, one cannot give life to oneself in this manner; the gift,
or burden, arrives from, or as, the past.

In this passage from "History for Life," Nietzsche's picture of the
self as an "uncannily active concept- and word-factory" in fact sounds
like Hamlet, with his wild and whirling words. In Nietzsche's revision of
the story of the founding of Thebes (Cadmus's sowing of the dragon's
teeth), it is "conceptual dragons," rather than warriors, that are spawned.
We ourselves are the sown and "stamped" field, a human "factory" that
makes echoing cries about creating a culture. Here, in contrast to *The
Birth of Tragedy,* the process of cultural (re)creation takes an individualist
form, with isolated selves calling to their similarly isolated counterparts,
instead of participating in a collective Dionysian ritual as in the *Birth.*

The paragraph I have just quoted from "History for Life" gestures
back to Emerson's "Self-Reliance," with its wish for originality and fullness of life, and forward to Nietzsche's own later variation on Descartes's *cogito ergo sum* topos in book 4 of *The Gay Science:* "I still live, I still
think: I still have to live, for I still have to think. *Sum, ergo cogito: cogito,
ergo sum*" (*GS* #276). Whereas the lines from "History for Life" depict a
thinking that is not yet sufficiently alive, those from *The Gay Science* give
us life and thought melded together. In *The Gay Science,* thinking and
living are poised in exact equation: *sum, ergo cogito; cogito, ergo sum.* Here
ego is playfully derived from *ergo:* as I argue in chapter 4, the symbiotic
balance of life and thought is part of the structured, architectonic perfection Nietzsche envisions in *The Gay Science.* Reading "History for

Life," by contrast, we find ourselves translated back into the unreal dominion of mere thought. Thinking ought to be the legitimate child of
life, but it has instead taken on an illegitimate, ghostly life of its own:
"Perhaps I still have the right to say of myself *cogito, ergo sum,* but not
vivo, ergo cogito."[38]

Nietzsche's play with the Cartesian *cogito* has its source in Emerson.
In "Self-Reliance," Emerson writes, "Few and mean as my gifts may be,
I actually am, and do not need for my own assurance or the assurance
of my fellows any secondary testimony" (E 263). A few pages later, in
the same essay, he remarks, "Man is timid and apologetic; he is no
longer upright; he dares not say, 'I think,' 'I am,' but quotes some saint
or sage" (*E* 270). As Cavell has noted, Emerson here cites Descartes in
the very act of denouncing such citation, the quoting of saint or sage.
But this is no mere self-referential gag, nor a (Derridean) gesture toward the all-pervasiveness of citation. Instead of surrendering to the
secondhand, Emerson rebukes it: he states the difference between
himself and Descartes. Cavell comments that "Emerson goes the whole
way with Descartes's insight—that I exist only if I think—but he there-
upon denies that I (mostly) do think, that the 'I' mostly gets into my
thinking, as it were."[39] In order to (actually) exist, I must claim or stake
my existence. But the price for this claim may be exorbitant, the giving
over of my being to a demand from the past: "Being asked to assume
the burden of another's existence as if that were the burden, or price,
of assuming one's own." Cavell speculates on the deed the past wants
from Hamlet, the death of Claudius. By killing Claudius, Cavell writes,
"Hamlet is asked to make a father's life work out successfully, to come
out even, by taking his revenge for him."[40] Yet this demand for the correction of the time, for setting it right, is exactly what enforces young
Hamlet's sense of oddity, making his emergence (or not) in the world
the shouldering of a wrongful burden. Cavell remarks:

> The emphasis in the question "to be or not" seems not on
> whether to die but on whether to be born, or whether to affirm
> or deny the fact of natality, as a way of enacting, or not, one's ex-
> istence. To accept birth is to participate in a world of revenge, of
> mutual victimization, of shifting and substitution. But to refuse
> to partake in it is to poison everyone who touches you, as if tak-
> ing your own revenge. This is why if the choice is unacceptable
> the cause is not metaphysics but history—say, a posture toward

the discovery that there is no getting even for the oddity of being born, hence of being and becoming the one poor creature it is given to you to be.[41]

Hamlet's odd theatricality is, then, for Cavell in this eloquent passage, an effort to take revenge on, but also an atonement for and an enactment of, the oddity of his historical, human place on this earth. Hamlet cannot come out even; Shakespeare's drama is, as Cavell asserts, deeply concerned with the sheer eccentric contingency of our individual positions. In Cavell contingency takes a cruel form as it does not in the liberal ethics of Mill, Rawls, and Rorty discussed in my Introduction. For Cavell, the fundamental fact of your being is that you are *this one* rather than another. You cannot see from the other's position, and the attempt to do so must be a doomed effort to deny the difference between your place and the other's.

Cavell's focus on the individual's contingent place in the world helps us toward Nietzsche's denser—because historically situated—treatment of this same question in "History for Life." Nietzsche's sense of our situation as poor creatures faced with the pressure of a past that threatens to usurp us is founded not merely in his awareness of our fragile contingency, but, more solidly, in the dynamics of our relation to our past, the way we reenact it even as we struggle to break free of it.

Here Nietzsche parts decisively from Emerson. For the agonistic Emerson of "New England Reformers," as we saw in chapter 1, truth is that which we resist precisely because it most profoundly inhabits our identity, influencing us beyond our will and beyond any historical scheme we might discover. We find what the Divinity School Address calls "the moral nature of man" "where the sublime is, where are the resources of astonishment and power" (*E* 63). What takes us aback, but also brings us forward, is the hitherto hidden, the unexpected access of imaginative force, a force that cannot be historically located or confined.

Emerson's trust in the mind's powers goes along with his freedom from the impulse toward ascesis that Nietzsche so profoundly lived and worked through.[42] But Emerson's exploration of a realm of iron fate that is also, and unexpectedly, the territory of hope does not help him measure the distinctive force of individual events and persons as Nietzsche can. Such attention to the historical effect of the particular influences that both orient and constrain us makes up the critical consciousness, Nietzsche's answer to the limitations of the monumental and antiquarian perspectives.

Following Nietzsche, we need to develop a critical order of rank, a reevaluation of the past influences on us that would make clear their distinct powers, and therefore free us, however partially, to exploit our place in, and beyond, history's continuing narratives. Nietzsche in his early development from *The Birth of Tragedy* to *Untimely Meditations* moves toward a form of critical attitude based on a canny awareness of one's inheritance from the past. In his last works, especially *Ecce Homo*, Nietzsche falls prey to what takes precedence over such historical awareness, in his subjection to the potency of the object *a*, a factor ungovernable by the critical consciousness.

Despite this capitulation in his last works to what Lacan calls the fundamental fantasy, Nietzsche remains a crucial champion of the critical, the focused study of how to achieve a liberating awareness of our present conditions. We need Nietzsche in order to resist the facile claims of relativism and mere rhetorical force. Nietzsche in "History for Life," Laurence Lampert reminds us, argues against the relativist advocacy of a fluidity of concepts that would establish the "sovereignty of becoming," a "true but deadly" doctrine.[43]

Our postmodern culture remains upset with its own addiction to relativism: witness the attachment of nearly all of what is currently called cultural criticism to a notion of its own disinterestedness. Cultural studies wants to expose and thereby rise above bias, prejudice, and mere opinion. As I argued in my Introduction, the cultural critic falls into the trap of assuming his own freedom from the prejudices ascribed to all others, who have apparently been indoctrinated as he has not. Moreover, cultural studies, for the most part, limits itself to the institutions and practices that enforce conformity. But cultural practices could not thrive without being embodied in singular, heroic phenomena. However dispassionate we are, we retain an obsessive and unjust valuing of certain well-nigh sacred texts and persons.

I am not speaking in favor of the idolatry of cultural presences, what Nietzsche labels monumental history. Instead, I am advocating an appreciation of our struggle with such presences. Nietzsche reminds us that the hero values his deed more than it is worth, and this prejudice toward one's own remains just as true of strong readers. As Bloom so shrewdly demonstrates, such readerly will exerts itself against the grain of individual past authors, in a profoundly Nietzschean historical agon, even when it thinks it is proving its loyalty to the past. The great authors of a tradition, like the memorable heroes of history, return to haunt us at their will, not ours.

In its posture of mythic celebration, the monumental attitude avoids struggle; it reduces the past to an indifferent blur. Even as it focuses on certain glorious figures, it perceives these figures weakly and vaguely, using them as practical sources of inspiration and encouragement. By relying on an occasional or casual use of heroes, monumental history fails to account for the constraining, and empowering, influence of remarkable persons, events, and texts: the presences that live in and through us, however unrecognized or repressed they may be. "How violently what is individual" in the past has to be overlooked by the monumental observer, "all its sharp corners and hard outlines broken up in the interest of conformity," Nietzsche exclaims (*UM* 69).

Monumental history gives the modern a free hand, the opportunity to use history however he wishes in order to enhance a belated existence and increase its share of life. Yet such misreading, or "free poetic invention" as Nietzsche calls it (*UM* 70), however profitable, denies the most urgent fact about history for precisely us moderns: the recurrent presence of powerful ghosts from the past who trouble our sleep. The relativist (or monumentalist) freedom to redescribe the world, and the self, endlessly reveals itself as a prison of indefinition. Richard Rorty in *Contingency, Irony and Solidarity* advocates a practice of inventive redescription that, in just this way, turns out to be too successful in its freedom from constraint. If we become overly adept at the creation of new worlds, we may prove too weak to bear the reality-testing that strong poetry must incur. And reality in this context means the pressure of the past.

As Nietzsche writes near the beginning of "History for Life," we cannot share the unhistorical happiness of animals, who live in the moment. Instead, for us "a moment," like old Hamlet in the essay on Schopenhauer, "returns as a ghost and disturbs the peace of a later moment" (*UM* 61). Nietzsche here reminds us of the *Birth*'s use of the return of Alcestis as an image for the presence of the god Dionysus to the tragic audience (*BT* chapter 8). But in the "History for Life" passage the past returns, not in order to free and unite us as Dionysus does, but to "disturb" us, to obstruct our "peace."

The past, when it returns upon us in this way, is neither living nor dead. We cannot consume the moment and be done with it; we are unable to sink into presence with the cow's vegetative consistency, "fettered to the moment and its pleasure or displeasure, and thus neither melancholy nor bored" (*UM* 60). Instead, we find ourselves borne by the stream of becoming, deprived of the bovine complacency of being. In short, we remain "an imperfect tense that can never become a perfect one" (*UM* 61).

Realization must take a different route. The perfection we can approach, according to Nietzsche in "History for Life," is of a radically different sort   anti-bovine, as it were. Nietzsche offers two alternatives: either to "sink down on the threshold of the moment [auf der Schwelle des Augenblicks] and forget all the past," to "stand balanced like a goddess of victory" in the moment "[auf einem Punkte] without growing dizzy or afraid" — or else to "transform and incorporate into oneself what is past and foreign, to heal wounds, to replace what has been lost, to recreate broken moulds [zerbrochene Formen aus sich nachzuformen]" (*UM* 62; *KSA* 1.251).

These are Nietzsche's two options for human flourishing: a Nike-like brilliance that achieves victory over the past by grappling with that past as its enemy, as the antagonist of the current moment; and a practice of *imitatio* that approaches wholeness by transforming and embodying history.[44] The uncompromising partiality that aims for success by riding the moment as it comes into being remains opposed, in "History for Life," to Nietzsche's architectonic aspiration, his gradual enterprise of healing and fulfilling the present by incorporating the past. Coming into one's own through a precarious embrace of the goddess of momentary triumph, through embracing oddness, the role cast for you by your time, stands against the alternative: evening that place out by recovering and transforming the past (a classic picture of humanist endeavor). In "Schopenhauer as Educator" another image arises: that of the philosopher as lawgiver whose eye "rest[s] upon existence" to "determine its value anew" (*UM* 144). The philosopher as judge recreates existence, justifying it and making it whole. As I describe later in this chapter, Nietzsche's unpublished *Philosophy in the Tragic Age of the Greeks,* from 1873–76, the same years in which he wrote the *Untimely Meditations,* significantly invests itself in the image of the philosopher as judge and fashioner of wholeness.

THE BODY IN PIECES

In the *Meditations* Nietzsche's pictures of fragmented life become those of a broken body, echoing Emerson's "American Scholar" and Hölderlin's *Hyperion*. Hölderlin writes that "I can think of no people more disintegrated [zerrissner] than the Germans. . . . [I]s it not like a battlefield, where hands and arms and limbs lie everywhere in pieces, while the life blood flows out into the sand?"[45] In Emerson, the dismembered ones show an unwitting self-parodic pride. They have no idea what they look like, Emerson remarks in "The American Scholar": "The state of society is one in which the members have suffered amputation from the trunk, and strut about so many walking monsters—a good finger, a neck, a stomach, an elbow, but never a man. Man is thus metamorphosed into a thing, into many things" (*E* 54). "A good finger," muses Emerson with the judicious air of the prospective buyer, ". . . but never a man," never the wholeness that signifies cultural truth. Emerson picks up the image of the dis-, or mis-, connected body in the "American Scholar"'s lament that "Our age is bewailed as the age of Introversion. . . . [W]e cannot enjoy any thing for hankering to know whereof the pleasure consists; we are lined with eyes; we see with our feet; the time is infected with Hamlet's unhappiness" (*E* 67–68). Hamlet's inward turn or introversion, the infection of enjoyment by a frustrated desire to know, appears as a jumbling of bodily functions. ("Unhappiness" here conveys its original sense of a temporal mismatch, as well; the time is out of joint.) Emerson's images themselves seem awkward attempts at expressing the malaise of which they are features: "we are lined with eyes"? "we see with our feet"? (He echoes Hamlet's strange words to Gertrude in 3.4: "Eyes without feeling, feeling without sight / Ears without hands or eyes, smelling sans all.")[46]

A lining is the inside of a cloak, or mantle, so to be "lined with eyes" is to sustain the delusion not that one can see into everything (Hamlet's bravado), but that one's self has been secretly laid open to surveillance, an Argus turned inside out. To see with one's feet suggests a blind, though perhaps bold, stumbling. Emerson's somewhat rude rebuke to doubt challenges our seeming desire for blindness, the self-impairment of our appetite. We have curtailed our wish to take or consume the world: "Is it so bad then? . . . Would we be blind? Do we fear lest we should outsee nature and God, and drink truth dry?" (*E* 68).

Hölderlin's passage is more gruesome, reminiscent of the paragraph from Hegel's *Jenaer Realphilosophie*, often cited by Zizek, in which Hegel stumbles across, in the night of negativity, "phantasmagorical representations": "Here shoots a bloody head—there another white ghastly apparition."[47] And Nietzsche, in book 2 of *Zarathustra* ("On

Redemption"), conveys his disappointment with the human scene by depicting the violence of the "battlefield or butcherfield" full of "fragments and limbs and terrible accidents—but no human beings!" (*Z* 160, translation modified). Nietzsche's image of the fragmented body implies that he continues to brood, with desire and with disgust, over phantasmic partial objects.[48]

Oddness and evenness, then, are opposing rhetorical options in Nietzsche (to adopt, and alter, Cavell's trope). The odd or partial, a polemical and contrarian announcement of the new and other, stands against the even: against a generosity that is willing to take on all of the past, good and evil, and value it in its variety. (Similarly, Emerson's poet "reattaches things to nature and the Whole"—but nature "detaches from him a new self," fragmenting him in the interest of dissemination [*E* 455, 457].) For all its vitality, the partial partakes of the unreal. Nietzsche's statement of the hope for critical consciousness makes it clear that what threatens the development of a truly critical power is our overinvestment in partial, unproven imaginations.

Nietzsche's work suggests that through testing our fictions, and proving their necessity, we might move beyond cultural studies' typical dualism, its opposition between bias or ideological falsification on the one hand and squint-eyed demystification on the other. This dualism, which has been handed down from a certain Marxism to cultural studies and new historicism, fails to explain the attractive force of bias. It turns bias into banality, viewing prejudice as an unavoidable and permanent aspect of our lives, but rarely as a field for genuine discovery or imaginative excitement. A Nietzschean statement of the matter will, in contrast, by seeing the question of bias in terms of influence, also see its excitement and its alluring necessity. Nietzsche's "History for Life" celebrates the interested struggle with influential precursors, whether they are persons or events. Such an agon leads to a truer estimation of past presences, and through this, to the increase of future life.

WAGNER AND THE UNCANNY

Nietzsche in his final *Untimely Meditation,* "Richard Wagner in Bayreuth," imagines Wagner as architect, founder, and judge of culture. Much of the drama of the essay stems from Nietzsche's own growing ambivalence about Wagner. The young Wagner, Nietzsche writes, was in danger of becoming a dilettante, of yielding to the chaos of talents and inclinations within him. Nietzsche remarks on Wagner's "spirit of restlessness, of irritability," his "nervous hastiness in seizing hold upon a hundred different things, a passionate delight in experiencing moods of almost pathological intensity, an abrupt transition from the most soulful quietude to noise and violence" (*UM* 200). Nietzsche's Wagner has the awkward, frustrated energy of Wagner's own young Siegfried.[49]

But Wagner, according to Nietzsche, has passed beyond the centrifugal, exploratory impulses of youth and accomplished a unity of self. At this early point, 1876, Nietzsche sees Wagner as having overcome his dangerous temptation toward incompleteness or partiality, toward an impetuous, Siegfried-like recklessness and arrogance. This danger haunts all of the *Untimely Meditations,* with their picture of German culture as a field for brash and immature spirits, whose distracted energy unfortunately suits this culture's status as a chaotic, tattered, and ostentatious collection of scraps rather than a unified whole.

Wagner's integration of self, according to Nietzsche, required the obedience of one "sphere of his being" to another: "the creative, innocent, more illuminated sphere" had to remain loyal "to the dark, intractable and tyrannical" (*UM* 203). Nietzsche shrewdly points to loyalty as Wagner's central term of value, what he demands from his characters as well as, Nietzsche knew all too well, from his disciples.

In "Richard Wagner in Bayreuth" Nietzsche, despite all his heroic praise for the great composer, for the first time recognizes Wagner as a dark, stubborn tyrant, whose intransigence and arrogance sometimes turned his life into a low comedy marked by a "grotesque lack of dignity" (*UM* 205). The Wagner depicted in Nietzsche's "Wagner in Bayreuth" unifies himself (so Nietzsche hints) only by subjecting the innocence of youth, the capering, joyous melodies of a Siegfried, to his Wotan-like narcissism, which inclines him toward a doom of self-destructive and self-aggrandizing isolation.

Wagner, then, represents, at moments in Nietzsche's essay, a somber example of unity of being achieved only at too great a cost. Like Schopenhauer's in "Schopenhauer as Educator," Wagner's strength seems at times inseparable from self-tyranny, from the distorted and strident way he forms himself against a resistant public. Elsewhere in "Wagner in Bayreuth," though, the stridency disappears, and Wagner's solitary grandeur takes on the definitive and irresistible cast of the maker of culture. Wagner, like the ancient Greeks, knows "what it means to found the state upon music," Nietzsche writes (*UM* 215).

Nietzsche now creates a solemn and hieratic tableau of Wagner the deity of artistic foundation, who makes culture the way the architect makes a building. "It is a joy to see," Nietzsche writes of Wagner. "He acquired and absorbed [cultural influences] from all sides, and the bigger and heavier the structure became, the firmer grew the arch of thought that was to order and control it" (*UM* 205). The solid fact of Bayreuth summarizes Wagner's grand ambition to build culture as a ruler builds an empire, unifying its elements just as Alexander the Great joined Asia and Europe:

> When on that day in the May of 1872 the foundation stone was laid on the hill at Bayreuth amid pouring rain and under a darkened sky, Wagner drove with some of us back to the town; he was silent and he seemed to be gazing into himself with a look not to be described in words. It was the first day of his sixtieth year: everything that had gone before was a preparation for this moment. . . . What may Alexander the Great not have seen in the moment when he caused Asia and Europe to be drunk out of the same cup? What Wagner beheld within him on that day, however—how he became what he is and what he will be—we who are closest to him can to a certain extent also see: and it is only from this Wagnerian inner view that we shall be able to understand his great deed itself—*and with this understanding guarantee its fruitfulness.* (*UM* 199)

In this passage the hermetic, meditative fixation of a Wagner "gazing into himself," attracting an audience through his somber air of mystery, functions as a ground or central source of power. Wagner proclaims his art by establishing a locus and an audience for it. The image of Wagner as Alexander "caus[ing] Asia and Europe to be drunk out of the same cup" contrasts with Brangäne's secret preparation of the love potion for Isolde in *Tristan,* just as it differs from Hagen's offering of an evil, Lethe-like drink to Siegfried in *Götterdämmerung,* whose taste makes Siegfried forget his heroic self and give up his secrets. One drink (Hagen's) instills a naive corruption, the other (Brangäne's) a naive ecstasy. Both potions are Dionysian: they cause a dramatic catastrophe, a breaking of the boundaries of accustomed self.

By contrast, Wagner's communion with himself, as Nietzsche depicts it in "Wagner in Bayreuth," is Apollonian. His closeness to himself enables his building of a musical *Gesamtkunst* based on the model of grand unity with his committed followers, who are like the minions of Alexander's empire. As the architect of sound who "unites what he has brought together into a living structure" (*UM* 209), he creates an audience of disciples "closest to him," a group that understands his message.

But near the end of "Wagner in Bayreuth," Nietzsche's argument takes a decisive, contrary turn, demolishing Wagner's status as the architect or Apollonian maker of a solid cultural reality. Now Nietzsche implies that Wagner's achievement is not a solid structure, but rather a furtive pursuit of keen and ghostly sounds.[50] At this point in his essay, Nietzsche has been condemning a (hypothetical, or unnamed) sensational artist who caters to his audience's hyped-up desire for "artificially engendered excitement," its wish to be "hunted, injured and torn to pieces" (*UM* 218–19).

Nietzsche here criticizes a vulgar version of his own Dionysian ideal, presaging as well the unthoughtful maenadism he will later associate with Wagner himself. At this early moment in Nietzsche's career, though, Wagner is presumably to be identified with the opposite of such sensationalism. The "better and rarer kind of artist," Nietzsche comments, avoids the "spectral chase" of special effects designed to please an excitable audience (*UM* 218). Instead he — Wagner — pursues a different kind of specter: "He hesitantly repeats in an uncertain tone ghostly words he thinks he hears coming from far away but cannot quite grasp" (*UM* 218).

Nietzsche quickly veers away from this description of the good artist as a dealer in the uncanny in order to assail at greater length the bad, sensationalist one. But he has recalled the emphasis of his essay's beginning: a "great event" requires a common bond between its creator and its audience, and the status of this bond may be uncanny or "ghostly," and therefore difficult to capture in words.

At this point in Nietzsche's essay, the bond between Wagner's work, its maker, and its listeners seems remarkably elusive. Nietzsche's counterexample to the permanent, architectonic union of artist and audience, on the first page of "Wagner in Bayreuth," was the deed done by a "man of force" that causes only a "brief, sharp echo, and all is over" (*UM* 197). The persistent, memorious sound that Nietzsche later shows Wagner listening to, the "ghostly words . . . coming from far away," evokes such an echo. This shadowy aspect of artistic production stands apart, in its dreamlike evasions, from the hearty authoritarian mystique Wagner exercises over his loyal disciples, a mystique that forms the other half of Nietzsche's essay, its contrasting theme. Nietzsche's Wagner is the composer as architect of force, firm in his rule over an audience, but he also (like Alberich teased by the Rhinemaidens in *Das Rheingold*) stands in for the tormented, desirous listener, chasing the elusive seductions of power.

In "Wagner in Bayreuth," then, Nietzsche oscillates between two images of Wagner's work, an architectonic and a musical one. On the one hand, writes Nietzsche, Wagner achieves incarnation, a unifying and graspable wholeness that makes us sense his imperial authority. On the other hand, Wagner creates a haunting, luxurious disorientation that eludes our grasp, and even his own: an uncanniness.

First, the Wagnerian solidity. "We feel certain," Nietzsche writes, "that in Wagner all that is visible in the world wants to become more profound and more intense by becoming audible, that it here seeks its lost soul; and that all that is audible in the world likewise wants to emerge into the light and also become a phenomenon for the eye; that it wants as it were to acquire corporality [Leiblichkeit]" (*UM* 223; *KSA* 1.467). In this description, sound and vision are perfectly matched and joined. The Apollonian or architectonic urge Nietzsche invokes here surfaces with Wotan's first appearance in *Das Rheingold,* near the very beginning of the *Ring* cycle. Wotan is the dreamer who wishes to dream on (a moment Nietzsche was apparently thinking of when he described the dreamer saying to himself "It is a dream! I will dream on!" in chapter 1 of *The Birth of Tragedy*). Wotan dreams of the solidity of the newly constructed Walhalla, its "Tür und Tor" (door and tower) — a guarded bliss (*Wonne*) that he defends against his wife Fricka's interruption, "Awake, husband, and reflect! [Erwache, Mann, und erwäge!]."

Walhalla is like Bayreuth, then, and Wotan is like Wagner. The father-god has realized his dream of a superbly founded realm, one achieved with self-seeking, businesslike ingenuity. Wish has emerged into actuality. As "Wagner in Bayreuth" continues, however (and as the *Ring* unfolds), the true slipperiness of this aesthetics of incorporation is revealed, and its Apollonian solidity melts away.

I have already cited the description of Wagner "hesitantly repeat[ing] in an uncertain tone ghostly words," words he "cannot quite grasp." But this ghostliness, too, can be transformed into a unified harmony. Nietzsche remarks that when we are under the spell of a "free artist," like Wagner, a composer who is also "the restorer of a unity . . . through a practical deed," "we swim in an enigmatic, fiery element, we no longer know ourself, no longer recognize the most familiar things; we no longer possess any standard of measurement, everything fixed and rigid begins to grow fluid, everything shines in novel colours, speaks to us in new signs and symbols" (*UM* 224). The solid melts into air. Instead of bringing us to a conscious incarnational fullness, as earlier in "Wagner in Bayreuth," Nietzsche's Wagner in this passage, despite his "practical deed," the building of Bayreuth, seems to derealize our condition, setting us out to sea in a fluid, ambient phantasmagoria. He "force[s] language back to a primordial state in which it hardly yet thinks in concepts and in which it is itself still poetry, image and feeling" (*UM* 237).

The derealization Nietzsche ascribes to Wagner may remind us of Lacan's definition of the gaze. "In our relation to things," Lacan says in his eleventh Seminar, the *Four Fundamental Concepts of Psychoanalysis,* "in so far as this relation is constituted by the way of vision, and ordered in the figures of representation, something slips, passes, is transmitted, from stage to stage, and is always to some degree eluded in it—that is what we call the gaze."[51] But the "primordial state" Nietzsche credits Wagner with evoking is, at least for this moment of "Wagner in Bayreuth," a liberation, a gift to the self rather than a tantalizing of the self of the kind that Lacan (and Nietzsche elsewhere in his Wagner essay) describes. At this point in Nietzsche's description of Wagner, desire is caught in the process of its formation, inchoate and novel, its essence a tentativeness that frees rather than entraps us. What we hear is the very beginning of *Das Rheingold* with its famously interminable E-flat chord, the raising of forms from undifferentiated chaos, before the teasing intrigue between Alberich and the Rhinemaidens. More delicately stated here than in *The Birth of Tragedy,* this is the promise of the Dionysian in music.

NIETZSCHE'S PHILOSOPHY IN THE TRAGIC AGE:
ARCHITECTONIC VS. MUSICAL

The magical subtlety and evasiveness of Wagner, invoked in "Wagner in Bayreuth," harks back to the tracking of Hamlet's ghost in "History for Life," which I have already discussed, and also suggests the governing thematic of another text of the 1870s, Nietzsche's unpublished *Philosophy in the Tragic Age of the Greeks.* In that work Nietzsche presents, in Anaxagoras, the figure of the philosopher as judge and founder, but also, in Thales, that of the philosopher as frustrated pursuer of elusive truth who fails to achieve a decisive role as philosophical maker. This difference between the solid builder Anaxagoras and the somewhat quixotic inquirer Thales resembles the one Nietzsche suggests in "Wagner in Bayreuth" between Wagner the bold architect of culture, founder of Bayreuth, and Wagner the refined quester after nuances.[52]

Philosophy in the Tragic Age of the Greeks begins by announcing its aim: to give a portrait of early Greek philosophy through a presentation of the philosophers' personalities. These remarkable characters, beginning with Thales, possess the "unity of style" that Nietzsche sees in the culture of pre-Platonic Greece and that is, as we have seen, sadly lacking in the Germany of the 1870s, according to the *Untimely Meditations* (*PTAG* 35). The ground or root of the pre-Platonic philosophers' character is their ability to judge existence (*PTAG* 33) and to animate the world with the singular, emphatic nature of their judgments. "Philosophy starts by legislating greatness," by "name-giving," writes Nietzsche (*PTAG* 43).

Nietzsche's first philosophical example, Thales, exemplifies the theme of name-giving. For Thales "all things are one" (*PTAG* 39), but this oneness takes a peculiar form, Thales' insistent insight that "all is water." Thales' philosophy resembles a fantastic, poetic kind of name-giving (*PTAG* 44). Nietzsche therefore applies to Thales an image we have seen in *The Birth of Tragedy*, that of the dramatic poet "who transforms himself into alien bodies and talks with their alien tongues and yet can project this transformation into written verse that exists in the outside world on its own" (*PTAG* 44).

Thales' "all is water," Nietzsche emphasizes, is not an allegorical or fabulous statement. Instead, it suggests an actual deed: philosophy's self-transformation, the translation of thought into real existence. Nietzsche characterizes Thales' dramatic capacity as "self-possession" [Besonnenheit], yet the case of Thales, with his strange aquatic obsession, suggests that the named object too much possesses the thinker, that he gets carried away by the image he has found. (A similar carrying away occurs in the destabilizing interchange of tenor and vehicle we witnessed in chapter 2 in Nietzsche's "On Truth and Lie.")

Nietzsche's discussion of Thales ends with a sharp, funny sentence: "Thales had seen the unity of all that is, but when he went to communicate it, he found himself talking about water!" (*PTAC* 45).[53] We might be reminded of a similarly comic picture of Thales, Diogenes Laertius's famous story (not recounted here by Nietzsche) that Thales was so lost in peripatetic contemplation that he fell into a well. For Nietzsche, Thales represents the thinker teased by his poetic inclination, by his desire to picture the universe, who therefore suffers a lapse: the gap between the *image* (water) and the *thought* (unity-as-truth).

"A sharp savoring and selecting, a meaningful discriminating, makes out the peculiar art of the philosopher, in the eyes of the people," Nietzsche writes (*PTAG* 43). But this same refinement leaves him open to the loss of consistent, convincing truth. He becomes a potential victim of his idiosyncratic judgment, of the futile Sisyphean bondage to an advanced taste (in this case, a taste for the image of water). According to Nietzsche, "The Greek word designating 'sage' is etymologically related to *sapio,* I taste, *sapiens,* he who tastes, *sisyphos,* the man of keenest taste" (*PTAG* 43). "The philosopher," Nietzsche writes, "seeks to let the entire sound of the world echo within himself [sucht den Gesammtklang der Welt in sich nachtönen zu lassen]," and to re-project this sound as a memorable image (*PTAG* 44; translation modified). But the memorable can lead him astray: like Wagner-as-Alberich, Thales represents the musical philosopher, the one who chases keen sounds and images, and loses his balance in the process.

The second philosopher in Nietzsche's *Tragic Age,* Anaximander, exemplifies a contrasting type, the philosopher as architect and lawgiver, a constructor of rigid judgments. After comparing him to Schopenhauer, Nietzsche pictures Anaximander fleeing this world of injustice into a metaphysical fortress from which he leans out, letting his gaze sweep the horizon. At last, after long pensive silence, he puts a question to all creatures: 'What is your existence worth? And if it is worthless, why are you here? Your guilt, I see, causes you to tarry in your existence. With your death, you have to expiate it.'" The speech Nietzsche puts in the mouth of Anaximander ends with a *Götterdäm-merung*-style image of apocalypse: "'Even now, fire is destroying your world. . . . But ever and anew, another such world of ephemerality will construct itself'" (*PTAG* 48).

Anaximander in fact resembles Schopenhauer more than he does Nietzsche, and his case illustrates the weakness of Schopenhauer's fortified, embattled posture. The severity and isolation of Anaximander's stance demonstrates the bathetic risk of the architectonic stance. In spite of his martial solidity and prophet-like self-assurance, it is not Anaximander's audience, but he himself, who fades from the scene. Instead of asking the individual to justify his existence, as Nietzsche does in "Schopenhauer as Educator," and as Emerson does in "Self-Reliance," Nietzsche's Anaximander asks that the world of the individual pass away, making room for a new, equally ephemeral world. But the sage too is transient. Nietzsche supposes that Anaximander's fellow citizens of Miletus nominated him to found a colony in order to at once honor him and get rid of him (*PTAG* 49). Accordingly, Anaximander's retreat to his metaphysical fortress mutates later in the *Tragic Age* into an even more regressive image, a flight into the womb (*PTAG* 58).

Nietzsche's next philosopher, Heraclitus, resembles Anaximander in that he describes a universe with a plot: it begins with lack, which then leads to satiety, which in turn leads to hubris, then to a crash, and then finally a rebirth, "another such world of ephemerality." The Heraclitean scheme as Nietzsche recounts it reminds the reader of Anaximander's gravity, his effort to load the universe with guilt (*PTAG* 60). But Nietzsche stresses that Heraclitus, unlike Anaximander, recovers from the weight of his cosmological vision by adopting a perspective both godlike and childlike, as a way of restoring innocence to the process of continual destruction and creation. Nietzsche here adapts the Emersonian-Heraclitean image of the child at play, as he did in his school essay "Fate and History" (see chapter 5):

> In this world only play, play as artists and children engage in it, exhibits coming-to-be and passing away, structuring and destroying, without any moral additive, in forever equal innocence. And as children and artists play, so plays the ever-living fire. It constructs and destroys, all in innocence. Such is the game that the aeon plays with itself. Transforming itself into water and earth, it builds towers of sand like a child at the seashore, piles them up and tramples them down. . . . The child throws its toys away from time to time—and starts again, in innocent caprice. But when it does build, it combines and joins and forms its structures regularly, conforming to inner laws. (*PTAG* 62)

Rather than trying with Anaximander to erect an invulnerable fortress out of prophetic moralizing, Heraclitus makes and topples castles in the sand. The stiff architectonic impulse yields to the resilience of play. But the playful does not, cannot, abolish the fated. Instead, play and fate partner each other: the Dionysian or musical text of becoming that Nietzsche invokes here bears witness to a balanced structuring of opposites. "Necessity and random play, oppositional tension and harmony, must pair to create a work of art." The artist is at once inside and outside, "contemplatively above and at the same time actively within his work," Nietzsche writes (*PTAG* 62). This detachment indicates Heraclitus's chilly isolation, a loneliness more radical and less melodramatic than Anaximander's, which forecasts the solitude of Nietzsche's future hero Zarathustra. Nietzsche says of Heraclitus,

> The feeling of solitude . . . that pierced the Ephesian hermit of the temple of Artemis, we can intuit only when we are freezing [erstarrend] on wild desolate mountains of our own. No all-powerful [übermächtiges] feeling of compassionate emotions, no desire to help, to heal, to save, stream[s] forth from Heraclitus. He is a star devoid of atmosphere. His eye, flaming toward its inward center, looks outward dead and icy, with but the semblance of sight. All around him, to the very edge of the fortress of his pride, beat the waves of illusion and of wrong-ness [die Wellen des Wahns und der Verkehrtheit]. Nauseated, he turns from them. But other men, too, those with feeling hearts, turn away in turn from such a mask, cast as it were in brass. (*PTAG* 67; *KSA* 1.834)

There is no love lost between Heraclitus and his *Nebenmenschen.* A cold star, he offers them no atmosphere in which to breathe. Whereas the *Untimely Meditations* ended, with "Wagner in Bayreuth," by invoking the building of an audience united in cultural or artistic consciousness, thereby returning to the collective emphasis of *The Birth of Tragedy,* the *Tragic Age* seems to be going in the opposite direction. Its portrait of Heraclitus turns the philosopher into a sacrificial outcast, eternally separated from his surrounding society.

But the split between the lonely philosopher and his social surroundings is cured at the end of the *Tragic Age,* when Nietzsche introduces the figure of Anaxagoras as a Periclean orator dazzling his audience (*PTAG* 114). Anaxagoras's *nous* starts creation by supplying a gesture or nudge, somewhat in the manner of Fichte's *Anstoss.*[54] This simple movement turns what has been chaotic into architectonic glory:

> The Spirit [*nous*] of Anaxagoras is a creative artist. It is, in fact, the most tremendous mechanical and architectural genius,

creating with the simplest means the most impressive forms and
orbits, creating a movable architectonic [eine bewegliche Architek-
tur], as it were, but ever from the irrational free random choosing [aus jener irrationalen Willkür] that lies in the artist's
depths. (*PTAG* 112; *KSA* 1.869)

Anaxagoras's *nous,* as Nietzsche describes it, sounds like the free individual who has dedicated himself to artistry. This is an advance beyond the gods of *The Birth of Tragedy,* made by man in his image. The
Birth's gods were mere spectators, whereas the *nous* is an active artist.
Nietzsche writes that

Anaxagoras assumed a free undetermined *nous,* dependent on
itself alone [nahm Anaxagoras den willkürlichen, von sich allein
abhängigen Nous an]. What he especially esteemed in it was its
quality of randomness [die Eigenschaft, beliebig zu sein], hence
its ability to activate unconditionally, undeterminedly, guided by
neither causes nor ends. (*PTAG* 117; *KSA* 1.872)

This passage ends Nietzsche's pamphlet on philosophy in the
tragic age. It also forecasts his work of the 1880s, in which the image of
the artist's work will be the presiding model for how we live our lives.
In *The Gay Science,* especially, the artistic ideal provides the crucial way
for Nietzsche to evoke a spontaneity that is at once "mechanical and architectural" and yet still capable of encompassing an "irrational free
random choosing"—still responsive to the ghostlier sounds and
keener demarcations evoked in "Wagner in Bayreuth." In *Daybreak* and
The Gay Science, Nietzsche, by combining architectonic solidity and musical susceptibility as he did in his portrait of Anaxagoras, will move beyond his ideal of the critical individual, the centerpiece of *Untimely
Meditations,* and toward a riskier version of individuality. He will also
discard his attachment to the idea of a remodeled and improved collective culture, the vision that remains substantially present at the beginning and end of *Untimely Meditations,* in its essays on David Strauss
and on Wagner. Nietzsche, in other words, will follow Emerson into
full-fledged individualism.

CHAPTER FOUR

Daybreak and The Gay Science

I HAVE GROUPED *Daybreak* and *The Gay Science* together because these are the works of the early 1880s in which Nietzsche explores his Emersonian inheritance most directly. Both these books represent a step beyond the ideal of the critical self as it was outlined in the *Untimely Meditations,* and toward a more precarious and daring model of the self's adventures, one that exceeds the stability Nietzsche associates with the critical. In this period of his writing, Nietzsche works toward his riskiest theoretical venture, first described in *The Gay Science:* the eternal return.

Abandoning the triad of monumental, antiquarian, and critical history he developed in "The Use and Disadvantage of History for Life," Nietzsche's *Daybreak* (1882) adopts instead the Emersonian division between conformity and originality. In this new polarization, conformity occupies the place previously allotted to both the monumental and the antiquarian postures, which now look much weaker than they did in "History for Life." According to the Nietzsche of *Daybreak,* both monumental and antiquarian modes rely on an attachment to convention and heritage that devolves into idolatry, into a dumb or arbitrary obedience to custom.

The other Emersonian term Nietzsche uses in *Daybreak,* the antidote to conformity—originality—can hardly be aligned precisely with his ideal of the critical as he expressed it in the mid-1870s, in "History for Life." In "History for Life" the critical relied on a careful sense of the influence of the past in order to promise a crucial freedom from that past. This was an unusual moment of idealism for Nietzsche, an uncharacteristically optimistic brief for the power of reflection to both conserve and liberate. By contrast, Nietzsche in *Daybreak* hopes for a form of newness stronger than the critical can supply: originality, the posing of a revolutionary turn against history. But at the same time he tries, in a way that is thoroughly Emersonian, to soften originality's break from the familiar, to sophisticate its radicalism. The Nietzsche of *Daybreak* recoils from the sublime violence originality can convey, a violence associated in *Daybreak* with St. Paul, and inclines instead toward the Emersonian ideal of refinement. The surprising, gently crepuscular machinations of lovers, and of the adept actors they resemble, offer models of refinement in the final books of *Daybreak*, ways of acknowledging and trying to tame the self's captivation by the mysterious cause of its desire (the object *a*). In this way Nietzsche overcomes the opposition between activity and passivity that torments the ascetic and that will return, with a vengeance, in the *Genealogy of Morals* and *Ecce Homo*.

FROM DRIVE TO DESIRE

Daybreak represents Nietzsche's first serious grappling with the ascetic attitude. For Nietzsche, the ascetic's is the most dramatic and severe form of originality, since it revolts against nature itself.

Nietzsche's thoughts on asceticism can be usefully referred to Lacan's opposition between desire and drive. The ascetic allies himself to drive; the lover and the artist, to desire. In *Daybreak's* book 1 Nietzsche recognizes the distinction between desire and drive when he explains how asceticism abolishes the structure of prohibition associated with desire, replacing it with the purity of drive. But love, in contradiction to the ascetic enshrining of drive, remains permanently enmeshed in the theatrical scenarios of desire (as Nietzsche will make clear in later sections of *Daybreak*).

The distinction between drive and desire is crucial in Lacan. Explicating this distinction, Jacques-Alain Miller writes that "The drive couldn't care less about prohibition; it knows nothing of prohibition and certainly doesn't dream of transgressing it. The drive follows its own bent and always obtains satisfaction. Desire weighs itself down with considerations like 'They want me to do it, so I won't,' or 'I'm not supposed to go that way, so that's the way I want to go, but perhaps at the last second I won't be able to do it anyway.'"[1]

Asceticism aims at freedom from the hesitancies and paradoxes of desire. For Nietzsche, the ascetic is the supreme example of drive, in Miller's terms: he always obtains satisfaction and cares nothing about the object's difficulty of access. Because drive takes itself for its own true object, it can disdain desire's practices of hide-and-seek, the mutual eluding and shadowing of lover and beloved. The second-guessing game-playing Miller describes as proper to desire remains, then, utterly foreign to drive, which insists in sublime manner on its own exalted status.

Nietzsche in book 1 of *Daybreak* is particularly concerned with asceticism's impulse toward grandiose exaltation: his prime exhibit is St. Paul's "anticipatory dwelling in divine glories" (*D* #58). Paul's theatrical grasp of a sublime self plays an important role in *Daybreak* because of the connection Paul claims between the cruelty of asceticism and liberation from the past, the killing off of the old law (see *D* #14, #58, #68).

In the book that immediately follows *Daybreak, The Gay Science* of 1882, Nietzsche formulates an architectonic building of self that can surmount ascetic cruelty, a formulation most fully visible in the "Sanctus Januarius," book 4 of *The Gay Science.* As I argue in the next chapter, though, asceticism comes into its own in the *Genealogy of Morals,* destroying Nietzsche's carefully achieved surpassing of drive by desire, asceticism by love, in *Daybreak* and *The Gay Science.*

Along with the opposition of ascetic drive and erotic desire, the connection between love and theater is the other preoccupation of *Daybreak* I explore in this chapter. In his comments on love as a theatrical phenomenon, Nietzsche turns away from the crude, violent originality (of drive) he associates with Paul, and toward a sophistication (of desire) that echoes Emerson's ideal of refinement in *The Conduct of Life.*

CUSTOM, ASCETICISM, AND THE SUBLIME IN *DAYBREAK*

Book 1 of *Daybreak* explores several variant explanations for the origins and motives of the human attachment to custom. Nietzsche's rhetorical practice here stands at the opposite extreme from his method in *The Birth of Tragedy,* where he insisted on a single, authoritative myth of origin that would incite our renewed belief, or at least our solemn attention. Here, by contrast, Nietzsche introduces fables of origin in a provisional way, making them available to be tested, tried out for their explanatory power. The optional or available character of Nietzsche's hypotheses of origin is allied to the piecemeal structure of *Daybreak,* Nietzsche's third book (after *Human All Too Human* [1879] and *The Wanderer and His Shadow* [1880]) to be divided into discrete paragraphs.

The reader is here on trial, along with Nietzsche himself: which possibility of origin will we, will he, find inspiring, which dull? Which one a beginning of promise, which a dead end?

It was, as we saw in chapter 3, a major intent of the *Untimely Meditations'* "History for Life" to turn a severe eye on the appeal of promising or inspirational origins, which Nietzsche associated with the monumental. The grandiose heroics of the monumental decline surprisingly quickly, in Nietzsche's account, into a dependence on indistinctly defined greatness, a vague state of social comfort in which the critical historian's aim of distinguishing between rumor and fact becomes an annoyance, if not a threat. In "History for Life," Nietzsche pictures the critical in opposition to the monumental: critical history inclines toward an increasing sophistication, rather than the accelerated banality monumentalism trades in.

Daybreak replaces "History for Life"'s opposition between monumental conformity and critical refinement (with the antiquarian hovering midway between the two, more precise than the monumental, but nonetheless uncritical). *Daybreak's* images of human custom can be divided into those that imply a softening into dumb reiteration (conformity) and those that raise the contrasting possibility of a sharp, accurate, and subtle voicing of one's place (refinement). Nietzschean refinement, with its images of sculptural and architectural solidity, owes much to Emerson's *Conduct of Life,* as I argue in chapter 5. Despite its rude beginning with the shock of "Fate," *The Conduct of Life* is a book that places subtlety at its center, as goal and orienting point.

Nietzsche in *Daybreak* confronts something far fiercer and more alluring than monumental banality or conformity, and more powerfully basic than the Emersonian sophistication he will espouse late in his book. Nietzsche describes a self-destructive ascetic sublimity, associated by him with that famous epileptic Paul, who, contaminated by indulgence in "enmity, murder, sorcery, idolatry, uncleanliness, drunkenness and pleasure in debauch," and most of all by "lust for domination," finds a way to satisfy that lust by destroying the law in the name of Christ (*D* #68). The offered ecstasy mimes the intoxication felt by Dionysus's worshippers in *The Birth of Tragedy,* but it asserts the self instead of dissolving it as Dionysus does. Paul, like Dionysus, frees us from the ordinary, from the pettiness and disgusting constraints imposed by custom. But Nietzsche is skeptical of the Pauline liberatory promise as he was not of the Dionysian one.

At this point in Nietzsche's career, the hope for an absolved, cleansed identity that the Dionysian festival represented in *The Birth of Tragedy* has been lost, obscured by Christianity's mock-humble exaltations. This is another way of saying that Nietzsche the critical historian has recognized the irrevocable character of the Christian-ascetic advent. Asceticism cannot be overcome without a struggle that acknowledges the persistent ascetic within even the gayest or freest self, voicing the secret compulsions that speak from within not only Nietzsche, but many of the rest of us. In *Daybreak,* asceticism can be worked through and overcome; in the *Genealogy,* it will prove definitive and ineradicable.

In book 1 of *Daybreak* Nietzsche aims to detect the mysterious development of the ascetic's secretive, imaginative self-cruelty from everyday custom, with its stolid and public triviality. The project does not begin well. Near the beginning of *Daybreak,* Nietzsche gives us an account of custom that is barely an account, and that therefore underlines custom's triviality. Here Nietzsche almost refuses the duty of explanation, in order to describe custom's similar refusal. He cites as the "first proposition of civilization" the "minute and fundamentally superfluous stipulations" that custom insists on: don't, on penalty of death, scrape the snow off your shoes with a knife (an example from the Kamshadales).[2] "Any custom is better than no custom," Nietzsche concludes (*D* #16).

The quiet poverty implied by such empty observances, or empty prohibitions, hardly enables Nietzsche to rise to the greatest theme of *Daybreak's* book 1, the sublime ecstasy of the religious visionary. Even considered on its own, paragraph 16 seems to be lacking a step or two. Why does the drastic punishment of death stand behind just this or that seemingly arbitrary practice, if the custom itself is as indifferent a thing as Nietzsche's paragraph assumes? The assumption of a founding arbitrariness here allows Nietzsche to diminish human culture. Such diminishing, such too rapid, too easy demystification, is a (temporary) obstacle to the true project of *Daybreak,* and of Nietzsche's whole career: the revaluing of humanness as something more, not less, worthy than the ascetic priests and philosophers, men like Paul and Schopenhauer, have deemed it.

One way of asserting the worth, the superior interest, of human culture is to emphasize its potential for sublimity. In *Daybreak* Nietzsche starts on his upward road to sublimity by considering sacrificial cruelty as the fundamental fact of human community.[3] "In the act of cruelty the community refreshes itself and for once throws off the gloom of constant fear and caution" (D #18). As we go on we will have to ask about this origin behind the origin: whence comes the "constant fear and caution" Nietzsche speaks of? First, though, we should go forward, toward Nietzsche's idea, in this paragraph, that ascetic self-torment is born from ritual observance, an idea that will flower in the *Genealogy*.

> Cruelty is one of the oldest festive joys of mankind. Consequently it is imagined that the gods too are refreshed and in festive mood when they are offered the spectacle of cruelty—and thus there creeps into the world the idea that voluntary suffering, self-chosen torture, is meaningful and valuable. Gradually, custom created within the community a practice corresponding to this idea: all excessive well-being henceforth aroused a degree of mistrust, all hard suffering inspired a degree of confidence. . . . Thus the concept of the "most moral man" of the community came to include the virtue of the most frequent suffering, of privation, of the hard life, of cruel chastisement— *not,* to repeat it again and again, as a means of discipline, of self-control, of satisfying the desire for individual happiness—but as a virtue which will put the community in good odour with the evil gods and which steams up to them like a perpetual propitiatory sacrifice on the altar. (D #18)

These moral men, Nietzsche goes on to write in the same paragraph of *Daybreak,* "ventured on to new paths" and were "as a consequence tormented by pangs of conscience and spasms of anxiety." The more they advanced into the new, "the more cruelly did they rage against their own flesh, their own appetites and their own health—as though to offer the divinity a substitute pleasure in case he might perhaps be provoked by this neglect of and opposition to established usages and by the new goals these paths led to" (D #18).

According to *Daybreak,* then, martyrdom is first a collective and only later an individual phenomenon. The community offers up a scapegoat in its own interest, for the delectation of the cruel gods. Almost invisibly, though, in this paragraph, a culture's collective rituals gradually become the property of the dedicated individual ascetic who opposes himself to "established usages," imposing a severe and unforgiving discipline on his existence. The self-outraging fanatic, spiritual leader, or priest now becomes recognizable to us in his "madness," his enthusiastic and "voluntary [self-]torture." The sublime exaltation the priest attains in his ascetic suffering enters into Nietzsche's notion, elsewhere in book 1, that, once custom is raised (*aufgehoben*) into heroic distinction, once certain individuals take it upon themselves to fulfill the law to the utmost, those individuals reach an ecstatic place in which they embody the law they have destroyed. "I have killed the law," Paul exults, and by this means, he becomes the law (*D* #68). Ascetic drive has triumphed, has declared itself as definitive.

The fact that Paul's sublime asceticism asserts individual distinction means that this form of self-torture stands in the way of the nobler sort of self-making Nietzsche wants to argue for in *Daybreak*. Paul's positioning of the self as outside the law, and therefore as the ultimate embodiment of a higher law, involves a morality of distinction or self-display calculated to show up others, to make them feel ashamed (*D* #30, #113). "The morality of distinction is in its ultimate foundation pleasure in refined cruelty," Nietzsche writes, because it aims to shame its audience, to impose itself on them (*D* #30). The cruelty of Paul's spectacular self-punishment, his weird, inventive ecstasy, stands in contrast to the everydayness of custom, the virtually automatic imitative habits Nietzsche often associates in *Daybreak* with the apes (as in *D* #25 and #34). Yet Paul also invents an ape-like practice of self-caricature for maximum effect.

Pauline exaggeration stands in high contrast to the subtle, hidden character of Nietzsche's self-portrait in his Preface to *Daybreak*. Nietzsche begins *Daybreak* by depicting himself as a Tryphonian initiate, an esoteric mole working underground, with diligence and subtlety. "In this book," he writes in his first sentence, "you will discover a 'subterranean man' at work, one who tunnels and mines and undermines [einen Bohrenden, Grabenden, Untergrabenden]" (*D* Preface; *KSA* 3.11).[4] *Daybreak's* development brings the book's project close to Nietzsche's aims as expressed in his Preface. Nietzsche traces a course from Paul's Christian sublimity to the sophisticated role-playing of lovers, marking a progression from the crude grandiosity of drive to the refinements of desire.

Within the rhetorical scheme of *Daybreak*, sublimity is linked to drive, but Nietzsche also sees the banality of custom as a product of drive. The seeming laxity of conventional belief, as well as the fierceness of Paul's iconoclasm, participates in the peculiar sort of investment that characterizes drive. Pauline Christianity, according to Nietzsche, shows a connection with the rhetorical practice, associated with Euripides in *The Birth of Tragedy,* of stirring up a certain mood so that the mood itself becomes an argument (*D* #28). Rational justification, dear to philosophers, turns out to be of limited use when the vulgar many declare that they believe what they believe because belief gives them a certain satisfying feeling of goodness or rightness.

The popular hypostatization of mood, which makes it a goal in itself, desirable in itself, displays the kind of repetition that characterizes drive. In Lacan's description, drive entails a continual return to the thing that always misses the thing, since it remains mere repetition or aiming-at, rather than a final experience of the thing itself: an experience that is by definition impossible, since it would annihilate the subject. But drive mimes this unavailable finality in, or through, the monotonous quality of its intent. In this way it hides the impossible character of the object. The obvious inertia or tedium of conformity, then, disguises its true, driven character as an emblem of drive.[5]

In one of his Paul passages (*D* #68), Nietzsche reflects on the distortion that goes along with the aggressive sublimity of drive. This ascetic egotism that transports itself in order to assert its privilege will occupy much of Nietzsche's attention in later works like the *Genealogy of Morals.* Ventriloquizing Paul's claim, Nietzsche writes,

> Guilt as such has been destroyed; now the law is dead, now the carnality in which it dwelt is dead—or at least constantly dying away, as though decaying [verwesend]. (*D* #68)

The "Christian's lot," Nietzsche continues, is to suffer this decay until he

> become[s] one with Christ, he arises with Christ, participates with Christ in divine glory and becomes a "son of God," like Christ.—With that the intoxication of Paul is at its height, and likewise the importunity [Zudringlichkeit] of his soul—with the idea of becoming one with Christ all shame, all subordination, all bounds are taken from it, and the intractable lust for power reveals itself as an anticipatory revelling in *divine* glories [der unbändige Wille der Herrschsucht offenbart sich als ein Vorwegnehmendes Schwelgen in *göttlichen* Herrlichkeiten]. (*D* #68)

At bottom, Nietzsche suggests, Pauline vengeance against Rome is vulgarly competitive; Christian righteousness resembles the strain of exaggerated aggression that characterizes the baboon's war-mask (*D* #25). Such aggression, like the strain of evil Brecht discerned in a Chinese statue, turns the elderly male baboon ugly. Feminine beauty, on the other hand, at least in this passage of *Daybreak*, remains inert:

> *Custom and beauty.*—Among the things that can be said in favour of custom is this: when someone subjects himself to it completely, from the heart and from his earliest years on, his organs of attack and defense—both bodily and spiritual—degenerate: that is to say, he grows increasingly beautiful! For it is the exercise of these organs and the disposition [Gesinnung] that goes with this exercise which keeps one ugly and makes one uglier. That is why the old baboon is uglier than the young one, and why the young female baboon most closely resembles man: is the most beautiful baboon, that is to say.—One could from this draw a conclusion as to the origin of the beauty of women! (*D* #25; *KSA* 3.36)

Nietzsche presents feminine beauty in paragraph #25 of *Daybreak* in a way that is for him very unusual: not as dangerous and alluring, but rather as the sign of an odd passivity, a surrender to conformist training. The subjection to custom, repetitive in nature, here seems to lack the fascinating character of drive. Instead of a high, mandarin discipline, beauty remains, in the case of the female baboon, a mere habit whose results Nietzsche disdains to describe, a blank, exhausting conformity.

Book 1 of *Daybreak* at first divides itself, then, in a kind of impasse, between the inert force of habit, the beauty that comes from near-automatic submission to custom, and the separating, sacred power of the demonic self associated with religious ecstatics like Paul. Feeling oneself sublime or exalted (*sich erhaben fühlen*), making oneself the representative of the drive, finds a response in the masses' admiration for holy madness (*D* #32; *KSA* 3.41). Already at this early point in *Daybreak*, though, there are hints of the subtlety or refinement that will become the reigning concept later in Nietzsche's book, when he moves on from drive to desire.

The subtlety of critical consciousness begins, Nietzsche implies, as an aspect of survival-oriented behavior, the animal practice of self-suspicion, of "lying in wait for oneself" (*D* #26). Fear has its dignity in Nietzsche as a factor of origin—in this case, fear of the self, a suspicious relation that for Nietzsche in #26 seems to be the origin of the critical mode: "One does not want to mislead oneself, one hearkens mistrustfully to the promptings of one's passions, one constrains one-self and lies in wait for oneself" (D #26). As book 1 of *Daybreak* contin-ues, fear of the incomprehensible, which is at first the stimulus for the merely customary (don't scrape the snow off your shoes with a knife), passes over into something more sublime, "the stimulus of the hard to comprehend" and of creativity itself:

> *Speculation on usages* [*Das Grübeln über Gebräuche*].—Countless prescriptions of custom hastily read off from some unique strange occurrence very soon become incomprehensible. . . . [P]recisely the most absurd aspect of a usage at length passed over into the holiest sanctity. . . . We have arrived here at the tre-mendous exercise ground of the intellect—it is not only that the religions were woven here: this is also the venerable if dreadful prehistoric world of science, here is where the poet, the thinker, the physician, the lawgiver first grew. Fear [Angst] of the incom-prehensible which in an ambiguous way demanded ceremonies of us gradually passed over into the stimulus of the hard to com-prehend, and where one did not know how to explain [er-gründen] one learned to create. (D #40; KSA 3.47)

Creativity, then, begins in the absurdity of custom and the allied free-dom of invention that derives from the lack of a reason, a *Grund*, for custom.

Here Nietzsche may well be answering Rousseau, who finds a dif-ferent beginning, in a different kind of fear, for human creative power. Derrida in *Of Grammatology* points to the passage of Rousseau's *Essay on the Origin of Languages* that evokes a primitive state in which hu-mans "believed themselves each other's enemies." Derrida comments that, according to Rousseau, cruelty (and the inventiveness associated with cruelty, in Rousseau as in Nietzsche) finds its origin in fear, in the frightening emptiness of the other's image: "The disposition to do evil finds its resource only in the other, in the illusory representation of evil that the other *seems* disposed to do to me."[6] The mimetic hypothe-sis of Rousseau insinuates a hollowness, a re-presentation and thus a lack of presence, into the encounter with the other, an encounter that takes a figurative or fantastic form. Captive to a metaphor that pre-cedes literal meaning, in Rousseau primitive man sees the fearsome other man as a giant.[7]

According to Derrida, the figurative, the basis of artistic creation, stands for Rousseau at (or before?) the very beginning of human experience. Figurative meaning is primary for Nietzsche, too, as we saw in chapter 2's consideration of "On Truth and Lie in an Extra-Moral Sense," but Nietzsche remains unafflicted by what Derrida describes as Rousseau's anxiety over the fact that "with imitation . . . duplicity . . . insinuates itself within presence."[8] On the contrary, Nietzsche will follow Emerson by exulting over the teasing, and promising, effects of such duplicity in our encounters with one another.

We have already seen, in *Daybreak* #40, the way Nietzsche establishes fear of the incomprehensible and unknown as the origin of creativity. Rather than becoming inert as a result of familiarity and the passage of time, customs can be elevated into a refined sublimity by creative practices of interpretation designed to engineer the continuation of veneration and holy dread. Here the opposition seen elsewhere in book 1 between Pauline crudeness (*D* #68) and Nietzsche's own mole-like cunning (Preface) begins to fade away, and Nietzsche's project comes into its own. For him, now, Christian subtlety becomes the sign of a newly sophisticated sublime, one born of centuries of customary practice.

In *Daybreak* #60, Nietzsche substantiates his statement on the authority of Christian tradition, its capacity to reach toward an embodied refinement:

> *All spirit in the end becomes bodily visible [leiblich sichtbar].—* Christianity . . . has . . . emerged from a rustic rudeness . . . into a very spirited [geistreiche] religion, with a thousand wrinkles, reservations and subterfuges in its countenance; it has made European humanity sharp-witted, and not only theologically cunning. From this spirit . . . it has *chiselled* out perhaps the most refined figures in human society that have ever yet existed: the figures of the higher and highest Catholic priesthood. . . . Here the human face attains to that total spiritualisation [Durchgeistigung] produced by the continual ebb and flow of the two species of happiness (the feeling of power and the feeling of surrender [Ergebung]). (*D* #60; *KSA* 3.60)

Nietzsche continues to remark that the noble priest "takes *pride* in obeying [Gehorchen], which is the distinguishing mark of all aristocrats; in the tremendous impossibility of one's task lies one's excuse and one's ideal [man hat in der ungeheueren Unmöglichkeit seiner Aufgabe seine Entschuldigung und seine Idealität]." We might be reminded of Georg Simmel's insight that Nietzschean discipline overcomes our habitual antithesis between obligation and hedonistic satisfaction.[9] The sculptural, chiseled majesty of the noble priesthood, with its godlike countenance and Michelangelesque "beautiful hands and feet," embodies a "total spiritualisation [Durchgeistigung]": a new kind of incarnation related to, but higher than, the kind imagined by the gospels (and certainly higher than Paul's vulgar thrills). The disciplined self-mastery Nietzsche admires here contrasts with the Emersonian abandonment, the yielding to illusion and the forsaking of self-fashioning, that Nietzsche will invoke as an ideal later on in *Daybreak*. But Nietzsche's point in *Daybreak* #60 is to blur the boundary between control and surrender, self-possession and self-abandonment, as Emerson also does.

At the end of #60 Nietzsche asks, with a delicacy or hesitancy not usually credited to him, whether the "harmony between figure [Gestalt], spirit and task [will] also . . . go to the grave when the religions come to an end? And," he continues, "can nothing higher be attained, or even imagined [ersinnen]?" The summit of spiritual refinement attained in Renaissance Catholicism may have a *Nachleben* in Nietzsche's own work, with its imagination of an embodied, purified existence, an existence that defends itself against vulgarity through its instinct for the pathos of distance. (Is this Nietzschean *Nachleben* the ideal's excuse or apology for itself, its *Entschuldigung*?) This Nietzschean imagination draws on the architectural discipline that discerns, or creates, a "harmony between figure, spirit and task." (How will this new spiritual discipline be higher than, how will it distinguish itself from, Christianity? The proof of this question lies, if anywhere, in the future of Nietzsche's words, whether they have a destiny.)

This Nietzschean discipline that inherits its subtlety from Christianity stands against the "rustic rudeness" of Paul and the other early Christians, their use of "holy madness" as a technique of sublimity, a way of abolishing distance, a subsuming of the self into the power that will save it. In *Daybreak* #58 Nietzsche writes that "the intoxication [Rausch] of Paul is at its height, and likewise the importunity of his soul—with the idea of becoming one with Christ," the "anticipatory reveling in divine glories." (*Zudringlichkeit*, "importunity," is an important word in *Daybreak*.) Similarly, the shaman imagined by Nietzsche in #14, a shameless, groveling diva, begs,

> Give me madness, you heavenly powers! . . . Give deliriums and
> convulsions, sudden lights and darkness, terrify me with frost
> and fire such as no mortal has ever felt . . . make me howl and
> whine and crawl like a beast: so that I may only come to believe
> in myself! I am consumed by doubt, I have killed the law, the law
> anguishes me as a corpse does a living man: if I am not more
> than the law I am the vilest of all men. (*D* #14)

The Pauline radicalism Nietzsche here portrays in the shaman's
words is at bottom a practice of vengeance. The shaman's fantasy is a
form of envy, a conviction that power has been stolen by another, and
that it can be recouped by punishing this other.[10] The ascetic first
creates a masochistic mood to inspire the soul and then "seeks for
those whom he has for long wished to torture with it" (*D* #30). The ascetic's use of imagination to invoke the polluting or corrupting closeness of one soul to another stands in contrast to what for Nietzsche
remains the proper, the noble or refined, use of imagination—to establish distances:

> The extent of the space between the highest happiness and the
> deepest unhappiness has been produced only with the aid of the
> imaginary things. This kind of feeling of space is, consequently,
> being continually reduced under the influence of science: just
> as science has taught us, and continues to teach us, to feel that
> the earth is small and the solar-system itself no more than a
> point. (*D* #7)

The vastness of space that imagination engenders may lead to the fantastic diminishing of "On Truth and Lie," in which, as we saw in chapter
2, humankind becomes almost invisible from the perspective of interstellar space, a mere mosquito's flourishing. Yet this expanding void
also enables the *Durchgeistigung*, the thorough spiritualization, that
Nietzsche evokes in *Daybreak* #60.

In *Daybreak* #8 Nietzsche depicts an archaic pathos of distance, one
that distinguishes three inadequate forms of life and thought, which he
identifies with the three levels of Raphael's *Transfiguration:* "Those that
suffer helplessly, those that dream confusedly, those that are entranced by things supernatural." (Nietzsche here revises a passage
from *The Birth of Tragedy* already discussed in chapter 2.) Nietzsche
adds to his invocation of Raphael's painting that "this is no longer how

we see the world"; we behold instead a "new transfiguration" (D #8). This new transfiguration replaces the old ways—the ascetic's helpless suffering, the idealistic dreamer's confused fantasizing, and the mystic's rapture—with a clearer, colder separation of the self from its surroundings. In this new hierarchy, thought, the middle level of the dreamer, is no longer confused. No more are we suffocated by the pressures of ascetic cruelty and mystic trance. Rather, we find ourselves freed into a new consciousness of ennobling distance.

The new mastery Nietzsche envisions depends on the opening up of a greater vista, on entering a path out of our traditional prison-houses. At the end of #44 Nietzsche comments, "Formerly, thinkers prowled around angrily like captive animals, watching the bars of their cages and leaping against them in order to smash them down: and *happy* seemed he who through a gap in them believed he saw something of what was outside, of what was distant and beyond" (D #44). The image of imprisoned consciousness, which Nietzsche developed in his early essay "On the Pathos of Truth," becomes in this passage of *Daybreak* an evocation of social law or custom as a kind of jail. Against this bondage stands the sublime Pauline rebellion against the law: a law that must remain bound to ascetic self-punishment. If we were to be released from this prison and pass beyond ascetic bondage, Nietzsche writes, we might hope to escape from the ugliness of the "human sacrifice which has at all times most elevated and exalted man" (D #45).

But the sacrificial idea is not so easy to overcome. In #45 Nietzsche supersedes the ascetic sacrifice of the individual only in order to speak of a promised, or hinted, sacrifice of humanity itself: "But to whom should mankind sacrifice itself? One could already take one's oath that, if ever the constellation of this idea appears above the horizon, the knowledge of truth would remain as the one tremendous goal [ungeheuere Ziel] commensurate with such a sacrifice" (D #45; KSA 3.52). This "tremendous [or monstrous, *ungeheuere*] goal" offers a coldly, cheerfully tragic end to the human quest for knowledge, something that, rather unexpectedly, "could drive mankind to the point of dying with the light of an anticipatory wisdom in its eyes." (This Nietzschean anticipation, it seems, establishes its difference from Socrates' anticipation of death in the *Phaedo* because Nietzsche looks to death as harbinger of a freeing difference from, rather than a freeing answer to, life.) Nietzsche concludes #45 by returning to the same futuristic *mise-en-scène* that he depicted in #7, by placing the human at a distance of light-years, of stellar eons. This time, though, Nietzsche offers a vision of intergalactic communication over these vast distances: "Perhaps, if one day an alliance has been established with the inhabitants of other stars for the purpose of knowledge, and knowledge has been communicated from star to star for a few millennia: perhaps enthusiasm for knowledge may then rise to such a high-water mark!" (D #45). *Daybreak* #45's science fiction of a vast, far-flung secret society that has transcended familiar, earthly limits returns when Nietzsche revises, at the very end of *Daybreak*'s book 1 (#96), the vision of Constantine: the IHSV (*In hoc signo vinces*, "in this sign you will triumph") that appeared in the sky, along with a crucifix, during the battle of the Milvian bridge, persuading the Roman emperor to convert to Christianity. So the project of mastery is extinguished or *aufgehoben* in a collective self-sacrifice that means a new, a newly transformed existence. With mankind having died out, the aliens who remain, our *übermenschlich* descendants, will exchange a novel *symbolon*, a sign of unbelief passed among the enlightened.

Nietzsche concludes book 1 of *Daybreak* by coming back to earth, while retaining the grand prospect of a secret society of the free, the illuminati, who will share a sign among themselves. He wishes for a development of Europe toward the "free-minded naivety" of the Brahmins who, according to Nietzsche, believed that the good things of religion derive from the mere faithful adherence to ceremony. Nietzsche here attempts to restore to ritual observance its original Brahmin innocence. He wants to redeem superstition through the rational consciousness that custom achieves its effects without being grounded in any greater or deeper power than its own self-perpetuation, than dumb ritual observance.

But Nietzsche, having lauded the Brahmin respect for ritual, rather surprisingly proceeds to envision its abolition. Once the law has been understood in the way the Brahmins understand religious ritual, as a mere matter of going through the motions, its power fades away: enlightenment conquers the power of convention. In effect, Nietzsche here proposes an advance in the opposite direction from the Pauline embrace/annihilation of the law. Instead of the sublime will to overthrow custom in the service of something greater (the powerful tautology of drive), custom becomes a mere sign, which will eventually disappear, virtually of its own accord. "Morality in the old sense," the ascetic sense, "will have died," to be replaced by the new sign of the free spirit:

> There are today among the various nations of Europe perhaps ten to twenty million people who no longer "believe in God"—is it too much to ask that they should *give a sign* to one another? Once they have thus come to know one another, they will also have made themselves known to others—they will at once constitute a power in Europe and, happily, a power between the nations! Between the classes! Between rich and poor! Between rulers and subjects! Between the most unpeaceable and the most peaceable, peace-bringing people! (*D* #96)

Daybreak #96, titled "*In hoc signo vinces*," imagines a political power based on enlightened lack of belief—a mediating power that, instead of eliminating opposites or making them as one in the manner of Christianity, will retain these differences, communicating between the "most unpeaceable and the most peaceable." Though it is unclear what kind of future might be brought into being by such association, it is certain that Nietzsche here refrains from his earlier suggestion, in *Daybreak* #45, that mankind's enlightenment will mean its dying out, a self-sacrifice illuminated by "anticipatory wisdom." Instead, Nietzsche here offers a pentecostal vision, an abstract communion that will serve continuing life. But this image at the end of *Daybreak's* book 1 still shares something of the attenuated, dispersed character attached to the earlier interstellar vision (the future alliance with "the inhabitants of other stars" described in *Daybreak* #45).[11]

Looking back at the last page of *Daybreak's* book 1, at Nietzsche's newly prophesied sign, we see the openness of the future, the illimitable enormity of space, the endless possibilities for knowledge. This Nietzschean vision measures itself, with a certain stress, against the fortified, resplendent self produced by the most refined examples of priestly artistry, the total, embodied spiritualization still associated in *Daybreak* with Catholic practice. The fading away of drive under the innovative sign of Nietzschean liberation from belief stands against the strenuous transformation of drive by the early Christian priesthood, and by the great painters and sly, powerful priests of Renaissance Italy who inherit and develop that early, fierce discipline.

The architectonic or Apollonian possibility for the self in book 1 of *Daybreak,* then, the potential for a taut, empowered refinement, finds itself superseded at the end of book 1 by Nietzsche's wish for a total freedom that he does not yet know how to envision incarnate: by a superseding, or sacrifice, of the human image we have known so far. Both these possibilities represent a defeat of the ascetic overintimacy of Pauline will, a will whose raw passion replaces, in *Daybreak*, the equally savage Dionysian ecstasy Nietzsche praised in *The Birth of Tragedy*.

Both Dionysus and Paul are, for Nietzsche, emblems of drive; both of them override the basic work of desire, its effort to state the enigma of the Other: to outline, and to compensate for, what is lacking in the Other. Commenting on Lacan's distinction between drive and desire in *Seminar XI,* Paul Verhaeghe writes that, in desire, "the subject, confronted with the enigma of the desire of the Other, tries to verbalise this desire and thus constitutes itself by identifying with the signifiers in the field of the Other, without ever succeeding in filling the gap between subject and Other."[12]

Nietzsche's exploration of love later in *Daybreak* corresponds to this riddling, conversational seeking out of the other in which the subject, as Verhaeghe puts it, "alternately appears and disappears." This is the play of desire, oriented by a lack insinuated between subject and other on both the Symbolic level (of "the other who speaks from my place, apparently, this other who is within me," as Lacan puts it) and the Imaginary level (the "other who is caught up with me in a relation of mirage").[13]

Verhaeghe goes on to say that unlike desire, drive responds to a different, anterior lack: the necessity of the individual's death as "the price life has to pay for the acquisition of sexual reproduction."[14] This lack, which Freud encounters most directly in *Beyond the Pleasure Principle,* gives drive a compelling force that precedes and, in the ascetic mode, seems to outweigh the enigmas of desire. Drive testifies to a human being's attempt to die in its own fashion, and thereby to imprint itself on life in supremely visible form, an attempt that is most obvious in asceticism.

As *Daybreak* continues, Nietzsche attempts liberation by moving from drive to desire, from the constant pressure exemplified in asceticism to the more mobile scene associated with the knowing self-delusion of lovers and actors. In later works, though, like the *Genealogy of Morals* and *Ecce Homo,* the imperative of drive returns, and with it the inescapability—at least for Nietzsche—of the ascetic attitude.

ARTISTS ONLY: LOVE AND THEATER

> . . . *wo die schönste Freiheit herrscht— Maskenfreiheit.*
> . . . *where the finest freedom reigns— the freedom of the mask.*
> —Heinrich Heine, *Briefe aus Berlin*[15]

> *Man wird fein genarrt, wenn man fein ist.*
> *If you are subtle and high-toned, you will be fooled subtly.*
> —Nietzsche, *The Will to Power* #808

"Illusions," the final essay in Emerson's *Conduct of Life,* begins with a journey to a cave, a familiar scene for philosophy. "Some years ago," Emerson writes, "in company with an agreeable party, I spent a long summer day in exploring the Mammoth Cave in Kentucky" (*E* 1115). The cave's "spacious galleries" and "sculptured and fretted chambers" culminate in the "'Star-Chamber.'" Emerson reports that "our lamps were taken from us by the guide, and extinguished or put aside, and, on looking upwards, I saw or seemed to see the night heaven thick with stars glimmering more or less brightly over our heads, and even what seemed a comet flaming among them. . . . I sat down on the rocky floor to enjoy the serene picture" (*E* 1115). In contrast to the be-nighted dwellers in Plato's cave, Emerson and his fellow tourists know that they are the audience for an illusion, one of nature's gimmicks or "theatrical trick[s]" (*E* 1116).[16] Emerson's sense of the world as a the-ater or a "spacious galler[y]," a place for knowing and exploiting illu-sions, parallels Nietzsche's images of the human types who, as it were professionally, engage in desire: the actor, the artist, and the lover.

In *Daybreak* and *The Gay Science* Nietzsche develops his images of theatrical and artistic deception more fully than in his other works and implicitly responds to Emerson's "good-natured" picture of life as theater: Nietzsche conveys a greater sense of risk, of potential trauma, than Emerson recognizes. For Emerson, what life requires is "a good-natured admission that there are illusions, and who shall say he is not their sport?" (*E* 1119). The Emersonian answer to the problem of fate often seems to be a smoothly ironic skating on surfaces.

For Nietzsche, theater is a model of artistic control in which we find ourselves deprived of the fortress-like defense against the other that the architectural image promises (for example, in a case like that of Anaximander from *Philosophy in the Tragic Age of the Greeks,* discussed in chapter 3). The actor must court an audience. The similarity of this theatrical courtship to that other work of desire, the machinations of erotic life, appears, with both stimulating and disorienting results, in *Daybreak*.[17]

For both Emerson and Nietzsche, the best theater of life is the kind that remains strictly controlled and yet also gives way: we surrender to the illusion we desire while knowing all the while that it is *mere* illusion. Love is the name Nietzsche gives, finally, to this half-trust in appearance. "Do you desire the most astonishing proof of how far the transfiguring power of intoxication [des Rausches] can go?" Nietzsche writes in *The Will to Power* (*WP* #808). "'Love' is the proof: that which is called love in all the languages and silences of the world."[18] For Nietzsche, love is a magical phenomenon that changes not only the beloved object but also the self that gazes on that object. Love, therefore, furnishes a model for the trust we give to versions of the world.

Love requires an acceptance of contingency. We happen to have met just this person, and seem rather unknowingly to have talked ourselves into playing just this role. Even the loneliness of the philosopher, whose isolation might appear to remove him from contingency, is swayed by such happy and unhappy chances. Especially in retrospect, the "looking back" that the Janus face of *The Gay Science* accomplishes, we are able to see our existence as pathos, as a mood dependent on lucky or unlucky accident, rather than as a fixed way of life derived from our character, or ethos:

> *Looking back.*—The true pathos of every period of our life rarely becomes clear to us as long as we live in this period; then we always assume that it is the only state [Zustand] that is possible and reasonable for us and—to speak with the Greeks and adopt their distinction—an ethos and not a pathos. A few musical chords reminded me today of a winter and a house and an extremely solitary [einsiedlerisches] life, as well as the feeling in which I lived at that time: I thought that I might go on living that way forever. But now I comprehend that it was wholly pathos and passion and thus comparable to this painful and bold music that was so certain that there was some comfort [vergleichbar dieser schmerzhaft-muthigen und trostsichern Musik]. That sort of thing one must not have for years or for eternities; otherwise one would become too "super-terrestrial" for this planet. (*GS* #317; *KSA* 3.549–50)

This passage is a portrait of an ethos, a character, Nietzsche's own, that is in danger of becoming otherworldly in its artful cherishing of moods. As in *Daybreak,* Nietzsche here runs the risk of desiring an escape from day-to-day embodiment in the name of an ecstatic concentration of self, turning his whole experience into the crystallizing of a single mood.

But Nietzsche will advance from this narrow, centripetal aestheticism to a less careful attitude. Like Emerson in *The Conduct of Life,* Nietzsche in *The Gay Science* tries for an architectonic solidity that will incorporate the fluctuation of mood, a mildly Dionysian ebbing and flowing. In Sanctus Januarius, book 4 of *The Gay Science,* Nietzsche tries to compose a self that is formed from moods and passions but nevertheless provides stability, a desired ethos that will unite time, place, and person. The security supplied by such a unified moment, however, threatens to bind the soul back to an inert place, a leaden and inflexible center. Nietzsche, in response to this danger of stasis, generates an opposing ideal of flying, or hovering, among possibilities, an ambient liberation.

Perhaps "the usual state" for "future souls" will be an ethos made of interwoven pathoi, rather like that of Stevens's Canon Aspirin in "Notes Toward a Supreme Fiction," who "was the ascending wings he saw / And moved on them in orbits' outer stars / Descending to the children's bed, on which / They lay." Nietzsche calls this sublime fluctuation "a perpetual movement between high and low, the feeling of high and low, a continual ascent as on stairs and at the same time a sense of resting on clouds [ein beständiges Wie-auf-Treppen-steigen und zugleich Wie-auf-Wolken-ruhen]" (*GS*#288; *KSA* 3.529). I have already discussed *Daybreak* #60, whose priest shifts in a self-sustaining manner between obedience and exaltation. Here Nietzsche expands this confluence of earthbound discipline and fantastic flight into a new freedom that is not bound to look back in a fixed direction—to the memorable coordinates of, for example, "a winter and a house and an extremely solitary life"—but is, instead, free to move around.

This superior mastery, then, also means triumphant mobility. The oscillation between opposite poles Nietzsche evokes in *The Gay Science* #288 is another way of looking both forward and back. In the title of Sanctus Januarius Nietzsche alludes to the opposing faces of Janus, as well as to the miracle of St. Januarius, whose clotted blood, preserved in a vial, transforms itself once a year into new, liquid life. (Is the saint's solid blood analogous to Nietzsche's writing, which revives and moves when faced by congenial readers?) Janus-like, book 4 of *The Gay Science* urges us to look forward and backward at once. This reversibility forms the basis of Nietzsche's detached and resilient comic vision.

When we are in a mood, we know it less truly than afterward, when we have lost it. True pathos appears only in retrospect, from a distance, after life has lost the pain of immediacy.[19] Nietzsche offers the comfort of a nostalgia that detaches and frees the self, making it "too 'super-terrestrial,'" *überirdisch,* "for this planet." The comfort also lies in an appreciation of contingency. A period of life is not an existential choice but a product of chance; its sheer occurrence alters everything before and behind it in ways we could hardly predict. But the chance origins of pathos render it fragile and therefore subject to our rearrangement. Pathos can be manipulated. If we know its illusory character and are able to rely on it while still realizing its fragility, Nietzsche suggests, we can make it convey the lightness of fiction, rather than the dullness of constraining fact. Nietzsche here proposes an Emersonian refinement: capitalizing on chance.

The aestheticizing distance from experience Nietzsche offers suggests the ungrounded nature of our moral earnestness.[20] Yet ungrounded does not mean transitory: the problem of existence returns incessantly, and this return, because it makes necessary the constant experimenting of the philosopher-quester, imposes a burden that continually threatens to turn tragic. The eternal return, when taken as a philosophical challenge, requires from the quester a severe isolation and self-examination. This trial, or *Untergehen,* is indicated in the final words of Sanctus Januarius, "Incipit tragoedia," and is dramatized at length in *Zarathustra.* But the final goal of Nietzsche's quest is the attainment of philosophical comedy, the mobility that hops from cloud to cloud, simultaneously at rest and in motion.

Like Nietzsche in *The Gay Science,* Emerson specializes in converting tragedy into comedy, while retaining the sense that this movement is reversible and that tragic experience is what motivates our wishes for, and our realization of, comedy. Emerson's *Conduct of Life* moves from the sublimely tragic insistence of "Fate," its first essay, to the tart comedy of "Illusions," its final one. Emerson in "Fate" views tragedy as the product of a splitting of perspective that opposes the cruelly determined to the free, fatalism to life. The split can only be overcome if the whole is reconciled, if it becomes a distant spectacle, the cool object of observation: the world "pleases at a sufficient perspective" (*E* 961). By the time we get to "Illusions," we have been reintroduced into the teasing, deceptive, alluring world Emerson distanced us from in "Fate." We are once again players, of a game that encompasses all our actions and desires.

Two passages from "Illusions" must have excited Nietzsche. In the first, Emerson pictures self-knowledge as a canny discipline of self-exposure. Describing a classic refinement of *sprezzatura*, Emerson suggests that an influential or brilliant character reveals itself only partially, in a teasing, transitory manner, not so much as to make itself vulnerable. By the end of the *Conduct of Life*, the model for Emersonian genius has become an actor's strategic self-display: "Men who make themselves felt in the world avail themselves of a certain fate in their constitution, which they know how to use. But they never deeply interest us, unless they lift a corner of the curtain, or betray never so slightly their penetration of what is behind it" (*E* 1119). The actor's turning up of a seam, a vulnerability, engages the audience more than the pose of untouchable power, and is therefore stronger. Moving others, one must *not* be as stone.

In the second passage, Emerson names women as the best actors, the creatures who know and manipulate illusion most fully. But now, in contrast to the first passage, which emphasized men's dominating usage of that "certain fate in their constitution," it is women's vulnerability, their need for illusion, that makes their manipulations effective. "Women, more than all, are the element and kingdom of illusion. Being fascinated, they fascinate. They see through Claude-Lorraines. And how dare any one, if he could, pluck away the coulisses, stage effects, and ceremonies, by which they live? Too pathetic, too pitiable, is the region of affection, and its atmosphere always liable to mirage" (*E* 1118). "Being fascinated, they fascinate": Emerson's lesson is that one must be susceptible oneself in order to exert the power of allure — one must play both audience and actor. There is a strength to this fragility: "the region of affection" that women inhabit defends its borders by being "too pitiable" to be demystified in the ruthless manner we see in (for example) Emerson's "Fate."

The studied imperfection and the real vulnerability Emerson attributes to women requires a mirror. Fascination relies on a sympathetic projection: its generosity is the impulse to "make the same" that Nietzsche in *Daybreak* identifies as crucial to love.

"Love makes the same." Love wants to spare the person to whom it dedicates itself every feeling of being other, and consequently it is full of dissimulation and pretence of similarity, it is constantly deceiving and feigning a sameness [sie betrügt fortwährend und schauspielert eine Gleichheit] which in reality does not exist. And this happens so instinctively that women in love deny this dissimulation and continually tender deceit and boldly assert that love *makes the same* (that is to say, that it performs a miracle!). — This process is simple when one party *lets himself be loved* and does not find it necessary to dissimulate but leaves that to the other, loving party; but there is no more confused or impenetrable spectacle [nichts Verwickelteres und Undurchdringbareres von Schauspielerei giebt es] than that which arises when both parties are passionately in love with one another and both consequently abandon themselves and want to be the same as one another: in the end neither knows what he is supposed to be imitating, what pretending to be. The beautiful madness of this spectacle [die schöne Tollheit dieses Schauspiels] is too good for this world and too subtle for human eyes. (*D* #532; *KSA* 3.304)

In this beautiful (and maybe a little mad) paragraph, seeking the desire of the other means the impossible effort to inhabit the other's terms, to appear by disappearing, by becoming the same as the other. What saves this effort from desperation and failure is not the restful interlude in which "one party *lets himself be loved*" (a phenomenon unusual in its simplicity, and which therefore marks a pause in love's theater rather than a definitive aspect of it), but rather the superior intricacy or confusion that leads to a kind of liberation in which one does not know "what one is supposed to be imitating, what pretending to be." (This is, perhaps, the emergence into the dawn of the subtle old mole invoked in Nietzsche's Preface.) In love, the effort to answer the other's desire, to model oneself on the other, turns reciprocal, in a hall of mirrors effect. I suit myself to the other's attempt to suit herself to me — or, rather, to my attempt to suit myself to her attempt to suit herself to my . . . and so on. As Lacan says of the Imaginary relation between self and other, "I can in no way expect to attain my accomplishment and my unity from the recognition of an other who is caught up with me in a relation of mirage."[21] Others are imperfectly second-guessing me just as I am second-guessing them, since each of us is working with an incomplete knowledge, rather than being pervaded or thoroughly constructed by knowledge, as in Foucault's version of things.

Through the reminder of our incompleteness it provides, Imaginary theatricality entails a knowingness that erodes the boundaries between myself and the Other. The Imaginary participation evoked by Lacan, and by Nietzsche in *Daybreak* #532, stands in its subtlety and doubtful knowledge at the opposite pole from the surrender to belief and to rhetorical effect that book 1 of *Daybreak* associates with Paul's sublime. This is a truly musical play of masks whose complication contrasts with the Pauline ascetic's drive to go behind or beyond the mask, to abolish the law in the name of newly incarnate reality.

In his translation of *Daybreak* #532, Hollingdale somewhat underemphasizes Nietzsche's references to theater and actors (*Schauspieler*). In the original text it is clear that Nietzsche is presenting love as a *Schauspiel*, or drama: a sublimely funny, though painful, form of theater, born from the marriage of looking (*Schauen*) and game-playing (*Spielen*). In this comedy of errors, we feel an impulse to repress the artistry that has made the other similar to ourselves, but we know all along that this impulse too is an artistic one. What is repressed is, above all, the fact that the similarity begins not from an analytic grasp (or "understanding") of the other's causes or motives, but from our own miming of her passion. As in *The Gay Science's* passage on "looking back," here ethos, upon reflection, finds itself transformed into a manipulable pathos. The analytic impulse that would search for the motives of an amorous case history in ethos, in the character of lover or beloved, is hopelessly derailed by the mirror-play of emotional gestures that goes on between a couple.

The section of *Daybreak* I have been discussing, #532, is titled "*Love makes the same.*" Nietzsche here relies on a moment from one of his favorite writers, Stendhal. In *The Red and the Black* Julien Sorel, about to begin his affair with Madame de Rênal, the provincial mayor's wife, notices that she has been condescending to him and angrily cites to himself a line of Corneille that he has recently learned: "Love makes equalities, it does not seek them." Stendhal's irony at this moment in *The Red and the Black* depends on the fact that Julien, even as he decides to seduce his social superior Madame de Rênal, has been casting about in search of "commonplaces with equality as their theme."[22] Stendhal bears witness to a downward spiral of amorous ridiculousness in which Julien's pretense to a distinguished ambition to conquer his beloved is instantly undone by the fact of this ambition's commonness, expressed in a common aphorism that makes all lovers the same. If Stendhal gives us low comedy, Nietzsche offers us high, with the gods looking down on a spectacle just as ludicrous as it is sublime. As Emerson writes in "Self-Reliance," "We pass for what we are" (*E* 266).

IMAGINARY MIMICRY AND REFINEMENT

For the Nietzsche of *Daybreak*, morality, like passionate love, finds its strange basis in a process of identification whose groundlessness appears in its confusing, theatrical intricacy. Our sympathies cannot be explained as the results of reasoned inquiry concerning others' emotional states. In a passage entitled "*Mitempfindung*" (Sympathy), Nietzsche argues against our usual notion that we sympathize with another because we understand the reason for her pain. Instead, Nietzsche writes, we "produce [a] feeling in ourselves after the effects it exerts and displays on the other person by imitating with our own body the expression of his eyes, his voice, his walk, his bearing (or even their reflection [Abbild] in word, picture, music)" (*D* #142; *KSA* 3.133). There is a historical origin for this mimicry, Nietzsche continues, perhaps following Rousseau (for whom, in the *Essay on the Origin of Languages,* that origin is the primal experience of fear), but the origin has been outgrown. Nietzsche argues that the instinct to imitate the gestures and sounds of sympathy precedes any actual occasion for this emotion: that, "like perfect fools, we grow sad without there being the slightest occasion for sorrow" (*D* #142). Here Nietzsche departs from Schopenhauer's idea of the grounded, authentic character of sympathy as well as his own early reading of the origin of the theatrical as a deep metaphysical communion with Being (in *The Birth of Tragedy*). Now, theater is the cause, not the effect, of sympathy, which is no longer primal, as in the *Birth,* but instead a product of Imaginary mimicry.

According to the Nietzsche of *Daybreak,* we produce a copy of a copy by aping the other's image, which is already a quasi-artistic representation whether it occurs in real life or "in word, picture, music." Here as elsewhere, the figure of woman preoccupies Nietzsche:

> One should observe especially the play on the faces of women and how they quiver and glitter in continual imitation and reflection of what is felt to be going on round them [vom unaufhörlichen Nachbilden und Wiederspiegeln dessen, was um sie herum

empfunden wird]. . . . The capacity for understanding—which, as we have seen, rests on the capacity for *rapid dissimulation* [sich rasch zu verstellen]—declines in proud, arrogant [selbstherr-lichen] men and peoples, because they have less fear: on the other hand, every kind of understanding and self-dissembling is at home among timid [ängstlichen] peoples; here is also the right-ful home of the imitative arts and of the higher intelligence. (*D* #142; *KSA* 3.134-35)

The agile sensitivity Nietzsche here attributes to women, like the Em-ersonian reception of impulses that reads new creation in, or into, these impulses (see chapter 1), yields just enough to reveal a symmetry between the self and its surroundings. Nietzsche here seems to echo Emerson's remark on women (cited earlier) from *The Conduct of Life:* that women's lives are the "kingdom of illusions." For Nietzsche, the quintessentially feminine weathervane of emotions masks its "rapid dissimulation," since woman believes that she does not create but merely receives.

How does Nietzsche know this about woman? Through his own ob-servation, and therefore mimicry, of their surfaces, through "ob-serv[ing] the play on the[ir] faces."[23] Woman, the supreme emotional aesthete, converts all her spectators into aesthetes like herself by re-taining her silent, defensive distance from them, even as her "continual imitation and reflection" signal her susceptibility to what surrounds her. Moving others, one must *not* be as stone.

Nietzsche in this paragraph does not express complete sympathy with woman, the object of his observation. Aesthetic refinement isn't everything. There is also the noble, predatory aloofness of the "proud, arrogant men and peoples," the male culture of the Roman masters. As Nietzsche's career continues, however, he will find himself more and more identifying himself as one of the feminine artists of sympa-thy, capable of recognizing any ethos, no matter how foreign or seem-ingly barbaric, as a legitimate way of being human: *nihil humani alienum est.* But—most important—he will not keep his distance from the other as this idealized woman does; while she watches and de-stroys, he will *be* destroyed (in *Ecce Homo*). Woman seems to represent exactly the freedom Nietzsche himself does not have.

But perhaps feminine and masculine mastery are not so different as Nietzsche's remarks imply. Nietzsche, later in his career, will further drive home the point he already recognizes in *Daybreak,* that despite his proud, isolate sublimity, the exemplary hero of advanced, distinguished morality plays to an audience just as the woman does: "*Refined cruelty as virtue.*—Here is a morality which rests entirely on the *drive to distinction*—do not think too highly of it! For what kind of a drive is that and what thought lies behind it? We want to make the sight of us *painful* to another and to awaken in him the feeling of envy and of his own impotence and degradation" (*D* #30). But this force of resentment, the will to power as a way of getting the other to see our strength and his weakness, fades away in the course of time, at least according to *Daybreak*'s theory of history. Nietzsche goes on, in *Daybreak* #30, to argue that the cruelty that originally motivates personal distinction fades away in succeeding generations, who instead discipline themselves in the name of "pleasure in the habit as such." This pleasure in habit is "the first stage of the good." The later stages of goodness, then, are born from the look and feel of the "drive to distinction" rather than the actual infliction of pain on another person: the enjoyment of masterful gestures and customs as such. Nietzsche is proposing the withering away of an original moral cruelty so that, instead of an intention to hurt others, later generations experience only a pleasure in the sharp style formerly associated with such cruelty.

In *The Gay Science* as in *Daybreak,* Nietzsche remains preoccupied by the question of mastery. Book 4 of *The Gay Science* speculates on the need to give up our usual treasured virtue of *Selbstherrschaft,* self-control. "Of course," Nietzsche writes, "one can achieve greatness" through iron self-control, but the person who does so "has certainly become insufferable for others, difficult for himself, and impoverished and cut off from the most beautiful fortuities of his soul. Also from all further *instruction.* For one must be able to lose oneself occasionally if one wants to learn something from things different from oneself" (*GS* #305).

Here we see the argument between Apollo and Dionysus, between an architectonic fortification of the self and a musical receptivity akin to Emersonian abandonment, a "los[ing] oneself" to inspiration. Sanctus Januarius turns in both these directions. Nietzsche wants to assert authorship, control over past and future, but also to give himself up to influence or sensation. As a result of such surrender to one's surroundings, he writes, the world's dimensions increase: "*The fancy of the contemplatives.*—... For anyone who grows up into the heights of humanity the world becomes ever fuller; ever more fishhooks are cast in his direction to capture his interest; the number of things that stimulate him grows constantly, as does the number of different kinds of pleasure and displeasure" (*GS* #301). "But," Nietzsche continues, the contemplative man "can never shake off a delusion" that he is merely the spectator, rather than the creator, of this ever-varying spectacle. Being aware that we are actually creators rather than mere spectators, Nietzsche suggests at the end of *The Gay Science* #301, would make us prouder and happier, secure in the knowledge of our workmanship. Yet the next aphorism, #302, implies the necessary frustration of the creator, the contemplative-as-artist who wishes to control fully the dimensions and meanings of his work, to plan its intricacies to the letter. Such fastidious crafting of one's *oeuvre*—and, therefore, of one's life—means that "One becomes ever more refined in pain and ultimately too refined; any small dejection and nausea was quite enough in the end to spoil life for Homer. He had been unable to guess a foolish little riddle posed to him by some fishermen" (*GS* #302).

Nietzsche's celebration of authorial control, then, finds itself reversed into a vulnerability to the details of his own work, and to whatever that work leaves out or resists. Paragraphs 301 and 302 of *The Gay Science* present a revision of *The Birth of Tragedy*'s image of the universe as a vast artwork in which we are the depicted figures who can magically turn around and look at ourselves (*BT* chapter 5, 32). In *The Gay Science*, we are the creators of the spectacle, and we ought to know it. This emphasis is in keeping with *The Gay Science*'s celebration of authorship. But this celebration discerns as well the frustrations the claim to authorship entails, just as *Daybreak* recognizes the mirroring that undermines the control of any master or lover. Nietzsche here seems to offer a reconciliatory dynamic, as in Emerson's "Illusions": the visible hand of the fabricator must yield to the imperfections that both frustrate and stimulate art. But this yielding may also force us into the vulnerability that "spoil[s] life for Homer," an over-sensitivity that (as we shall see in *Ecce Homo*) is capable of being wrecked by the unexpected presence of that sharp "fishhook," the object *a*.

When he wrote *The Gay Science*, Nietzsche's faith resided in the possibility of restating the individual's artistic manipulation of his world as his loyal service to, his near-religious sustaining of, this world. Nietzsche images such service as the carrying of a goddess across "the river of becoming." When we finish or "round off" life, appreciating it as we would an art object we are in the process of creating, we lift the (feminine) figure of perfection above the unfinished stream of existence. Nietzsche speaks of "art as the *good* will to appearance":

> We do not always keep our eyes from rounding off [auszurunden] something and, as it were, finishing the poem; and then it is no longer eternal imperfection [die ewige Unvollkommenheit] that we carry across the river of becoming—then we have the sense of carrying a *goddess,* and feel proud and childlike as we perform this service. As an aesthetic phenomenon existence is still bearable for us, and art furnishes us with eyes and hands and above all the good conscience to be able to turn ourselves into such a phenomenon. At times we need a rest from ourselves by looking upon, by looking *down* upon, ourselves and, from an artistic distance, laughing *over* ourselves or weeping *over* ourselves. (*GS*#107)

Nietzsche's description in *The Gay Science* of standing above and looking down on oneself develops from his image in *The Birth of Tragedy* of the world as a work of art, and of us as fairy-tale creatures who can turn around and look at ourselves. The rescued goddess embodied in a distant sight of perfection is, in turn, related to Nietzsche's picture of Nike in "History for Life": the victory over time's amorphousness, unerringly balanced in the moment. But here, in *The Gay Science*, it is we who carry the goddess across the river of becoming, an image related to Orpheus's task in rescuing Eurydice. It is ourselves that we bring back from the dead, and we do so by maintaining a proper distance as Orpheus did not, the "artistic distance" that, as so often in Emerson, enables us to put a finish, a finality, on life's appearances.

Massimo Cacciari sees Nietzsche's favoring of brief habits in *The Gay Science* as his means of *Ausrunden,* of finishing off the world, and of staying safely removed from experience. Such a practice of closure is also, Cacciari continues, Nietzsche's answer to Wagner's recursive melancholy, the Wagnerian way of dwelling seemingly infinitely on a phrase.[24] Nietzsche's phrase in paragraph #107, "die ewige Unvollkommenheit," is in fact not a bad description of the Wagnerian style of infinite incompletion. The eternal return described at the end of Sanctus Januarius will offer an alternative to this Wagnerian eternity or *Ewigkeit*. But it also differs decisively from the means of eternalizing ourselves that Nietzsche himself proposes in paragraph #107, his notion of rounding off or completing experience, carrying the goddess safely across the stream of becoming, like a successful Orpheus bearing his Eurydice.[25] Instead of this proud and childlike service to the goddess, the perfecting of our existence, the eternal return proposes a decision to embrace the moment in its imperfection.

Such embracing of the temporary and imperfect as we see in the eternal return is heralded earlier in book 4 of *The Gay Science*. In Sanctus Januarius habits become the forms, both necessary and transitory, of self-fashioning. Nietzsche writes of one's truths as a snakeskin, a necessary sheath that must nevertheless be shed periodically (*GS* #307). The image occurs often in his earlier works—for example, in "Schopenhauer as Educator"—but in *The Gay Science* it acquires an unprecedented comic tone:

> Now something that you formerly loved as a truth or probability strikes you as an error; you shed it and fancy that this represents a victory for your reason. . . . What killed that opinion for you was your new life and not your reason: *you no longer need it,* and now it collapses and unreason crawls out of it into the light like a worm. . . . We negate and must negate because something in us wants to live and affirm—Something that we perhaps do not know or see as yet.—This is said in favor of criticism. (*GS* #307)

Nietzsche here depicts not the melodrama of a conversion experience, not a fervent turning against one's earlier beliefs, but a happy shedding of them. The past is easily disposed of, and the future, just now coming to birth, cannot be defined or named, refusing to be known or fully seen. But this future deserves to live as *potentia.* The ascetic self-struggle that absorbs Nietzsche in *Zarathustra* and the *Genealogy,* and that most readers associate with his name, has vanished into thin air, killed, as so often in Emerson, by a simple, casual ray of truth.

Self-criticism in Sanctus Januarius takes the form of a clear-eyed, calm, and honest appraisal of one's actual experience, in contrast to the severe and devious pathways of the *Genealogy*. Nietzsche in *The Gay Science* presumes that experience is available to be observed, and even transformed. Only the rigid and pious, the anti-thinkers, need to avoid lucid self-skepticism. In *The Gay Science,* faith is so fragile that it threatens to collapse at the mere touch of scientific attitude (*GS* #319); in the *Genealogy* its tenacity is almost too much to be suffered.

The Gay Science is concerned not just with the fragility of habitual faith, but also with the enduring habit of study, the slow process of our learning to know a new object, person, or text. In *The Gay Science* Nietzsche provides an affecting image of the humble, yet sublime, reward of study: we must learn how to love what is new to us just as we get used to, and take increasing pleasure in, the details of a musical score. The beloved object or person finally drops its veil and thanks us for our quiet energies: "In the end we are always rewarded for our good will, our patience, fairmindedness, and gentleness with what is strange; gradually, it sheds its veil and turns out to be a new and indescribable beauty. That is its *thanks* for our hospitality. Even those who love themselves will have learned it in this way; for there is no other way" (*GS* #334). Nietzsche, at the end of #334, circles back to the issue of self-knowledge and self-fashioning with a casualness that colors the entire paragraph. Usually in Nietzsche the image of the veil signifies that which is superficial and yet essential, both surface and depth, and in any case profoundly permanent. Yet here, uncharacteristically, the veil falls away like the snake's skin of #307. Gratitude, which frequently seems convoluted in Nietzsche, and sometimes poisoned by resentment, now appears simple and conclusive. Such is the perfection of Nietzsche's mood in Sanctus Januarius, the sunny afternoon of his soul.

Paragraph #310 of *The Gay Science* proposes a different image. Like many passages in the book, it makes a riddle that refuses to yield itself fully to our reading:

> Will and wave.—How greedily this wave approaches, as if it were after something! How it crawls with terrifying haste into the inmost nooks of this labyrinthine cliff! It seems that it is trying to anticipate someone; it seems that something of value, high value, must be hidden there.—And now it comes back, a little more slowly but still quite white with excitement; is it disappointed? Has it found what it looked for? Does it pretend to be disappointed?—But already another wave is approaching, still more greedily and savagely than the first, and its soul, too, seems to be full of secrets and the lust to dig up treasures. Thus live waves—thus live we who will—more I shall not say. (*GS* #310)

The enigmatic quality of this page of Sanctus Januarius is its way of keeping faith with Nietzsche's private happiness and his melancholy. With tact and admiration, the Nietzschean spectator questions the crashing waves that form the protagonist of this passage; and with a kind of adroit projection too, that sees in the waves a sharp, full-blooded pleasure in malice, a healthy delight in war that mirrors Nietzsche's own.

"Thus live waves—thus live we who will—more I shall not say . . ." Despite his gesture toward an esoteric meaning that must not be divulged publicly, Nietzsche goes on to "say more." He continues #310 for another, lengthy paragraph, which concludes, "Mark my word!—I know you and your secret, I know your kind! You and I—are we not of one kind?–You and I—do we not have one secret?" (*GS* #310). What has he discovered?[20]

Nietzsche's waves do not just keep secrets. They also uncover them, and their "lust to dig up treasures" seems to be a reference to the Nietzschean investigator's sometimes shocking excavations. The waves' greedy hunger for existence, as they "roar with overweening pleasure and malice," images a universal eagerness, an eternal return of the ever-different and ever-the-same. But the spectacle also draws forth our appetite for projective anthropomorphism and projective misreading. Nietzsche here whimsically recalls Schopenhauer's daemonizing of the will as an anthropomorphic creature of fierce, insatiable appetite. He turns Schopenhauer's frightful image into a perfect picture of eternal return in which no regret for the past, and no tormented choice of a future, could ever be possible: any potential time of crisis would be washed away before it could even appear. Yet the desire to find the secret is also embodied in this passage, and this desire returns us to crisis. Nietzsche implies a view of the waves not just as the signs of a limitless ocean of becoming, but also as a Sphinx-like monster that can be confronted and addressed.

AESTHETICISM, ITS HAZARDS AND REWARDS

Aesthetic fashioning of the world receives its most persuasive statement in Sanctus Januarius when Nietzsche once again invokes the image of the artist: detached and yet involved, neutral and yet committed.

> *What one should learn from artists.*—How can we make things beautiful, attractive, and desirable for us when they are not? And I rather think that in themselves they never are. . . . Moving away from things until there is a good deal that one no longer sees and there is much that our eye still has to add if we are still to see them at all; or seeing things around a corner and as cut out and

framed; or to place them so that they partially conceal each other and grant us only glimpses of architectural perspectives; or looking at them through tinted glass or in the light of the sunset; or giving them a surface and skin that is not fully transparent— all this we should learn from artists while being wiser than they are in other matters. For with them this subtle power usually comes to an end where art ends and life begins; but we want to be the poets of our life—first of all in the smallest, most everyday matters. (*GS* #299)

Artfully arranging the vista of one's life, beautifying it: this requires a conscious and deliberate addition to the object, to the "everyday matters" which in themselves are lacking. It also requires a hiding of certain things, a tinting or coloring. The *Dichter* (poet or writer) becomes the master of the *dicht*, the dense or concealed. Schopenhauer in his *Aphorismen zur Lebensweisheit* makes a similar point when he celebrates the ability of poets to make something beautiful out of everyday occurrences.[27] But Schopenhauer makes it clear that for him such transformative poetic ability remains secondary to the fact that individuality is a prison. "No one can escape his individuality [Aus seiner Individualität kann keiner heraus]," in the Schopenhauerian view, and a person, like a pacing animal in a cage, remains confined within the narrow circle of his character.[28]

In Schopenhauer, the possibilities for an artistic transformation of individual existence remain limited. He puts his faith in the traditional philosophical task of knowing the limits of one's being, rather than knowing the potential of that being as material for creative metamorphosis. Nietzsche states a different faith, in transformative possibility. By doing so, he attacks Schopenhauer's belief that self-possession requires a calm reduction of human expectations and of our tendency to self-deception, which is allied with these expectations.

Schopenhauer's proto-Nietzschean Wanderer in the *Aphorismen* looks back from the heights toward the experiential path that led him to this summit. But the retrospect that Schopenhauer's Wanderer engages in tells us his difference from, as much as his affinity to, Nietzsche's character. "Just as the Wanderer when he reaches the summit," Schopenhauer writes, "for the first time surveys and recognizes the twists and turns of the path behind him in all their connections [im Zusammenhange], so we at the end of a period of our life, or even at the very end of our life, first recognize the true connections among our actions, results and works, their exact consequences and links, even their worth itself."[29]

Unlike the Wanderer in book 4 of *The Gay Science*, Schopenhauer's figure is filled not with a melancholy awareness of the self's continual need for illusions, but with a coolly assured sense of the difference between profit and loss, reality and fantasy. Schopenhauer states that resolve, *Besonnenheit*, requires looking back and reflecting, attaining an accurate retrospect.[30] But for Nietzsche, as for Emerson, our life of illusions cannot be made to submit to such measures. Does retrospect produce a reliable and healthy disillusion (Schopenhauer) or a newly cultivated understanding of how deeply we need illusion (Nietzsche)? Whereas Schopenhauer urges philosophical patience, a discarding of masks in favor of analytic solidity, Nietzsche holds to the continuing necessity of theatrical and creative strategies. His truth is that art is worth more than the truth. But Nietzsche is also aware of the hazards contained in this perception: for him, unlike Pater, an aestheticized existence requires a yielding to experience, a *lack* of mastery. Something escapes the aesthete's impulse to control the contours of his life—and, in *Ecce Homo*, that thing finally wrecks these contours.

In one of its most memorable paragraphs, Sanctus Januarius portrays the hazards involved in aestheticizing one's life. According to Nietzsche, an existence that values refinement in everyday experience is bound to be frustrated by the flaws and gaps the world imposes. The Homer of *The Gay Science* differs from the Homer of *The Birth of Tragedy*. In *The Gay Science*, Homer's art becomes a study of his own affect, his own response to his creations and their melancholy beauty; the heroic impersonality the *Birth* granted Homer has disappeared in favor of a poet teased by inaccessible secrets and fragile in his sensibility. Homer, according to Nietzsche in *The Gay Science*, is an aesthete of "refined senses" who "go[es] through life with a calm eye and firm step, always prepared to risk all—festively, impelled by the longing for undiscovered worlds and seas, people and gods." But as Nietzsche goes on, the resolve that characterizes Homer's heroic aestheticism falls apart:

> in the most profound enjoyment of the moment, to be overcome by tears and the crimson melancholy of the happy: who would not wish that all this might be his possession, his state! This was the happiness of Homer! The state of him that gave the

Greeks their gods—no, who invented his own gods for himself!
But we should not overlook this: with this Homeric happiness in
one's soul, one is also more capable of suffering than any other
creature under the sun. This is the only price for which one can
buy the most precious shell that the waves of existence have ever
yet washed on the shore. As its owner one becomes ever more
refined in pain and ultimately too refined; any small dejection
and nausea was quite enough in the end to spoil life for Homer.
He had been unable to guess a foolish little riddle posed to him
by some fishermen. Yes, little riddles are the danger that confronts those who are happiest. (*GS* #302)[31]

In #310 the emeralds of the sea were continually lost in the "infinite
white mane of foam and spray"; here, the sea's treasure takes on a
taunting, secretive power. Instead of arriving again and again, with
ever-increasing motions of joy, the ocean teases and eludes the poetic
seeker. Homer, instead of the heroic *Schöpfer* who has created humanity's gods, becomes a *Geschöpf*, a poor creature exhausted by his ceaseless sensitivity.[32]

Nietzsche in *The Gay Science* #302 will transform the flaw that
Homer weeps over into a more energetic emblem of the quest. In several markedly Emersonian passages in Sanctus Januarius, he writes
that we should be grateful for our flaws and imperfections (#295 and
#303). In another crucial paragraph he develops this idea:

> *In media vita.*—No, life has not disappointed me. On the con-
> trary, I find it truer, more desirable and mysterious every year—
> ever since the day when the great liberator came to me: the idea
> that life could be an experiment of the seeker for knowledge—
> and not a duty, not a calamity, not trickery.—And knowledge
> itself. . . . for me it is a world of dangers and victories in which
> heroic feelings, too, find places to dance and play. (*GS* #324)

In this very affecting passage, so wholehearted in its hope, life becomes
an experiment marked by happy misfirings and wanderings. The "dangers and victories" Nietzsche speaks of here represent the Emersonian
transformation of life into a bold experiment. The boldness is an exor-
cism of the truer danger that will appear full-blown in the *Genealogy,*
the "calamity" of asceticism that binds us to a particular object and a
particular scene. Whereas *Beyond Good and Evil* (*BGE* #231) invokes the

bedrock or "unteachable 'right down deep'" of each person's inalienable character which he cannot alter, and whereas *Ecce Homo* will founder on just this bedrock, *The Gay Science* manifests a hope for endless revision. Nietzsche in *The Gay Science* claims as the "great liberator" an interest in brief habits and changes of life that combines the experimental attitude of the scientist with the improvisational one of the actor.

THE ARCHITECTURE OF HOME

But for Nietzsche such mobility must be anchored; it must have a home. In a memorable paragraph of *The Gay Science,* Nietzsche clarifies the advantage that the image of architecture, of building a home, can offer:

> *Genoa.* — For a long while now I have been looking at this city, at its villas and pleasure gardens and the far-flung periphery of its inhabited heights and slopes. In the end I must say: I see faces that belong to past generations [Gesichter aus vergangenen Geschlechter]; this region is studded with the images of bold and autocratic human beings [mit den Abbildern kühner und selbstherrlicher Menschen übersäet]. They have *lived* and wish to live on: that is what they are telling me with their houses, built and adorned to last for centuries and not for a fleeting hour; they were well-disposed toward life, however ill-disposed they often may have been toward themselves. I keep seeing the builder, how his eyes rest on everything near and far that he has built, and also on the city, the sea, and the outline of the mountains, and how he, with this gaze, keeps practicing violence and conquest [Gewalt und Eroberung ausübt]. All this he wants to fit into his plan and ultimately make into his *possession* by making it a part of his plan. This whole region is overgrown with this magnificent, insatiable selfishness of the lust for possessions and spoils [mit dieser prachtvollen unersättlichen Selbstsucht der Besitz- und Beutelust überwachsen]; and even as these people refused to recognize any boundaries in distant lands [in der Ferne] and, thirsting for what was new, placed a new world beside the old one, each rebelled [empörte sich] against each at home, too, and found a way to express his superiority [seine Überlegenheit] and to lay between himself and his neighbor his

personal infinity. Each once more conquered his homeland for himself by overwhelming it with his architectural ideas and re-fashioning it into a house that was a feast for his eyes [indem er sie mit seinen architektonischen Gedanken überwältigte und gleichsam zur Augenweide seines Hauses umschuf].

In Genoa, Nietzsche concludes, one finds

> a human being who abhors the law and the neighbor as a kind of boredom and who measures everything old and established with envious eyes. With the marvelous cunning of his imagina-tion [mit einer wundervollen Verschmitztheit der Phantasie] he would like to establish all of this anew at least in thought, and put his hand to it and his meaning into it—if only for the mo-ments of a sunny afternoon when his insatiable and melancholy soul does feel sated for once and only what is his and nothing alien may appear to his eyes. (*GS* #291, translation modified; *KSA* 3.532)

Here, in Nietzsche's vision of Genoa, possession, the conquering of a place for oneself, means setting a distance between oneself and one's neighbor—and constantly reestablishing that distance, retaking that place. The imaginary Genoese conqueror Nietzsche describes fashions a home for himself by means of an architectural scheme, "mit architek-tonischen Gedanken." Just as Columbus's voyages "placed a new world beside the old one," the Genoese at home enact individual difference even in the crowded scenes of the city. But the tinge of melancholy that inflects Nietzsche's paragraph on Genoa implies the illusory nature of the Genoese citizen's victory, of the mirage in which "only what is his and nothing alien may appear to his eyes." The Genoese are "ill-disposed . . . toward themselves" because they know that disquiet and strife with their neighbors, rather than quiet self-possession, animates them. The narcissism of minor differences, as Freud called it in *Civili-zation and Its Discontents,* appears here: the neighbor is always suspected of stealing or ruining one's own enjoyment. As Emerson writes in a simi-lar moment in "Self-Reliance," "They cannot imagine how you aliens have any right to see,—how you can see; 'It must be somehow that you stole the light from us'" (*E* 277).[33]

A few pages earlier in Sanctus Januarius, Nietzsche imagines a more expressive and calm setting for self-knowledge. Instead of the martial rivalries encoded in Genoa's landscape, he dreams of a proudly located contemplative individualism utterly at ease with, or in, itself, and unaware of any threats from without: "*Architecture for the search for knowledge.*—One day, and probably soon, we need some recognition of what above all is lacking in our big cities: quiet and wide, expansive places for reflection. . . . [B]uildings and sites that would altogether give expression to the sublimity of thoughtfulness and of stepping aside." The monuments and sanctuaries of the church, Nietzsche continues, speak a "language . . . far too rhetorical and unfree" for the new contemplative life. "Even if they were stripped of their churchly purpose," they would still

> remind us that they are houses of God and ostentatious monuments of some supramundane intercourse; we who are godless could not think our *thoughts* in such surroundings. We wish to see ourselves translated into stone and plants, we want to take walks *in ourselves* when we stroll around these buildings and gardens. (*GS* #280)

Here Nietzsche responds to Emerson's bold comment in "Self-Reliance," "I like the silent church before the service begins, better than any preaching" (*E* 272). Nietzsche goes Emerson one better: for Nietzsche, even the empty church still echoes with disagreeable history. The Nietzschean solution, a newly invented landscape, is more similar to Auden's "In Praise of Limestone," which carries forward Nietzsche's idea of taking walks in oneself, than to Emerson.

In a later passage from book 5, Nietzsche specifies the rhetorical character of the churchly, which needs a "witness" and always plays to an audience: "For the pious there is as yet no solitude; this invention was made only by us, the godless" (*GS* #367). Nietzsche poses against Christianity's habits of rhetorical display the contemplative obliviousness to audience attained only by the godless: "the music of forgetting" (*GS* #367). This forgetting is related to the Emersonian abandonment Nietzsche evokes elsewhere in *The Gay Science* against stringent moralists who preach the value of self-control: "One must be able to lose oneself occasionally if one wants to learn something from things other than oneself" (*GS* #305).

But this Emersonian abandonment, inherited by Nietzsche, still takes place in a landscape that expresses the self. There is a dramatic contrast here to the radical, disoriented modernity that finds itself at

sea in the madman's parable of the death of God, the best-known passage of *The Gay Science* ("Is there still any up or down? Are we not stray-
ing as through an infinite nothing? Do we not feel the breath of empty
space?" [*GS* #125]). The architectonic goal of placing oneself, of building a home, that we have observed in book 4 of *The Gay Science* provides
an antidote to the disorientation caused by the death of God.

Orientation also comes back with the idea of the eternal return,
voiced near the end of Sanctus Januarius. Nietzsche's eternal return is
not the good repetition, self-enclosed and secure, that it has sometimes
been read to be. Instead, it offers a challenge to embrace one's life in
all its irrevocable incompleteness. For the thought of eternal return,
what has happened in one's life is merely the work of occasion, not the
work of error or original sin: not destined or fated, and therefore not
guilty. In this way, Nietzsche answers Christian morality's imagining of
time as culpable, as the agency of our guilt. He also differentiates his
path from perfectionism's usual visions of self-making. Embracing our
lives as occasional and imperfect, but deeply consequential for all that,
means *not* wishing to perfect ourselves. The eternal return asks us to
give up the aspiration for a completed, aesthetically finished existence,
achieved through continual self-revision and self-fashioning. This is the
goal that critics like Rorty and Nehamas esteem in Nietzsche, and that
Nietzsche himself explored, with ambivalence, earlier in Sanctus Januarius, in his image of the frustrated Homer. Now Nietzsche, as he
thinks the thought of eternal return, writes, "If this thought gained possession of you, it would change you as you are or perhaps crush you.
The question in each and every thing, 'Do you desire this once more
and innumerable times more?' would lie upon your actions as the
greatest weight. Or how well-disposed would you have to become to
yourself and to life *to crave nothing more fervently* than this ultimate eternal confirmation and seal?" (*GS* #341).

With the eternal return, Nietzsche embraces the imperfection of
life, "once more and innumerable times more." The embrace includes
tragedy. As we saw in the passage from *Zarathustra* I cited near the end
of chapter 1, tragedy wants the new, which can only be born in suffering.
The eternal return, for Nietzsche, means the ability to repeat that suffering, to ask for it again, and by doing so to transform it into joyful affirmation. The eternal return is in this sense the opposite of the disease
suffered by Borges's Funes the Memorious, whose perfect recall of every
single moment he has experienced offers a view of life as something

already achieved, and therefore as permanently and profoundly past.[34] (Nietzsche's comment in "History for Life" that, according to the Pythagoreans, "Whenever the stars stand in a certain relation to one another a Stoic again joins with an Epicurean to murder Caesar, and when they stand in another relation Columbus will again discover America," in fact sounds rather like Borges's Funes [*UM* 70].)[35]

Instead of evening out time and rendering it past, the eternal return as Nietzsche envisions it in *The Gay Science* dares to accept the present tense as decisive. The eternal return challenges the antiquarian consciousness, which wants to encompass and preserve every name in history, as well as the monumental consciousness, which also mirrors itself in an already composed, nonrepeatable past. The Apollonian (or, in my terms, architectonic) building of unity can only be achieved, Nietzsche claims through his idea of eternal return, if we accept the Dionysian (or musical) surrender to the moment. The unpredictable course of time dictates the impulse toward a compelling or necessary repetition.

This last notion, of necessary repetition, deserves further explanation. In Lacanian terms, the eternal return represents an embrace of repetition that argues against the internal principle of change, the perfectionist teleology, that Aristotle attributes to living creatures. Lacan favors the automaton, the principle of compelling chance or coincidence, over the holistic development toward a sovereign good outlined in Aristotle's description of the individual's growth.[36] The entire subject matter of psychoanalysis is generated by the anti-Aristotelian fact of ruling coincidences, which work on a machinelike, anti-human principle, interrupting our lives in untimely fashion.[37] Psychoanalysis suggests that our imaginings of a unified, coherent self often depend on the repression of, or flight from, events that come at their will rather than our own, disturbing the harmony of the organic being. The obsessive preoccupations and traumatic memories that tend to master us are the representatives of this disturbance, interfering with the wholeness and assurance we want for ourselves. The permanently incomplete character of selfhood shows up in the continual, unexpected return of the object-cause of desire, the object *a* that fascinates because it has been left out of the Symbolic order.

What does all this mean for our understanding of Nietzsche? The eternal return, as it is pictured in *The Gay Science* as well as *Zarathustra*, suggests that we might be able to face our incompleteness by confronting repetition in all its cruelty, and all its promise, instead of merely being afflicted by it. Similarly, Nietzsche, earlier in Sanctus Januarius, faces the cruel, secretive rage of the ocean waves. Nietzsche envisions welcoming his fundamental fantasy, that stupid and ineluctable bedrock of the self, as something that continually returns to and—almost unthinkably—*reaffirms* his existence, throwing up against him events that are ever new and ever the same. But the *Genealogy of Morals* and *Ecce Homo,* by making clear the nature of Nietzsche's fantasy, will show why, finally, "traversing" it (to use Lacan's term) results in the destruction of the subject. For Nietzsche, the fundamental fantasy is centered on his mother and his sister: his helplessness at the hands of the feminine (or, in *The Gay Science*'s hopeful version, his service to the feminine principle of affirmation through artistry). This fantasy finally becomes not the sign of eternal return, not the work of a benevolent goddess, but, as he puts it in *Ecce Homo,* the final objection to the eternal return: the permanent, inalienable thing in him that *cannot* be embraced.[38]

CHAPTER FIVE

Emerson's "Fate," the *Genealogy of Morals, Ecce Homo*

NIETZSCHE'S WORK ASKS A QUESTION about the possibility of freedom that is still urgent for us. How might we move beyond a self-frustrating irony in which we fight against, only to wind up reenacting, the roles and meanings from the past that most intimately determine our lives? The critical stance Nietzsche describes in "On the Use and Disadvantage of History for Life" suggests a way out: a perfectly balanced awareness of how our rebellion against the ancestral powers that have influenced us itself depends on stances derived from these ancestors. This awareness enables a measured triumph over the anxiety of influence, a new degree of freedom. In later works, as we have seen, the struggle between context and newness envisioned in "History for Life" becomes a polarity. Nietzsche now is attracted both to the architectonic perspective that locates itself firmly in a particular place and time (in *The Gay Science*) and to a more open stance akin to Emersonian abandonment, the cultivation of a persona that awaits the arrival of a new world, one that dares experiment (in *Daybreak* and, again, *The Gay Science*). The proudly located self proves too defensive, too constrained by the desires it guards against. It must therefore yield to the Dionysian or musical self that welcomes the thought of eternal return, and with it the fracturing of located, architectonic identity.

As Nietzsche's career continues through the *Genealogy of Morals* and *Ecce Homo,* the architectonic self that engages with its own particular past will develop into a severe ascetic, captive to this personal history. The musical self fares no better: its tragic openness will be revealed as noble but reckless, a trap for the philosopher who becomes a Dionysus torn to pieces by the hands of women.

Nietzsche's development toward asceticism was not inevitable. In this book, by presenting Emerson as an alternative to the ascetic stance that finally takes over Nietzsche's work, I suggest as much. But Nietzsche's decision not to, or his incapacity to, follow Emerson is suggestive as well. Where does knowledge of the ascetic dilemma get us? Cultivating a wry distance from the ascetic's pain belies our own investment in ascetic strategies. But dwelling on the allure of ascetic posturing does not help much either, and may shortchange the liberating power of Emerson, our own American Gnostic, as Harold Bloom has described him. In this chapter I weave a path between Emersonian freedom and Nietzschean asceticism, following Nietzsche's trajectory to its end with frequent reference to what was for Nietzsche Emerson's most significant essay, "Fate" (the first essay in *The Conduct of Life*).

INSPIRATION AND REFINEMENT IN EMERSON

For the early Emerson, abandonment to the daemon, to the work of inspiration, offers liberation. In an essay on Emerson from the 1970s, Harold Bloom writes that Emerson in "Circles" (from *Essays: First Series* [1841]) is "telling us—as Yeats did—that the daemon is our destiny. Our longing for the wider circumference is daemonic, and belongs to personality as against character. . . . The daemon knows how we do it or why it is done; we are along for the glory, and the sorrows, of the ride."[1] By implying that the daemon or Gnostic spirit takes us for a ride, inducing us to surrender ourselves to the sudden rule of an alien force, Bloom captures Emerson's sense of the daemon as an otherness that cares nothing for our conscious efforts at control. It is not something we choose, not a way for us to refashion ourselves, but rather a way to let our destiny, usually repressed by everyday commitments, at last take hold.

The surrender to wild, prophetic voice is a recognizable aspect of Emerson: it strains against an antithetical but equally Emersonian emphasis on the job of refashioning and sophisticating one's character ("We begin low with coarse masks, and rise to the most subtle and beautiful," he writes in "Illusions" [*E* 1119]). The same split, I have suggested, occurs in Nietzsche, between the musical self, dispersed and given over to its roles, and the architectonic, carefully defended self. In Nietzsche, though, the split masters him as it does not master Emerson. The architectonic or Apollonian attitude, despite its best efforts, finds itself prey to the object *a*, thwarted by a tiny bit of the Real—like the riddle that reduces Homer to weeping in *The Gay Science* (*GS* #302, discussed in chapter 4). By contrast, the musical or Dionysian attitude tends to a dissolution of coherence that culminates in *Ecce Homo,* with its capitulation to the Real. In Emerson, unlike Nietzsche, the Dionysian can be harnessed to Apollonian purpose, the founded self enhanced by the alien, wavelike circuits of the force that (as Pater, another of Emerson's inheritors, will put it) "rusts iron and ripens corn."[2]

What argues against the inescapability of ethos, the violent necessity of fate, in *The Conduct of Life* is the growth into amelioration or sophistication that Emerson claims. Growth or *Bildung* occurs as an enterprise of learning one's own peculiar necessity: ethos can be, must be, known and manipulated. Emerson writes that "a man's power is hooped in by a necessity, which, by many experiments, he touches on every side, until he learns its arc. . . . As we refine, our checks become finer" (*E* 952). The educated person "yields to a current so feeble as can be felt only by a needle delicately poised" (*E* 965). Receptivity, in Emerson as in Pater, leads to refinement: "We begin low with coarse masks, and rise to the subtle and beautiful," though often still trapped in the earthy and, like the "tawny lion" rising from the dirt in Milton's account of creation (*Paradise Lost* 7.464), "pawing to get free" (*E* 1033).

BURKE ON TRAGEDY AND COMEDY

Emerson's striving for a more refined vision, and thereby a sophisticated pragmatism, passes into his inheritors: not just Nietzsche in "History for Life," with its ideal of the critical, but also, for example, Kenneth Burke. In a neglected book from 1937, *Attitudes toward History,* Burke describes Democritus's "trench humor" ("the jokes whereby men, in the face of danger, dwarf the danger"):

> It is said of Democritus, that when he imagined a universe made of tiny atoms bumping and combining with one another, he *laughed.* Why did Democritus laugh? Perhaps he laughed because, by his materialist doctrine, he had "debunked" the gods. He "accepted" the world by ruling out the threats of ghostly vengeance. He was in the trenches of metaphysics, and materialism was the humor for his trench morale.[3]

Burke selects comedy over tragedy as a superior way of reading history, one that offers freedom rather than confinement. But this freedom is a perilous one, as he shows with his vignette of the laughing Democri tus (traditionally counterposed to the tragic Heraclitus, who was depicted in Nietzsche's *Philosophy in the Tragic Age of the Greeks*). In his joke about Democritus, comedy, Burke's chosen "frame" for the world, appears in response to the dire necessity of trench warfare: Democritus's is a nervous laughter indeed. Fighting the gods of conformity, Democritus's laughter bears witness to the potent character of their "threats of ghostly vengeance." Similarly, Emerson in "Fate" introduces the perspective of freedom or "power," which makes light of limitation, as a badly needed remedy for his opening vision of cruel, fateful limits. The alternative is itself a refinement. Neither perspective—neither fate nor freedom—can succeed in erasing the other; but their contrast engenders a subtlety of perception that rises to the comic through its reliance on (to use a Burkean term) incongruity.

Burke in *Attitudes toward History* claims to distance himself from both Emerson and Nietzsche, but as he later realized, his stance incorporates aspects of both. His Nietzscheanism appears most clearly in his plan to pluck a comic perspective out of a tragic one by rising above the common, moralizing readings of human character. Burke writes that "the progress of humane enlightenment can go no further than in picturing people not as *vicious,* but as *mistaken.*"[4] Even within the tragic dynamics of the *Genealogy,* as I will point out, Nietzsche wished for a richly comic society, one that, freed from resentment, could afford not to punish evil: in essence, one that could afford to regard crime as mistaken rather than evil.

But Burke differs from both Emerson and Nietzsche in his desire to moderate the clash of perspectives. He writes in "War, Response, and Contradiction" that, instead of a hysterical, savage depiction of war, we ought to aim at a "total, restful attitude" toward it, "precisely such a response as might best lead one to appreciate the preferable ways of peace."[5] In this important essay, as in his discussion of Hitler's *Mein Kampf,* Burke plays the rhetorician who rebels against rhetoric's investment in hyperbole, in the intense and serious caricature. He rejects the habits of political melodrama. In the world of the 1930s and 1940s, Burke's posture makes enormous sense. But Burke also knows that rhetoric's war, its practice of extreme, exclusive position-taking, cannot be banished. (Burke's sometimes wild or eccentric readings are his own warlike gestures.)

The extreme character of rhetorical postures, whether the high solipsism of Emersonian enthusiasm or the self-cruelty of Nietzschean asceticism, *should not* be banished. We need to overcome our current sense that democracy depends on the moderating, rather than the severe, dramatic ennobling, of our chosen values and attitudes. Perspectives do exclude one another, and their exclusivity must be granted so that they can attain their full power. The mobility of the self, its capacity to move from one perspective to another, becomes all the more useful and potent when these perspectives are allowed to appear in their full strength. Only by allowing incongruity to exist in all its ferocious multiplicity can we achieve the capacity for identification, the actor's receptivity, that will let us comprehend history actively.

Yet we cannot identify completely with a radical or sublimely primitive attitude, exactly because our identification is experimental. We have learned the distance that the primitive does not possess. In "Power," from *The Conduct of Life*, Emerson writes that education relies on relishing from afar examples of "aboriginal might," which "gives a surprising pleasure when it appears under conditions of supreme refinement" (*E* 981). The spectacle of crude power gives pleasure when refinement is added, in the form of a sophisticated viewer's detached perspective.

THE LESSON OF EMERSON'S "FATE"

While advocating such detachment in "Fate," Emerson remarks, rather shockingly, "The whole circle of animal life — tooth against tooth, — devouring war, war for food, a yelp of pain and a grunt of triumph, until, at last, the whole menagerie, the whole chemical mass is mellowed and refined for higher use, — pleases at a sufficient perspective" (*E* 960-61). The roundabout form of Emerson's sentence, which frames as an excursus the savagery he depicts, testifies to his arm's-length treatment of the subject. Our worry might be that the distance here introduced, as the "sufficient perspective" that measures a "mellowed and refined" understanding, may encourage a complicity with brutal forces and prevent identification with those who are subject to this brutality: most pressingly in Emerson's era, African American slaves.

Crudeness and sophistication are the twin poles of *The Conduct of Life,* and Emerson in the course of his book often encourages us to see design rather than war, artistry rather than disgusting violence, in the workings of the world. We are hedged round not by iron fate but by elusive, delicate laws the discerning can exploit (*E* 1119). Emerson argues against the pessimistic belief that "life is an affair to put somewhat between the upper and lower mandibles" (*E* 1060). Yet it is no accident that the raw images of "Fate," which crush puny human life beneath them, are more memorable than Emerson's emphasis elsewhere on the cultivated human power that can temper such rough visions. Even when we appreciate other persons' individual force, we exploit them in disturbing fashion by attending to our real interest, the authority behind the person, rather than the distinctive profile they present to us. "We do not care for you," Emerson writes, "let us pretend what we will:—we are always looking through you to the dim dictator behind you" (*E* 1069). This is not exactly the picture of a conversation. We find ourselves thrown on the universe's side, against ourselves, just as we are thrown against others, when we see individual actors as mere vehicles of universal force. The logical conclusion occurs in the famous ending of "Fate": why not rejoice at being "crushed by savage elements" (*E* 967), since we and these elements share the same hard substance?

Like Emerson in "Fate," Schopenhauer is determined to confront us brutally with the ugly proportions of the will, which cannot be morally ameliorated or aestheticized. Schopenhauer's daemonization becomes a way of facing the sheer, rude facts: "Teeth, gullet, and intestinal canal are objectified hunger; the genitals are objectified sexual impulse; grasping hands and nimble feet correspond to the more indirect strivings of the will which they represent" (*WWI* 1.108). Emerson memorably echoes Schopenhauer's image of brutal animal life in "Fate": nature is "the tyrannous circumstance, the thick skull, the sheathed snake, the ponderous, rock-like jaw" (*E* 949). But in a later essay from *The Conduct of Life*, "Worship," nature and its law have become, instead of an anthropomorphic and palpable tyranny, a smooth, invisible suasion. Emerson cites from the "Hindoo Scriptures a definition of Law": "'Law it is, which is without name, or color, or hands, or feet; which is smallest of the least, and largest of the large; all, and knowing all things; which hears without ears, sees without eyes, moves without feet, and seizes without hands'" (*E* 1065–66). The rough personification of "Fate" has its limits. It cannot capture the spider-thread laws of the world as the spiritual aesthete's quick subtlety, evoked in "Worship," can.

NIETZSCHE'S "FATE AND HISTORY"

Nietzsche wrote his school essay of 1862, "Fatum und Geschichte [Fate and History]," after reading Emerson's "Fate," but long before he grasped Emerson's idea of refinement as stated later in *The Conduct of*

Life. "Fate and History" is nevertheless telling for the way it indicates, even so early in his intellectual life, Nietzsche's interest in Dionysian transformation. The essay is the work of an eighteen-year-old wrestling with questions of religious faith and his own imminent loss of that faith, but it also looks forward to Nietzsche's mature preoccupation with the possibility of liberation from the conformist reality principle that nature, law, and history tend to signify for us.

In "Fate and History" Nietzsche asks what will turn out to be the prompting question of *Zarathustra:* after life develops from stone, through plant and animal, into the human, will the sequence stop there? Is there a transformation beyond the human — "Is the human only a means, or an end? [Ist der Mensch nur Mittel oder ist er Zweck?]"[6] As Nietzsche continues his essay he occupies himself with the Emersonian notion that we are ringed round by invisible influences, that history constitutes us without our even realizing it. But "Fate and History" then takes a dramatic turn, picturing a realization of our present position that would set the self against the past — and topple it:

> As soon as it were possible to overturn, through a strong will, the world's entire past, we would immediately enter into the series of autonomous gods, and world-history would then be for us nothing but a dreamlike self-delusion [träumerisches Selbstentrücktsein]; the curtain falls, and man finds himself again to be like a child playing with worlds, like a child who awakes in the glow of dawn and, laughing, wipes the fearful dreams from its brow.

In this revolutionary fantasy, Nietzsche imagines an overthrow of all history, the reduction of the past to a bad dream, supplanted by the infant reality that creates us anew. The image of the child playing with worlds should remind us of some memorable passages in Emerson that praise our instantaneous, infant powers.[7] From "Montaigne," for example: "Each man woke in the morning with an appetite that could eat the solar system like a cake" (*E* 708); and from "Fate" itself, "The world of men show [*sic*] like a comedy without laughter:—populations, interests, government, history;—'tis all toy figures in a toy house" (*E* 955).[8] But Nietzsche's passage, which introduces a newly momentous laughter into the comedy by declaring it to be over once and for all, also represents a striking revision of "Fate" on the question of transformation.[9] In "Fate," Emerson writes, "If we thought men were free in the sense, that, in a single exception one fantastical will could prevail over the law of things, it were all one as if a child's hand could pull down the sun" (*E* 967).

In the next paragraph of "Fate and History," Nietzsche seems to remember Emerson's limiting point: he turns his image of the child playing with worlds into just another deceptive dream. "We would be the playthings [Spielbälle] of our own fantasies," Nietzsche writes, were it not for the dominion of fate, which he expresses in the form of an Emersonian ruling tautology: "'Events are that which events themselves determine' ['Die Ereignisse sind es, die die Ereignisse bestimmen']."[10] Nietzsche ends the essay with an unadulterated homage to Emerson: free will is nothing but fate raised to the highest power, he writes; everything flows together in an oceanic union where all levels of world history find themselves "united, melted together, all-one [vereinigt, verschmolzen, all-eins]."[11] The creative frivolity of the newly awakened child, a central presence in *Zarathustra,* in this early essay yields up his Dionysian play to a controlling harmony, the law of fate.

Childlike grace gives way, then, to a larger, more mature rule, in both Emerson and Nietzsche. But this rule takes on a fierce aspect in Emerson that is not reflected in Nietzsche's youthful essay, with its image of a universe "united, melted together, all-one." Emerson writes in "Fate" that "Fate slides into freedom, and freedom into fate" (*E* 961). But this higher unity bears witness to a necessity that, at the end of "Fate," appears far cruder and more threatening than it does to the young Nietzsche in "Fate and History": "Let us build altars to the beautiful Necessity," Emerson writes. "Why should we fear to be crushed by savage elements, we who are made up of the same elements?" (*E* 967).

In the sublime conclusion to "Fate" Emerson comes as close as he ever will to a paean to the universe's enormous violence. In Emerson's passage, the violence is natural, not produced by the self working desperately against the body, as in the asceticism that will be Nietzsche's chief concern in the *Genealogy.* For Emerson, we prove our own durability by identifying with the universe's savage elements, even if it means our dissolution. For the ascetic such proof is not available: his existence is partial, not capable of sublime identification with the universal in its power. The ascetic individual feels himself impaired from the start. Haunted by an originary loss that links the fact of mortality to sexual reproduction, asceticism seeks the second death invoked by Lacan: the utter destruction of the individual, beyond the mere ending of one's lifetime. The ascetic self stands, therefore, as a contrast to the Emersonian self that swallows, and is swallowed by, the universe.

NIETZSCHE AND SCHOPENHAUER ON DESIRE

> *The greatness of Nietzsche is not that he was right in any sense*
> *but that he paid so dearly for being wrong. He never got away*
> *with anything, which is the closest thing to being right.*
>
> —René Girard[12]

As we saw in chapter 3's discussion of "On the Use and Disadvantage of History for Life," Nietzsche's project for a critical history, rather than a merely monumental, or mythically inventive, revision of the past, demands that we submit to the pain of self-critique, in order to know how far we can afford to rebel against our origins and our ancestry. In "History for Life" a promised victory stands at the end of this process: the production of a new "first nature." This victorious originality is still based in a firm reconciliation with the past, a successful coming to terms with, and acceptance of, what cannot be changed in the fundament of the self. In *Daybreak* and *The Gay Science,* a careful triumph over the past is still possible, through the building of an architectonic identity secure in its place, yet open to the disorienting novelties of desire, the crises that reveal a strong individuality to itself.

By the time of the *Genealogy of Morals* and *Ecce Homo,* this measured victory has disappeared. To investigate the origins of the self now means to encounter the traumatic Real that determines what is both alien to and inalienable in the self, what cannot be accepted but nevertheless remains: the decisive kernel, the object *a.*

In *Ecce Homo,* the object *a* is woman; in the *Genealogy,* it is more broadly defined as the secret guilt that motivates the ascetic's discipline. In both cases, the uncanny return of the object *a,* in its automatic, inexorable character, thwarts the critical project outlined in "History for Life," disrupting the hermeneutic ambitions of the self-fashioning consciousness. In the *Genealogy* the revolt against the hermeneutic is fully visible: the self turns fatally against its sources, wishing for an utter, apocalyptic break from the entire history of ascetic practice. But the self's wish for liberation, for the freedom of the Dionysian or musical mode, serves only to confirm more solidly its ascetic captivity.

The question of asceticism in philosophy and culture inevitably recalls for Nietzsche the work of Schopenhauer, as Nietzsche struggles to define his own stance against Schopenhauer's. Schopenhauer is an exemplary figure for Nietzsche because, in contrast to Nietzsche himself, he represents the stand of philosophy against wishful fiction-making and against desire, and (therefore) against our attachment to particular events and persons we fantasize about, or imagine for ourselves. Schopenhauer wants to escape the torment that desire incurs in its clinging to the individual beloved. He writes in *The World as Will and Idea:*

> The process of nourishment is a constant generation; the process of generation is a higher power of nourishment. The pleasure that accompanies procreation is a higher power of the agreeableness of the feeling of life. On the other hand, excretion, the constant exhalation and throwing off of matter, is the same as what at a higher power is death, namely the opposite of procreation. . . . [F]rom this point of view, it seems just as absurd to desire the continuance of our individuality, which is replaced by other individuals, as to desire the permanence of the matter of our body, which is constantly replaced by fresh matter. It appears just as foolish to embalm corpses as it would be carefully to preserve our excreta. . . . Deep sleep, while it lasts, is in no way different from death. . . . Death is a sleep in which individuality is forgotten; everything else awakens again, or rather has remained awake. (*WWI* 1.277–78)

In Schopenhauer's version, individuality and the fact of its passing have receded into oblivion, since, from this perspective of frozen light years, we no longer know or want any particular object of desire. In order to distance himself from desire and its implication in death, Schopenhauer must idealize disinterested knowledge in a Platonist manner: everything essential "has remained awake." But the distancing does not work, it is not genuinely disinterested, because it represses so much more grimly and insistently than Plato does. Whereas Diotima in the *Symposium* incorporates both sickness and erotic attraction in her song of praise, and even cheerfully blurs the line between the two, Schopenhauer turns all desire to ill, reducing it to a vulgarity, to (in Augustine's memorable phrase) fornicating with the world.

Schopenhauer tries to eliminate the uncanny or spectral character of experience, the way the dead return upon the living. He wants the idealist's aeons-long view because he remains terrified of contingency and the automatism associated with it. He fears, desperately, the singular fascination attached to erotic objects. Whereas Diotima insists on the need to commemorate heroic action, Schopenhauer is ready to forget the dead Achilles, since even the hero's godlike individuality looks "foolish" from a cosmic perspective. What use could a real philosopher have for an exemplary past? Why not just forget it, wipe it away as time itself will in any case? "The form of life is the endless present," Schopenhauer announces a few pages after the long passage quoted above. "It matters not how individuals, the phenomena of the Idea, arise and pass away in time, like fleeting dreams" (*WWI* 1.281). Schopenhauer here both represses and voices the possibility of the uncanny return of the past: if we are fleeting dreams, perhaps these dreams are capable of haunting, *and thereby constituting*, waking life.[13]

Schopenhauer's need to ward off the individual as the object of our respect or attraction, to reduce even the most remarkable memories of beloved persons to insubstantial, transient dreams or "excreta," is born from his fear of *eros*, to him a lively-yet-deathly reminder of ephemerality—and of the persistence, allied to *eros*, of the Lacanian object *a*. Schopenhauer's claims, voiced with such striking eloquence, stand permanently and perversely against our deepest intuitions. Schopenhauer would have agreed with William Burroughs's line that love is a venereal disease: the compulsive attachment of a decaying animal to that which must also decay. But, *contra* Schopenhauer and Burroughs, *eros*, unlike the body, remains immortal; it is not imprisoned by its fleshly object: both Plato and Freud teach us its amazing mobility. Sexual desire is not a heightened version of the pleasure of eating, a "higher power of nourishment." And the deaths that mark our past, surviving within us and guiding our present lives, are not disposable.

The weird revulsion apparent in Schopenhauer's slighting of the startling forces of sex and death bears witness, as Nietzsche will emphasize, to the strength of the *eros* from which the philosopher wants to escape. In this strange passage from *The World as Will and Idea* we see the vicious energy of Schopenhauer's repudiation:

> The knowledge of the contradiction of the will-to-live with itself can, through great misfortune and suffering, violently force itself on us, and the vanity of all endeavour can be perceived. Hence men who have led a very adventurous life under the pres-

sure of passions, men such as kings, heroes, or adventurers, have often been seen suddenly to change, resort to resignation and penance, and become hermits and monks. To this class belong all genuine accounts of conversion, for instance that of Raymond Lull, who had long wooed a beautiful woman, was at last admitted to her chamber, and was looking forward to the fulfillment of all his desires, when, opening her dress, she showed him her bosom terribly eaten away with cancer. From that moment, as if he had looked into hell, he was converted. (*WWI* 1.394–95)

Schopenhauer here draws on the medieval topos of the *Frau-Welt,* in which a woman who represents worldly life reveals beneath her beautiful semblance a disgusting putrefaction.[14] According to Schopenhauer, what Raymond Lull realizes is the contradiction between the forever agitated, unforgiving character of the desire that spurs him on and his hope for "the fulfillment of all his desires," a fulfillment that would put desire itself to rest. For Schopenhauer, clarity about this issue comes only in the form of monastic renunciation, and renunciation comes only as the result of a look into the hell that Schopenhauer here, as elsewhere, names "woman." The knight becomes a true wise man when he comes up against, when he realizes and refuses, the elusive character of desire woman so persistently figures: the tantalizing resistance that attracts, the no that seems to say yes, yet finally smiles enigmatically instead of delivering the promised goods. Schopenhauer, along with Raymond Lull, finds himself nauseated by the specter of a Gorgon-like, monstrous *eros,* but this nightmare itself represents, like Spenser's foul Duessa, the taming into easily rejected, repugnant shape of something far less lurid, and far less visible. The fantasized revelation of palpable monstrosity is not, itself, the Real, which remains resistant to representation.[15]

In Schopenhauer's story, the knightly seducer becomes a philosopher when the seducer realizes that courtly love is in fact designed to shield us from a monstrous fulfillment, from the Thing itself: the obscenity of the (female) body. This prospect of ultimate obscenity then sustains the philosopher by becoming basic to his formulation of a new reality that can claim thoughtful independence from the obscene fact. The female Thing in this way becomes, for Schopenhauer, a support for the philosopher's fantasy, whereas in Nietzsche's *Ecce Homo* the Thing or object *a,* which is precisely *not* representable as it is in Schopenhauer, will interrupt, even as it causes, the fantasy.

Another way of putting this is that, in Schopenhauer's fable of Raymond Lull, it is not the Lacanian Real, the traumatic kernel of experience, that is brought out into the open, but rather a fantasy of it. The Real, by definition, cannot be exhibited, and thereby robbed of its power, in this way. As we shall see, the female Thing in *Ecce Homo,* the presence of Nietzsche's mother and sister, is—unlike Schopenhauer's decayed courtesan—the sign of the Real itself, because the trauma it signals cannot be converted into a lesson about the necessity for sublimation, and thereby eased.

But Nietzsche, unlike Schopenhauer, does try to sublimate, to recast the female Thing (sometimes, at any rate) as an elusive principle of feminine artistry. Nietzsche, in contrast to Schopenhauer, courts the seductiveness of life by praising its unrivaled beauty: life is a woman. In much of his work, Nietzsche insists that we need to reach out toward the feminine principle of desire. Existence, in its elusiveness, its translucent, shadowy nature, will never be wholly ours. We need tragic art, an art that recognizes and values, even *over*values, the fragility of our existence, so that we do not perish from Schopenhauerean pessimism.

Nietzsche, then, justifies art by defining it as the poetic revision of reality that makes our desires worthwhile. Schopenhauer, by contrast, despite his praise of art, finally degrades it by turning it into an escapism incapable of transforming the world. In Schopenhauer, the world resists art because, for him, the world in its (female) ugliness has become the phantasmic support for philosophy.

For Nietzsche, unlike Schopenhauer, the way existence resists us takes an utterly particular form. In *Ecce Homo,* the object *a* is unveiled as that piece of the Real that Nietzsche's fantasy of self is unable to transform. Nietzsche will, by the end of his career, be forced to recognize his own bondage to particularity in the form of the unexpected, obstructing appearance of his mother and his sister, whose presence is the final, definitive objection to the eternal return. The self's origins capsize its fantasy, rather than supplying a site of individuation, as was suggested in the works immediately following *The Birth of Tragedy* (the *Untimely Meditations, Daybreak,* and *The Gay Science*). Already by the time of *The Gay Science,* the contingencies of desire were able to frustrate the architectonic, defended self (the fishermen's riddle that spoils life for Homer in *GS* #302). In the *Genealogy* and in *Ecce Homo,* the contingent piece of the past that remains lodged within the self will overturn the entire Nietzschean program of strenuous architectonic individualism, his way of at once being receptive to the world and carefully monitoring it, warding off potential trauma.

NIETZSCHEAN GENEALOGY AND SELF-KNOWLEDGE

The Preface to the *Genealogy of Morals* offers the story of an individual coming into his own. The relation between this Preface and what follows, as always in Nietzsche, is a dramatic one. Nietzsche's prefaces qualify his work as a series of perspectives linked by the similarities, but also the differences, among his philosophical narrators, each of whom presents himself as "Mr. Nietzsche" (*GS* Preface). As in the case of the *Birth*, with its beginning invocation of the author imagining Wagner's reaction to his book, of *Daybreak* with its picture of the author as mole, and of *The Gay Science* with its self-excruciating Herr Nietzsche, in the *Genealogy* we are forced to consider how the character introduced to us in the Preface writes the text that follows.

The first section of the *Genealogy*'s Preface presents an image of the progress of philosophy. Nietzsche moves from a posture of untimely distraction to one of obedience to a newly discovered law or command: an obedience that is also a kind of tacit lawgiving.

> Like somebody divinely absent-minded and sunk in his own thoughts [wie ein Göttlich-Zerstreuter und in-sich-Versenkter] who, the twelve strokes of midday having just boomed into his ears, wakes with a start and wonders "what hour struck?," sometimes we, too, afterwards rub our ears and ask, astonished, taken aback [ganz erstaunt, ganz betreten] "What did we actually experience then?" or even, "Who are we, in fact?" and afterwards, as I said, we count all twelve reverberating [zitternden] strokes of our experience, of our life, of our being,—oh! And we miscount ourselves [und verzählen uns dabei]. (*GM* Preface 1, translation modified)

Nietzsche's Preface constitutes a mysterious, newly self-critical collective entity, "we" industrious seekers of knowledge, who "have never really been 'with it' [bei der Sache]," never attuned to self-analysis and internal "experiences [Erlebnisse]," despite being "sunk" within ourselves. Like Emerson in "History," Nietzsche intends to "remed[y] the defect of our too great nearness to ourselves" (*E* 238), which is really an abstraction from ourselves. We have been passed by or passed over by the sounding of what Zarathustra will call the Great Noon, the *kairos* of history.

By the end of the first section of Nietzsche's Preface, the experience of distraction has become a law: "We remain strange to ourselves out of necessity, we do not understand ourselves, we must confusedly mistake who we are, the motto 'everyone is furthest from himself' applies to us for ever,—we are not 'knowers' when it comes to ourselves." Nietzsche here reverses a familiar German proverb that implies that one knows instinctively what is good for oneself: "Jeder ist sich selbst der Nächste."[16] *The Gay Science* proposed that we do know ourselves, and that we both knowingly and instinctively cultivate self-ignorance as well as self-knowledge, so that we will not be destroyed by sudden revelations. The *Genealogy*, by contrast, begins with the idea that we are unknown to ourselves, and necessarily so, that the secret reasons behind our lives must remain hidden if we are to survive. Nietzsche suggests that our storing up of treasures out of what Robert Pippin, in a comment on the *Genealogy*, calls "self-induced, slavish anxiety and fear" serves a necessary defensive function.[17] But the *Genealogy of Morals* makes the further point that, for the purposes of Nietzsche's own quest, his storeroom must be searched—even ransacked, as the *Genealogy* does in its consummate project of self-attack.

PUNISHMENT AND RESPONSIBILITY

> *Is it possible that just as grey-haired libertines inflame their flagging flesh with whippings to renewed capacity for enjoyment, aging Rome wanted to let itself be scourged in monkish fashion in order to discover subtle pleasures in the torture itself and ecstasy in suffering? . . . Can it be that assassinated Judea, in presenting the Romans its spiritualism as a gift, meant to take revenge on the victorious enemy as did once the dying centaur who so craftily succeeded in passing on to Jupiter's son the fatal garment poisoned with his own blood? It is a fact that Rome, the Hercules of nations, was so effectively devoured by the Jewish poison that helmet and armor dropped from its withering limbs, and its imperial battle cry sank to the praying whimper of priests and the trilling of eunuchs.*
>
> —Heinrich Heine, "The Romantic School"[18]

Heine's passage contains all the ingredients of Nietzsche's *Genealogy*: the staging of healthy and heroic Rome against devious, vengeful

Judea; the condemnation of ascetic Christianity as a decadent, at once perverted and castrated phenomenon; and finally, the description of the Christian faith as a "Jewish poison," a seeming love potion that, as in a reversal of the plot of *Tristan and Isolde,* is revealed as an agonizing and deathly medicine. In another essay, "Concerning the History of Religion and Philosophy in Germany," Heine pictures the sickness of medieval Christianity, with its apocalyptic urge to divide good from evil, as a sickness from which the present age is recovering:

> [According to Christianity, Heine writes,] it is necessary to torture our body, Satan's fief, so that the soul may soar upward all the more gloriously into the bright heaven, into the radiant kingdom of Christ.
>
> This cosmogony, the real idea of Christianity, had spread over the entire Roman empire with incredible rapidity, like a contagious disease, at times a raging fever, at times exhaustion, lasted all through the Middle Ages, and we moderns still feel spasms and lassitude in all our limbs. Though many of us have already recovered, we cannot escape the all-pervading hospital atmosphere and feel unhappy in being the only healthy persons among all the diseased. Someday when mankind regains its complete health, when peace is restored between body and soul, and they blend again in their original harmony, we will scarcely be able to comprehend the unnatural discord that Christianity has sown between the two.[19]

Nietzsche, drawing on his fantasized Polish heritage, liked to ally himself with the Jewish Heine as superior to "mere Germans," and his invocation of classical health against the Christian poison owes something to Heine's cheerful paganism. But the first essay of the *Genealogy* tellingly departs from Heine's optimism when Nietzsche gives the floor to an interlocutor, a "free-thinker" who comments that "the passage of this poison through the whole body of mankind seems unstoppable. . . . We loathe the Church, not its poison. . . . Apart from the Church, we too love the poison" (*GM* 1.9). This passage is an early hint in the *Genealogy* that Nietzsche intends to accuse himself of loving the poison of asceticism, that he means to picture his own soul as a "battle ground for these opposites," Rome and Judea: "There is, today, perhaps no more distinguishing feature of the '*higher nature*,' the intellectual nature, than to be divided in this sense and really and truly a battle ground for these opposites" (*GM* 1.16).

Increasingly, as the *Genealogy* continues, Nietzsche shows this internal "battle ground," his self-division, by allying himself to slave as well as master morality, to the cunning and vengeful spirits as well as the proud, independent, and noble ones. As Geoffrey Harpham writes, Nietzsche in the *Genealogy* "repeatedly and pointedly characterizes himself in precisely the terms applied to the base and ignoble—silence, cleverness, and the tendency to caricature enemies as evil."[20] The problem with the ethnological interpretation offered by the *Genealogy*'s first essay, which famously divides mankind into two tribes—the strong, self-sufficient masters (Romans) and the weak, resentful slaves (Jews/Christians)—is, Harpham remarks, that "it cannot account for the triumph of the weak—something has to happen to the strong in order for them to be defeated, but their strength should preclude such disasters."[21] Only, Harpham continues, if each individual is seen as a potential battleground of strength and weakness can Nietzsche's theory make sense: and this is why Nietzsche moves from the grand pseudohistorical scheme of the first essay to the ascetic individualism of the third.

The second essay occupies a transitional function in Nietzsche's progress toward individual asceticism. It begins with a famous picture of the fully formed human individual who prides himself on his ability to make promises:

> We . . . find the sovereign individual . . . like only to itself, having freed itself from the morality of custom, an autonomous, supra-ethical individual . . . in short, we find a man with his own, independent, durable will, who has *the right to make a promise*—and has a proud consciousness quivering in every muscle of *what* he has finally achieved and incorporated, an actual awareness of power and freedom, a feeling that man in general has reached completion. (*GM* 2.2)

This passage presents a full-blown perfectionist vision of the human as completely achieved, completely self-assured and autonomous, and completely satisfied in his conscience of his own rightness. But this idealized vision will not last long. It is revealed as early as the essay's next chapter, 2.3, that bad conscience is required in order to breed the promising animal whose proud autonomy has just been celebrated, and that the horrors of bad conscience are uniquely memorable:

> Perhaps there is nothing more fearful and strange [furchtbarer und unheimlicher] in man's pre-history than his *technique of mnemonics*. "A thing must be burnt in so that it stays in the memory": only something which continues *to hurt* stays in the memory—that is a proposition from the oldest (and unfortunately the longest-lived) psychology on earth. You almost want to add that wherever on earth you still find ceremonial, solemnity, secrecy, gloomy colors [Feierlichkeit, Ernst, Geheimniss, düstere Farben] in the lives of men and peoples, something of the terror [Schrecklichkeit] with which everyone, everywhere, used to make promises, give pledges and praise, is *still working* [*nachwirkt*]: the past, the most prolonged, deepest, hardest past, breathes on us and rises up in us when we become "solemn" ["ernst"]. When man decided he had to make a memory for himself, it never happened without blood, martyrs and sacrifices. (*GM* 2.3, translation modified; *KSA* 5.295)

This fascinating passage has a recursive relation to the picture of the proud, promising sovereign individual from the previous chapter of the *Genealogy:* it turns back on, even aggressively turns on, that earlier picture, in order to contradict it. Instead of the mere "pre-history" of promising, self-torture turns out to be, by the time we get to the end of Nietzsche's passage, something that remains within us. "The dread with which everyone, everywhere, used to make promises, give pledges and commendation, is *still working*": this is a far cry from the calm self-assurance of the sovereign individual. Apparently, now, one can only be sovereign if one is terrified by the memory, and the still-present feeling, of excruciating pain.

But this conjunction of bad conscience and autonomous individuality cannot really be accepted; and so Nietzsche separates these two facts of consciousness. The second essay concludes by suggesting that Nietzsche's idealizing vision of human autonomy, the breeding of a noble animal with the capacity to make promises, requires a decisive and willful *looking away* from asceticism, from the infliction of bad conscience—and from the connection between bad conscience and promising that the second essay has already exposed.

In order to sustain hope, which resides in the second essay's separation of the noble promise-maker from the wretched creature punished by conscience, Nietzsche must struggle against the human inclination toward asceticism. In the midst of a fervent denunciation of "man's will to find himself guilty and condemned without hope of reprieve," Nietzsche writes near the end of the second essay,

> Alas for this crazy, pathetic beast man! What ideas he has, what perversity, what hysterical nonsense, what *bestiality of thought* immediately erupts, the moment he is prevented, if only gently, from being a *beast in deed!* . . . This is all almost excessively interesting, but there is also a black, gloomy, unnerving sadness to it as well, so that one has to force oneself to forego peering for too long into these abysses. (*GM* 2.22)

In place of the noble animal imagined at the very beginning of the second essay, inhabited by a "rare freedom and power over himself and his destiny," and in place of the sovereign, collected, self-controlled Roman masters of the first essay, we have been given a radical alternative: the mindless rampaging of the blond "beast in deed" is posed against the sickness of ascetic conscience, with its all-too-fascinating "bestiality of thought."

Nietzsche's hope in the second essay resides in a looking away from this grim alternative, and toward the possibility of an exception to bad conscience: a justice that would take the form of a society's disdainful indifference to its enemies (or its benign "parasites," as Nietzsche renames them).

> It is not impossible to imagine [a] society *so conscious of its power* that it could allow the noblest luxury available to it, — that of letting its malefactors [Schädiger] go *unpunished.* "What do I care about my parasites [Schmarotzer]," it could say, "let them live and flourish: I am strong enough for all that!" . . . Justice, which began by saying "Everything can be paid off, everything must be paid off," ends by turning a blind eye [durch die Finger zu sehn] and letting off those unable to pay, — it ends, like every good thing on earth, by *sublimating itself* [*sichselbstaufhebend*]. The self-sublimation of justice: we know what a nice name it gives itself — mercy; it remains, of course, the prerogative of the most powerful man, better still, his way of being beyond the law. (*GM* 2.10, *KSA* 5.309)

What is the background to Nietzsche's image of the "self-sublimation of justice"? In the *Genealogy* Nietzsche makes it clear that, as Bernard Williams remarks, the crucial aspect of resentment is its will to get the other, its target, to *see,* to realize his responsibility for an unfortunate state of things.[22]

Such a will to impose responsibility on the other did not exist from the beginning. The original aim of punishment, Nietzsche claims, was a kind of innocent pleasure in the spectacle of suffering; only later did punishment become degraded into a way of getting the victim to realize his guilt. (But how—why—did this corrupting development occur?) This later will to impose guilt is allied to the tainted idea of responsibility itself: that "'someone or other must be to blame that I feel ill'" (*GM* 2.15).

Nietzsche aims to correct such illusory assigning of responsibility, whether to the other (as in resentment) or the self (as in bad conscience): not by returning to the original scene of punishment as sheer innocent spectacle, but by developing a more knowing stance toward the fact of punishment itself. The newly sophisticated society's *staged* decision to forgo punishment involves a "self-sublimat[ed]" sense of justice, one based on a neutral medical or economic model. Instead of being bound to the moral model based on getting the self or the other to see (its own or the other's) guilt, society will simply ask itself whether it can afford the damages inflicted by its criminal "parasites," or whether these damages must be curtailed through punishment. With the body politic, as with the individual body, Nietzsche hopes that a scientific, resentment-free approach—how many parasites can we tolerate?—will supersede the moralizing impulse to turn the parasite into a scapegoat for all our ills.

The just judge's looking away from the criminal, his decision not to insist on making the criminal see his own blameworthiness, sublimates the image of justice as a keeping of economic accounts by forgetting, or letting go of, the original "debt" the criminal owes, and instead casting society as a more generous host, the source of a wealth whose function is to be continually given away. In Nietzsche's view, the judge ought to ask coolly whether or not society can afford the presence of criminals, instead of afflicting the criminal with the force of conscience as if such affliction were a self-sustaining good in itself. Nietzsche, then, proposes or forecasts a new justice-as-economic, beyond the original, pure state of justice-as-spectacle. He hopes for a regaining of innocence in which, instead of enjoying the suffering of those who offend against it, society can give up that privilege, taking sufficient pleasure in its knowledge that it has the "luxury" of allowing criminality. In doing so, society has shown itself mercy as well, given itself the privilege of "being beyond the law."

For Nietzsche, then, unlike Foucault, a decisive practice of restraint, a development beyond the claustrophobic regimes of power and justice, is not only possible, but even natural.[23] There is an important debate here, involving Nietzsche's insistence on the fundamental wrongness of a justice that relies on the need to inflict remorse or bad conscience. Nietzsche claims the natural character of what I have called an economic justice, one based on a neutral, quantitative model, which reckons how much crime a society can afford to forgive and still remain healthy.

This model is only possible, according to Nietzsche, because justice began in a neutral or innocent, rather than a vengeful, enjoyment of violence. Nietzsche in the *Genealogy* and elsewhere argues against Dühring's claim that the origin of justice lies in society's justified resentment against the criminal. Instead, Nietzsche portrays as fundamental the original festive use of violence, the barbarian forms of punishment he catalogs with such ambivalent relish as he illustrates the primordial law "No cruelty, no feast" (*GM* 2.6).[24]

Nietzsche's troubling insistence, in the *Genealogy*'s first and second essays, that there is no feast without cruelty is intended to restore cruelty's innocence. The blond beast, after his hideous bouts of murder and rape, far from being afflicted by the pains of conscience, was convinced only that he had provided some great new material for the poets (*GM* 1.11). Yet the somewhat clinical or neutral pleasure in the infliction of suffering that Nietzsche uncovers here, and that is borne out by the heroic ethos of the Homeric poems or the *Song of Roland*, will be overshadowed by the more intense guilty pleasure that is so central to our current idea of justice: inflicting bad conscience, making the criminal feel worthless.

If bad conscience is an unnatural deviation from a proper, original form of justice conceived as cruelly pleasurable theatrical display, as Nietzsche argues, then how and why does the significant and pervasive pleasure of bad conscience arise at all? This seems an insoluble question of origins—or a question that remains insoluble if discussed in terms of origins. We only know that we are here, in a moral jail of our own making; we cannot explain why the ascetic will to punishment arose, exactly because its very excess, its extreme character, uproots all natural origins.

Nietzsche stresses that the sudden, violent force exerted by the strong against the weak takes the form of a trauma or inexplicable accident, an interruption, rather than a development understandable in historical terms (2.17). Bad conscience, asceticism, begins when the weak, traumatized by the violence directed against them, find their desire for freedom "forced back, repressed, incarcerated" and begin to punish themselves, constructing a compensatory, internal theater of power.[25]

Nietzsche's useful interest in establishing a regime of justice disjoined from ascetic resentment and remorse can become a kind of avoidance. However attractive it may be, the notion of society giving up the idea of inflicting bad conscience either on the "good" law-abiding individual soul or the "evil" criminal also seems hopelessly optimistic. Asceticism, by insisting that we all deserve the extreme pains of conscience, has confused or leveled the differentiations a regime of economic justice would need in order to free itself from resentment. Instead of a secure knowledge that we, as a "society . . . *conscious of its power*," have little in common with our criminal parasites, we are haunted by a profound, guilty identification with them.

In Lacanian terms, this difficulty concerns the difference between desiring the other's desire as a familiar means of self-assurance—the guilty identification with the criminal that makes us punish him in order to punish ourselves—and recognizing the other as a separate subject of desire, as genuinely different and therefore inaccessible to identification.[26] Paradoxically, the criminal other really is like us: for example, in no sense is he an ineluctable force of nature, a disastrous, psychotic machine of death whose being is inherently, and therefore dangerously, assured. Rather, he lacks knowledge in just the way we do (in Lacanian terms, he looks to the Other and sees the Other's lack). What we resist in him is his uncomfortable closeness to us, his threatening way of reminding us of our own habits and interests. (Freud in *Civilization and Its Discontents* calls this phenomenon the "narcissism of minor differences.")

Punishing the criminal by forcing him to feel remorse appears to be a way of making him recognize his humanness, so that society can overcome the monstrous specter of an inhuman, cold-blooded barbarism.

But what the infliction of bad conscience on the criminal actually does is quite different. It enables us to put ourselves safely, in fantasy, in the criminal's place, by putting him in a place essentially different from ours. It fences off this place from our own so that the over-closeness, the threat of the narcissism of minor differences, is avoided. This is a kind of theatricality intended to reassure us, to let us remain who we already are. Here Freud's insight into the narcissism of minor differences intersects with Cavell's idea of positionality as basic to our lives, and of our desire to stage our differing positions, to turn them into theatrical scenes, in order to avoid seeing where we are, acknowledging our place.

Perhaps an individual might overcome the allure of bad conscience, might rescue himself from asceticism, even if society cannot. This is why Nietzsche moves, in the paragraph I have quoted, from the picture of a strong society able to afford this new justice (a "society . . . *conscious of its power*") to that of a strong individual who pleases himself by exercising justice (which remains, after all, "the prerogative of the most powerful man"). This "most powerful man" is a revised version of the noble type from the *Genealogy*'s first essay, the proud Roman conqueror who has now become strong enough to forget and forgive, to forgo the keeping of punishment's strict records.

The appeal of this transformation on the individual level is twofold. First, the noble type *hebt sich auf,* sublimates itself, by naming this new justice "mercy." Here as in *Zarathustra,* Nietzsche implies that the value of giving (what Aristotle calls magnificence) supersedes that of mere independence and autonomy. At some point, the proud individual feels the need to descend from his isolation, his mountain cave, and give to others. The second attraction of the new justice is the sense it gives of being "beyond the law." Rather than finding satisfaction in the legal, in the careful keeping of obligations, like the noble promise-maker invoked at the beginning of the second essay, this sublimated version of the strong type enjoys a high freedom. He accomplishes the pathos of distance by looking down on society's enemies as mere microscopic parasites, and yet at the same time gives these lowly creatures what they need.

Nietzsche strangely claims that the strong individual's new justice is not mere neutrality, but a form of care, of active engagement (*GM* 2.11). The *Genealogy*'s third essay, however, will testify that this nobility of distance, unlike the interstellar spaces that Emerson so often invokes when he images the Gnostic light, fails to provide sufficient engagement. The self needs an intimacy that the arm's-length pride of the noble cannot supply. Only asceticism, we learn in the third essay, can fill this gap by eliminating the pathos of distance in favor of an overly intimate pathos of self-examination and self-punishment. Only by undergoing ascetic self-punishment can a future, freer self emerge; seen this way, the ascetic individual is "just a path, an episode, a bridge, a great promise" (*GM* 2.16).

But Nietzsche retreats from this optimism, from the sense of ascetic self-punishment as a transition to something nobler. In a later section of the second essay, Nietzsche contradicts his earlier idea that, as a society's strength or spiritual wealth increases, it will be able to afford a newly generous form of justice that can overcome the oppressive infliction of ascetic suffering. Nietzsche now writes:

> The *dread* of the ancestor and his power [Die *Furcht* vor dem Ahnherrn und seiner Macht], the consciousness of debts toward him increases inevitably, in direct proportion to the increase in power of the tribe itself, that is, in proportion as the tribe [das Geschlecht] itself becomes ever more victorious, independent, honored and feared. And not the other way round! . . . Through the hallucination [die Phantasie] of the growing dread itself, the ancestors of the *most powerful* tribes must have grown to a monstrous stature [in's Ungeheuere gewachsen] and must have been pushed into the darkness of a divine uncanniness and inconceivability [in das Dunkel einer göttlichen Unheimlichkeit und Unvorstellbarkeit]. (*GM* 2.19, translation modified; *KSA* 5.328)

In this version, origins increase in power as time passes, rather than declining (as in the economic-justice passage I quoted from the second essay, or as in *Daybreak*). Here Nietzsche forecasts the pessimism of Freud's *Civilization and Its Discontents*, with its insistence that the ascetic ideal, born from the consciousness of an originary, unpayable debt, exacts from us ever more extreme sacrifices.[27] "The *dread* of the ancestor and his power," as the source of ascetic guilt, vaguely suggests the version of events that Freud developed in *Totem and Taboo*, the overweening father whose death at the hands of his sons haunts all posterity.

Whether we can name the traumatic origin that must be at the core of ascetic suffering is a question to which Nietzsche keeps returning until the very end of the *Genealogy*, when he famously suggests that ascetic self-torture was, as it were, called forth by the meaninglessness of existence, the fact of the Real itself. It is not suffering itself, but the meaninglessness of suffering (i.e., the Real), that afflicts us, Nietzsche concludes at the end of the third essay (*GM* 3.28). Man's mission is to give suffering meaning: in Lacanian terms, to turn it toward the Symbolic. But the meaninglessness, the left-over character of the Real as what cannot be symbolized, continually returns to nauseate us and poison human existence.

This idea of the Real as that which inherently resists making sense accords with Lacan's notion of cause as a particularity that is not lawful or comprehensible but, for this very reason, has an inevitable effect, an effect stronger or more primary than that of the law. And Lacan's description of cause, in turn, illuminates Nietzsche's reflection on resentment's will to root itself in a piece of the past that is irrevocable and ineradicable, whether that piece is located within the self (as an other, an enemy inside us) or in an external enemy.[28] "From this magician, the ascetic priest," Nietzsche writes, the human being "receives the first tip as to the 'cause' of his suffering: he should look for it within *himself*, in *guilt*, in a piece of the past" (*GM* 2.20). *Ecce Homo* will link the cause of suffering to the cause of desire, the object *a:* Nietzsche's particular relation to the feminine in his own history.

ASCETIC IDEAL AND ASCETIC STYLE

> *The ascetic treats life as a wrong path which he has to walk along backwards, till he reaches the point where he starts; or, like a mistake which can only be set right by action—ought to be set right: he demands that we should accompany him, and when he can, he imposes his valuation of existence.* (GM 3.11)

> . . . *this hatred of the human, and even more of the animal, and even more of the material, this horror of the senses, and even of reason itself, this fear of the happy and the beautiful, this demand to get away from all appearance, change, becoming, death, wishing, demanding itself* . . . (GM 3.28, translation modified)

The ascetic who begins by demanding a correction of existence, who judges the world and imposes his valuation on it (that it is fundamen-

tally lacking), ends by demanding an impossible escape from existence, a "get[ting] away" from every aspect of the actual world, and even
from his own importunate demand. Turned round from an active to a
passive posture, the ascetic, who started off by finding existence want-
ing, by the final words of the *Genealogy* finds himself subjected to want
or lack itself. Is this sacrifice of mastery an inevitable aspect of asceticism? Is the plot of the *Genealogy* an irreversible journey toward desperate denial of one's own experience and senses? Or is it possible to
retain the side of asceticism that is conducive to "higher spirituality,"
and with it a healthy relation to life, the discipline of the noble soul: a
"hard and hearty renunciation with a good will [eine harte und heitere
Entsagsamkeit besten Willens]" (*GM* 3.9; *KSA* 5.356)?

Relying on a passage like the one I have just cited, which praises ascetic habits as the natural hygiene of the philosophical spirit, Tyler
Roberts argues that Nietzsche in the *Genealogy* draws a distinction between this practice of ascetic style and the ascetic ideal, with its sacrifice
of human life in the name of an otherworldly purity. Nietzsche reflects
appreciatively on the ascetic style in order to (in the words of a note in
The Will to Power) "make [asceticism] natural again."[29] Nietzsche writes:
"I also want to make asceticism natural again; in place of the aim of denial, the aim of strengthening; a gymnastics of the will . . . an experiment with adventures and arbitrary dangers" (*WP* #915). In section 7
of the *Genealogy*'s third essay Nietzsche does indeed aim to make asceticism natural, following Emerson's suggestion of a human genius that
frees or serves itself through its ethical and customary practices.
Nietzsche praises the philosophers who "think of the ascetic ideal as the
serene asceticism of a deified creature which has left the nest and which
is more liable to roam above life than rest" (*GM* 3.8). Nietzsche in this
passage presents asceticism as the philosopher's natural strength, the
necessary condition of his creativity, a kind of strenuous spiritual hygiene that enables him to float above life. Here Nietzsche champions
the conversion to a discipline of Emersonian abandonment. He now
advocates taking the way "from man, not to man," as Emerson himself
puts it in "Self-Reliance" (*E* 271). Nietzsche writes in the *Genealogy* that
"The ascetic ideal points the way to so many bridges to independence
that no philosopher can refrain from inwardly rejoicing and clapping
hands on hearing the story of all those who, one fine day, decided to say
"no" to any curtailment of their liberty, and go off into the desert: even
granted they were just strong asses and the complete opposite of strong

spirits" (*GM* 3.7). The possibility that the ascetic choice of exile, of the desert over the city, might end in the ludicrous, that it might be the act of a strong ass instead of a strong spirit, is explored most fully in book 4 of *Zarathustra*. But Nietzsche, later in the *Genealogy*'s third essay, recovers from the potential for farce that marks the end of *Zarathustra*. In chapter 26, near the end of the third essay, he forecasts the appearance of "comedians of the ascetic ideal" who will make the ass's obstinacy spiritual and creative (*GM* 3.26).

In his comments on asceticism in the third essay, Nietzsche links his praise of the philosopher's natural affinity for the desert, for an isolation that "dislikes being bothered with animosities or even with friendships," with a thesis on artistic and philosophical pregnancy that is indebted to Diotima's speech in Plato's *Symposium*. Chastity, Nietzsche writes, is a way of exploiting sensual energy to create "a bit of immortality" rather than mere mortal children. "When they are pregnant with something great," artists and philosophers avoid sex in favor of their work: "Sensuality is . . . transfigured and no longer enters consciousness as a sexual stimulus" (*GM* 3.8).

But these descriptions of the philosopher's natural asceticism, which hark back to the organic integrity of the tree image in Nietzsche's Preface, are exceptions in the third essay. Instead, asceticism most often appears, here at the end of Nietzsche's book, as determined self-destruction. The third essay dwells on the disastrous grip of the ascetic ideal, rather than on the disciplined, life-strengthening choice of an ascetic style. (Here I adopt Roberts's persuasive distinction between ascetic ideal and ascetic style in order to argue against his conclusion that the style wins out over the ideal.) The ascetic ideal, Nietzsche writes, is an unavoidable abomination, a perversion, a reversal of what is proper or natural:

> The idea we are fighting over here is the valuation of our lives by the ascetic priest: he relates this (together with all that belongs to it, "nature," "the world," the whole sphere of what becomes and what passes away), to a quite different kind of existence which is opposed to it and excludes it *unless* it should turn against itself and *deny itself*: in this case, the case of the ascetic life, life counts as bridge to that other existence. The ascetic treats life as a wrong path which he has to walk along backwards, till he reaches the point where he starts; or, like a mistake which

can only be set right by action — *ought* to be set right: he *demands* that we should accompany him, and when he can, he imposes his valuation of existence. (*GM* 3.11)

Unlike the philosopher who has committed himself to loneliness, the ascetic priest demands our company in his backward march to origins, his futile but unstoppable will to correct, or reverse, existence. Throughout his writings, Nietzsche argues against the posture of the ascetic priest who would impose on us the sense of life as a "wrong path." He insists, instead, as Emerson does, that our experience is always open to new creation. Yet since our lives are not infinitely revisable, they are finally, for Nietzsche, subject not to the hermeneutic refinement Emerson proposes but rather to the determining kernel of an individual's existence, the object *a*. As a result, the sense of wrongness the ascetic seizes on, a wrongness banished by Emerson, remains active in Nietzsche. *Ecce Homo* will surrender to the implication that the cause of Nietzsche's life has permanently injured it, placed it beyond repair. As we shall see, the name of this cause is "woman."

NIETZSCHE'S EXPLODING SELF

> *Refined cruelty as virtue. — Here is a morality which rests entirely on the drive to distinction — do not think too highly of it! For what kind of a drive is that and what thought lies behind it? We want to make the sight of us painful to another and to awaken in him the feeling of envy and of his own impotence and degradation; by dropping on to his tongue a drop of our honey, and while doing him this supposed favor looking him keenly and mockingly in the eyes, we want to make him savor the bitterness of his fate.* (D #30)

Nietzsche, in this aphorism from *Daybreak*, opens up a surprising vista, an alternative genealogy to the one he will produce later in his career, in the *Genealogy of Morals*. "The morality of distinction is in its ultimate foundation refined cruelty." That is, such morality is reactive; in order to thrive it requires an audience, an other which it affects and compels to see. *Daybreak* offers exactly the reverse of the reading of the morality of distinction Nietzsche will later propose in the *Genealogy*'s first two essays, where the master's nobility resides in his self-concern, his disdainful lack of need for the reactions of those he looks down on. In *Daybreak,* the master *produces* the slave's resentment: how else could one have dominion over slaves except by provoking their bitterness?

Daybreak #30 deprives the noble master of the autonomy the *Genealogy* grants him. Somewhat paradoxically, though, the greater independence that the *Genealogy* claims for the master actually undermines his authority. Nietzsche's idealization of master morality in essays 1 and 2 of the *Genealogy* catapults him into a disappointed counter-idealization of slave morality in essay 3. In essay 3, it is half-revealed to us that the idealization of masters could only have been the product of slaves, of contemporary priestly ascetics like Nietzsche himself. But *Daybreak* offers a way out of the dilemma that accompanies the polarizing of master and slave morals in the *Genealogy.* The *Genealogy*'s implication of a permanent moral deadlock, embodied in the persistence of an asceticism that exacts ever greater payment from us, stands against the possibility of Emersonian refinement and enhancement of power envisioned earlier in Nietzsche's career, in *Daybreak* and *The Gay Science.*

The *Genealogy* insists that origins persist and take their revenge on the belated sophistication that claims to have gone beyond them. As I argued, though, *The Gay Science* wants just this capacity to transfigure origins beyond their cruel beginnings; and the power to accomplish such transformation is forecast as early as *Daybreak.* Nietzsche writes in *Daybreak* that the morality of distinction, despite its origin as a means of creating the oppressive feeling of envy and resentment in others, redeems itself when it becomes a self-concerned habit of noble manners that has forgotten its reason for being. In contrast to the proud autonomy of the promising animal proclaimed in the *Genealogy*'s second essay, whose nobility lies in a singular, inaugural act, *Daybreak* champions a certain discipline of repeating noticeable or excellent actions so that they become habits: a discipline that naturally develops into refinement.

> For when the habit of some distinguishing action is inherited [Denn wenn die Gewohnheit irgend eines auszeichnenden Thuns sich *vererbt*], the thought that lies behind it is not inherited with it (thoughts are not inherited, only feelings): and provided it is not again reproduced by education, even the second generation fails to experience any pleasure in cruelty in connection with it, but only pleasure in the habit as such. *This* pleasure, however, is the first stage of the "good." (*D* #30; *KSA* 3.40)

In the opening pages of the *Genealogy*'s first essay, Nietzsche will deride such faith in habit, associating it with the English psychologists for whom human virtue is inert, the product of dumb obedience. In *Daybreak* the conventional and habitual seemed more vivid to Nietzsche, the site of invention rather than numb rule-following.

Emerson's goal of refinement, then, present in *Daybreak,* has disappeared from the *Genealogy*. But Nietzsche continues, even after *Daybreak* and *The Gay Science,* to reflect on the Emersonian picture of human mastery as a graceful practice of style exercised on, and by, the self. In an Emersonian vein, a note from 1884 collected in *The Will to Power* defines the essence of human cultivation as a balance of drives: since "moralities are the expression of locally limited orders of rank in his multifarious world of drives . . . man should not perish through their contradictions. Thus a drive as master, its opposite weakened, refined, as the impulse that provides the stimulus for the activity of the chief drive" (*WP* #966). In this note, Nietzsche envisions the kind of architectonic balance that will be violated by the explosive conclusion of his career. In fact, the Nietzschean sublime as we have seen it at work in the *Genealogy* seems to embrace an increasing severity or extremity, rather than balance. Daniel Conway remarks that "Nietzsche's model of self-overcoming is strongly Apollonian, insofar as it promotes the mastery within a single soul of as many tensions and contradictions as possible. But this model is also undeniably Dionysian, for it promotes internal mastery only as a means of further expanding the capacity of the soul, an ever-escalating process that must eventually culminate in the destruction of the soul."[30]

The side of Nietzsche influenced by Emerson's vision of architectonic refinement embraces the sort of "asceticism *ironice*" that carefully moderates drives, even in their contention (*WP* #113). But the ongoing thrust of Nietzsche's meditation in the *Genealogy* will be toward asceticism as an increasing, and increasingly dismaying, (seeming) inevitability of our nature. To the extent that this sense of inevitability involves a sublime dispersion of the self (the Dionysian expansion Conway invokes), it will also mean the tranformation, in *Ecce Homo,* of Herr Nietzsche the meticulous builder of his existence into Nietzsche the momentous exploding self and the prophetic sign given to posterity.[31] In the terms I have adopted in this book, Nietzsche will definitively move from the architectonic to the musical mode of selfhood.

Several other notes contained in *The Will to Power* communicate an Emersonian aim to build the self, constructing it in its very contradictions:

to establish a mean between divergent drives. "Who will prove to be the strongest" in the crisis betokened by European nihilism? Nietzsche asks in a note from June 1887. His answer is

> The most moderate [die Mässigsten]; those who do not require any extreme articles of faith; those who not only concede but love a fair amount of accidents and nonsense [einen guten Teil Zufall, Unsinn]; those who can think of man with a considerable reduction of his value without becoming small and weak on that account; those richest in health who are equal to most misfortunes and therefore not so afraid of misfortunes—human beings who are sure of their power and represent the attained strength of humanity with conscious pride. (*WP* #55)

Nietzsche goes on to ask, of this strong and moderate type, "How could such a human being think of the eternal recurrence [Wie dächte ein solcher Mensch an die ewige Wiederkunft]?" (*WP* #55).[32] The question seems oddly double-edged. On the one hand, Nietzsche appears to mean that the eternal recurrence, a cruel burden to those who want to take revenge on life for the misfortunes it has inflicted, becomes a trivial matter indeed for those who "represent the attained strength of humanity with conscious pride." On the other hand, though, the thought of eternal return might be an unwelcome reminder for precisely these proud individuals: their autonomy could be based on repression of their own, and others', weakness or sickly nature. The eternal return might therefore threaten them with the Dionysian destruction Conway invokes. They might be "equal to most misfortunes," but not to (biological or destined) misfortune itself, which is sealed into permanence by the thought of eternal return.

The *Will to Power* passage seems as good a place as any to enter the territory most ruthlessly explored by the *Genealogy:* does the entertaining of contradictory drives necessarily lead to a tearing apart of the self? In other words, is the movement from architectonic containment to disastrous musical dispersion that Conway describes an inevitable one?

At times in the *Genealogy*, Nietzsche hopes for an architectonic identity that could avoid the ruin courted by the ascetic. This identity, he thinks, would build on asceticism. In the third essay of the *Genealogy* Nietzsche draws on the self-wounding ascetic reversal of perspective. Here, he considers this reversal essential preparation for a new architectonic knowledge, for a firmly contained and planned way of being oneself:

Finally, as knowers, let us not be ungrateful towards such reso-
lute reversals of familiar perspectives and valuations with which
the mind has raged against itself for far too long, apparently to
wicked and useless effect: to see differently, and to *want* to see
differently to that degree, is no small discipline and preparation
of the intellect for its future "objectivity"—the latter understood
not as "contemplation without interest" (which is, as such, a non-
concept and an absurdity) but as *having in our power* our "pros"
and "cons." (*GM* 3.12)

Now, in Nietzsche's idealizing vision, instead of a battlefield of contraries
the self has become a cool manipulator of them, "able to engage and
disengage" contradictory perspectives. But this image, true to Emerson's confidence in the empowered self, will prove overly optimistic as
Nietzsche ends his writing life with the increasingly strident and disqui-
eted books of the late 1880s. I turn now to the last of these books,
Nietzsche's final account of himself: *Ecce Homo.*

ECCE HOMO: WOMAN AS OBJECT *A*

"The ascetic ideal expresses one will," Nietzsche writes late in the *Genealogy*'s third essay, and goes on to wonder, "where is the opposing will,
in which an *opposing ideal* might express itself?" (*GM* 3.23). Several
pages later, Nietzsche finds his answer: "The ascetic ideal has, for the
present, even in the most spiritual sphere, only one type of real enemy
and *injurer:* these are the comedians of this ideal" (*GM* 3.27).[33] *Ecce Homo,*
for all its laughs, is not the comedy of the ascetic ideal that Nietzsche
wanted. The work that concludes Nietzsche's career is a story not of
freedom but of bondage.

In a recent book, *The Fragile Absolute,* Zizek presents the Lacanian
version of the critical ideal: the ability to recognize oneself in the "excremental remainder," the Real fragment, that has been left out of
(but that also "secretly sustains") the Symbolic image of self. "On the
one hand," Zizek writes,

there is the Master-Signifier that delineates the contours of the
subject's Ego-Ideal, his dignity, his mandate; on the other, there
is the excremental leftover/trash of the symbolic process, some
ridiculous detailed feature that sustains the subject's surplus-
enjoyment—and the ultimate goal of psychoanalysis is to enable

the subject-analysand to accomplish the passage from S1 to *objet petit a*—to identify, in a kind of "Thou Art That" experience, (with) the excremental remainder that secretly sustains the dignity of his symbolic identification.[34]

Zizek here speaks to our sense that our Symbolic, social identity, our "dignity" or "mandate," remains hollow because it requires us to hide from or cover over an embarrassing, exceptional element. This element, the object *a*, motivates us to appear to the world as something other than the embarrassing feature. The image of our lovability and dignity is made possible by the very object *a* this image must exclude. According to Lacan, Zizek explains, the imperative given to the analysand to identify, and identify with, the object *a*, the senseless, humiliating, or traumatic center of his being, makes psychoanalysis a discourse of revolutionary intimacy and revelatory force. Nietzsche in *Ecce Homo*, which might in some respects be considered his self-analysis, uncovers the place of the object *a*, but for him identifying with it will mean destruction rather than critical self-consciousness.

This drama of pathology I am pointing to, driven by the role of woman as object *a*, is not present from the beginning of *Ecce Homo*. At the start of Nietzsche's book, Emersonian refinement and balance reign. Nietzsche begins *Ecce Homo* by maintaining the status of the moment as a comprehensive stillness that centers his life and work. The Janus-faced day of perfect autumn, self-harvest, that Nietzsche depicts so memorably near the beginning of *Ecce Homo* holds to the moment as a kind of frame for his being: "On this perfect [vollkommnen] day, when everything has become ripe and not only the grapes are growing brown, a ray of sunlight [Sonnenblick] just fell onto my life: I looked behind me, I looked before me, never have I seen so many and such good things together. . . . *How should I not be grateful to my whole life?*— And so I tell myself my life" (*EH* 7, translation modified; *KSA* 6.263). Here Nietzsche is supremely thankful for the gift of his whole life: for his life as a wholeness, eternized and concentrated in a perfect day, and in a perfect page of a perfect book. But the Pilate-like skepticism suggested by the title of *Ecce Homo*—which, as Sarah Kofman argues, counters within Nietzsche's text itself this text's practice of Rousseau-style tell-all confession—disintegrates this wholeness.[35] It is not just possible, but necessary, for the reader to exercise the same skepticism toward the book *Ecce Homo* that Pilate showed toward the inscription

"INRI." (Such skepticism does not reduce Nietzsche's book to self-parody; on the contrary, it provides a means of guarding against self-parody.) Is *Ecce Homo* the alpha or omega of testaments, kingly or beggarly? does it show us the first or the last of men? As Kofman remarks, Pilate, by unmasking the human being behind the Symbolic entity *king/son of God,* makes possible the unmasking of the divine within the human.[36] So Pilate does the work of Jesus: skepticism opens toward fate.

In Nietzsche's famous warning that we should not confuse him with what he is not, his "*ich bin der und der*" substitutes for the Eucharist's "*hoc est corpus meum.*" But what is he pointing to? His singular, fundamental wound (the cause), as in Zizek's "Thou Art That," or—given the implied sequence of identifying *ders*—his endless legacy of text (the effect)? How is Nietzsche's remark, "*ich bin der und der,*" indicative?

Ecce Homo, then, begins by reinforcing the aesthete's embrace of the moment that *The Gay Science* enshrined in its statement that "life is a woman," unveiling itself only once, but unmistakably, in a "lucky accident" (*GS* #339). This engraving of the perfect moment is extended by the idea of eternal return, the tragic joy of accepting our *im*perfect existence.

The fact that, for Nietzsche, redeemed life has a feminine gender is crucial. In Faust's Helen or Wagner's Isolde, as they are remembered in *The Birth of Tragedy,* the image of woman survives and becomes the vehicle for the male poet's own survival. But in *Ecce Homo,* woman will come to represent the tearing of the moment, and therefore of the self: not survival, but ruin.

THE NIETZSCHE FAMILY ROMANCE

> *Wie sah mein Vater wohl aus?*
>
> *Ha! Gewiss, wie ich selbst!*
>
> *Aber—wie sah*
>
> *Meine Mutter wohl aus?*
>
> *[What did my father look like? Ha! Surely like me myself.*
> *But . . . what did my mother look like, then?]*
>
> —Wagner, *Siegfried,* Act 2

Like Dionysus, and like the Christ, Nietzsche is a wounded god, despite his effort to produce a *noli me tangere,* a pathos of distance. In the notorious passage of *Ecce Homo* destroyed by Nietzsche's sister but recovered in the 1960s from a copy kept by Heinrich Köselitz (Peter Gast), Nietzsche admits,

> When I look for my profoundest opposite, the incalculable pettiness of the instincts, I always find my mother and my sister—to be related to such *canaille* would be a blasphemy against my divinity [eine Lästerung gegen meine Göttlichkeit]. The treatment I have received from my mother and my sister, up to the present moment, fills me with inexpressible horror [flösst mir ein unsägliches Grauen ein]: there is an absolutely perfect hellmachine at work here [hier arbeitet eine vollkommene Höllenmaschine], operating with infallible certainty at the moment where I can be bloodily wounded [über den Augenblick, wo man mich blutig verwunden kann]—at my highest moments . . . then, there, every strength fails to defend against a poisonous serpent . . . physiological contiguity renders such a *disharmonia praestabilita* possible. . . . But I confess [bekenne] that the deepest objection to the "Eternal Recurrence," my real idea from the abyss [mein eigentlich *abgründlicher* Gedanke], are [*sic*] always my mother and my sister. (*EH* 11, translation modified; *KSA* 6.268)

Here form echoes theme. These violent words attack Nietzsche, he attacks himself, at his highest moment, when he has just been boasting about his angelic father and about the fact that he is "a pure-blooded Polish nobleman, in whom there is no drop of bad blood, least of all German" (*EH* 11). Here the perfection of the perfect day ("vollkommner Tag") invoked at the beginning of *Ecce Homo* uncannily returns, reversed into—memorable invention!—a perfect hell-machine ("eine vollkommene Höllenmaschine"). Thanks to woman, a "poisonous serpent" hidden in his garden, Nietzsche is always wounded at precisely his highest moment, which means that the moment itself as an emblem of being has been damaged beyond repair. As a result, the eternal return becomes a thought without foundation, a thought of the lack of foundation: *ein abgründlicher Gedanke*. The hell-machine makes high moments into abysses, inexpressible regions in which Nietzsche's singularity disappears, swallowed by the women who surround him.[37]

It is as if the three Marys were tormentors rather than comforters for the Christ. Unlike the women who cluster around the dead Jesus, Elisabeth and Franziska had already started during Nietzsche's sane lifetime to make him over, bloodying his corpus in the process of preserving it for posterity. Looking for his "profoundest opposite," Nietzsche here necessarily finds only himself. Bloodlines blur into a "physiological contiguity," the copresence of divinity and *canaille,* the duality that inhabits the philosopher who has admitted himself to be both a decadent and the opposite of a decadent.[38]

Nietzsche's next close encounter with women occurs in the section of *Ecce Homo* that follows "Why I Am So Clever"—"Why I Write Such Good Books." Here Nietzsche writes that, in contrast to the "Circe of humanity, morality," which has falsified all psychology "to its very foundations [in Grund und Boden]," he has set himself on a firm foundation: "One has to be set firmly upon oneself [Mann muss fest auf *sich* sitzen], one has to stand bravely upon one's own two legs, otherwise one cannot love at all" (*EH* 45; *KSA* 6.305).

"The perfect woman tears to pieces when she loves [das vollkommne Weib zerreisst, wenn es liebt]," Nietzsche writes in this same section of *Ecce Homo* (*EH* 45; *KSA* 6.306). This feminine monster is perfect, *vollkommen,* like the day that originally oriented Nietzsche in *Ecce Homo,* but the monster's perfection has an automatic, machine-like quality that converts the mood of blessing to one of inexorable curse. Nietzsche's highest day has become the day of his sacrifice to the "amiable Maenads [liebenswürdigen Mänaden]" (*EH* 46; *KSA* 6.306).

Near the end of section 5 of "Why I Write Such Good Books," Nietzsche accuses Ibsen of "*poisoning* . . . the naturalness [die Natur] in sexual love" (*EH* 46; *KSA* 6.307). But Nietzsche himself seems to have a sufficiently poisonous view of the matter, despite his claim to possess a Dionysian "Mitgift" (sympathy) with the little woman or "Weiblein" (*KSA* 6.305). Nietzsche suggests that Ibsen's notion of correcting, of making healthy, sexual relations between man and woman is in fact a way of poisoning these relations, a *Vergiften,* whereas Nietzsche's own *Mitgift,* his sympathy, with woman recovers a naturalness, a fair antagonism, between the sexes. But how is fairness, how is justice, still possible here, given Nietzsche's images of sexual love as trauma and exclusion, and incestuous ruin?

WAGNER AND THE RETURN OF THE ARCHITECTONIC IDEA

It is important to note that at the end of "Why I Write Such Good Books" Nietzsche does recover from the interruption of the Real, the trauma represented by mother and sister. This recovery will be continued, in the rest of *Ecce Homo,* by Nietzsche's identification with Wagner's work. As in "Wagner in Bayreuth," so here the elusive, shivery infinity of Wagner's music suggests a fascinating shipwreck of the self. Wagner provides a fleeting and ecstatic sense of the object *a,* in contrast to the traumatic sense of this object imposed on Nietzsche by his hell-machine. On Wagner's musical effects, *Ecce Homo* suggests, something solid can be built.

After the hell-machine passage, then, Nietzsche overcomes his panic at the prospect of *sparagmos* at the hands of women. He cites at length the end of *Beyond Good and Evil,* a passage in which Dionysus is reborn after being "broken open, blown upon and sounded out [ausgehorcht]," made an instrument of ecstasy as well as divination (*EH* 47; *KSA* 6.308). Nietzsche here smoothes over, even covers over, his traumatic wound through the invoking of musical effects whose manifold and mysterious character may remind us of Wagner's. In section 4 of "Why I Write Such Good Books," Nietzsche refers to his own "multiplicity of inner states [Vielheit innerer Zustände]" matched by his "manifold art of style" (*EH* 44; *KSA* 6.304). This "Vielheit innerer Zustände" echoes what Nietzsche, earlier in *Ecce Homo,* admits are "the tremendous things Wagner was capable of, the fifty worlds of strange delights to which no one but he had wings" (*EH* 31).

It is not accidental, I think, that Nietzsche in this passage from "Why I Am So Clever" refers to Wagner's *Tristan* as the height of his achievement: the opera in which a pair of lovers, a man and a woman, become consubstantial mirrors of each other. Nietzsche in *Ecce Homo,* seeking a model of the sexual relation, implicitly looks toward Wagner's mirroring of Tristan with Isolde in Act 2 of *Tristan.* In this final book, Nietzsche recovers from the risk of destruction by taming the wild femininity that threatens to tear him to pieces, turning it into something similar to the daring, assured, and sly Nietzschean self of *Ecce Homo,* who now seems, at least for a moment, to have found his exact counterpart. Answering his own question, "What I really want from music," he writes, "That it be one's own, wild, tender, a small, sweet female of low cunning and charm [Dass sie eigen, ausgelassen, zärtlich, ein kleines süsses Weib von Niedertracht und Anmuth ist]" (*EH* 32, translation modified; *KSA* 6.290).

Nietzsche here turns that feminine creature, music, into a compact being matching the images of sculptural or architectonic solidity with which *Ecce Homo* abounds. "A human being who has turned out well [ein wohlgerathner Mensch]," Nietzsche remarks, "is carved out of wood at once hard, delicate and sweet-smelling" (*EH* 10; *KSA* 6.267). The idea of the eternal return, Nietzsche reports, first occurred to him when he "stopped beside a mighty pyramidal block of stone which towered up not far from Surlei" (*EH* 69, translation modified). For Zarathustra "man is formlessness, material, an ugly stone which requires the sculptor" (*EH* 80).

The architectonic, the crafted or sculpted, self invoked in these comments represents a perfectionism that is also the consummate form of self-defense. "And in what does one really recognize that someone has turned out well? [Und woran erkennt man im Grunde die *Wohlgerathenheit?*]" Nietzsche asks (*EH* 10; *KSA* 6.267). The answer: precisely in his groundedness, in his crafted or built nature. The man who has turned out well is the "Gegenstück," the opposite piece, to the decadent (*KSA* 6.267). He has learned the art of blocking off the world. At one point in *Ecce Homo,* in the section "Why I Am So Clever," Nietzsche describes his shrewd art of self-defense as a building of fortifications, a way of walling himself in ("eine Art Selbst-Vermauerung" [*KSA* 6.284]). The first, most important cleverness is "Not to see many things, not to hear them, not to let them approach one" (*EH* 33). Like Socrates the torpedofish warding off the world with his stinging defenses, so Nietzsche sees himself as an "Igel," or hedgehog (*KSA* 6.292).

But the rather tense architectonic self-defense, the nervous quilled solidity, that Nietzsche proclaims in the passages I have just collected wars against a competing interest: the fully Emersonian impulse toward abandonment, toward the self-forgetfulness that leads to victory. The subtitle of *Ecce Homo* is "how one becomes what one is." In order to become what you are, Nietzsche tells us, it is absolutely necessary not to have the slightest idea what you are. Here, then, is a new imperative to compete with the Delphic oracle's "know thyself" (*gnôthi seauton*): Don't know thyself!

> That one becomes what one is presupposes that one does not have the remotest idea *what* one is. From this point of view even the *blunders* [die *Fehlgriffe*] of life . . . have their own meaning and value. They are the expression of a great sagacity, even the supreme sagacity [Darin kann eine grosse Klugheit, sogar die oberste Klugheit zum Ausdruck <kommen>]: where *nosce te*

> *ipsum* would be the recipe for destruction [zum Untergang], self-forgetfulness, self-*misunderstanding,* self-diminution, -narrowing, -mediocritizing [Vermittelmässigen] becomes reason itself. (*EH* 34; *KSA* 6.293)

The Emersonian aspect of *Ecce Homo* is notable, here and in other passages. In the lines I have quoted, Nietzsche echoes Emerson's defense of a deliberate self-misunderstanding and self-forgetting, and his ideas about the usefulness of mistakes. Earlier in *Ecce Homo,* he agrees with "Self-Reliance" on the disposability of "great" literature. In an Emerson-like gesture, Nietzsche remarks on the ruinous effect of reading books, especially early in the morning, at the height of one's strength (*EH* 34).

In Nietzsche's ideal vision, as in Emerson's, abandonment to one's genius allows the discovery of the organic law of the individual, a grounding of self. The proper mode of self-defense, the real secret, is, it now seems, a healthy self-misunderstanding. In contrast to the *Genealogy*'s Preface, self-mistaking here opens into a meaningful accident of self-discovery and an ensuing strength, the individual growing plant- or fetus-like according to his own law: "In the meantime the organizing 'idea' destined to rule [die organisirende, die zur Herrschaft berufne 'Idee'] grows and grows in the depths" (*EH* 35; *KSA* 6.294).

In this Nietzschean sentence, the biological organizing impulse, growing into slow, patient power, is called forth in religious fashion from the deep. Here we have a near-perfect combination of the architectonic idea of the individual, organizing its security in decisive manner, and the idea of a plant-like organism developing spontaneously but determinedly according to its own sovereign good. In his championing of what looks like Aristotelian growth, Nietzsche here claims a contrast between himself and those living abortions, the preachers of vengeance who strike Nietzsche as "the refuse of mankind, abortive offspring of sickness and vengeful instincts [Ausschuss der Menschheit, Ausgeburten von Krankheit und rachsüchtigen Instinkten]" (*EH* 37; *KSA* 6.296).

But Nietzsche's wish for a natural growth in the direction of architectonic solidity is suddenly overturned by his apocalyptic impulse, his desire, not to build, but to tear down, when he writes, a few pages later in *Ecce Homo* (also in "Why I Am So Clever"),

> What is being built today will in three years' time stand no more. [Das, was heute gebaut wird, steht in drei Jahren nicht mehr.] —

If I measure myself by what I am *capable* of, to say nothing of what will come after me, an overturning, a taking down without comparison, then I have more than any mortal the claim to the word "great." [Wenn ich mich darnach messe, was ich *kann,* nicht davon zu reden, was hinter mir drein kommt, ein Umsturz, ein Aufbau ohne Gleichen, so habe ich mehr als irgend ein Sterblicher den Anspruch auf das Wort Grösse.] (*KSA* 6.296, my translation)[39]

The well-turned-out Nietzsche has now been replaced by the Nietzsche who is a sheer sign of momentous, world-historical conflict without bounds.

Scattered into his texts, Nietzsche becomes "Nietzsche," a new sign or password for the enlightened ones, just as the author envisioned in *Daybreak* (see chapter 4 of this volume): *In hoc signo vinces.* This time around, however, the sign promises not victory, but ruin, the catastrophic taking apart of what we had built for ourselves. *Ein Umsturz, ein Aufbau ohne Gleichen:* and on the other side of this revolution, perhaps, a new face of individualism.

CONCLUSION

NIETZSCHE WAS A LIBRA, with Scorpio rising. Or so I was told some years ago, at a conference, by a graduate student from (predictably?) Santa Cruz. Taking a cue from Nietzsche's own observation in *The Gay Science* that superstition is not only more interesting but more sophisticated than belief, that *Aberglaube* is superior to *Glaube* (*GS* # 23), I embrace the astrological hint and see Nietzsche as Libra-like in his oscillation between two extremes: an attraction to solidity and balance, to the architectural—a shoring up of the self—and a contrasting impulse to dissolve the self in a plurality of masks and motifs, in musical or theatrical play.[1] These extremes cannot finally be balanced, and the revolutionary volatility of the Scorpio takes over as Nietzsche ends his writing career in the prophetic, explosive conclusion of *Ecce Homo,* which establishes the triumph of musical/theatrical dispersion over Nietzsche's architectonic ambition for a guarded, safe self.

I have not been able to track down Emerson's astrological chart. But we know that he was a Gemini, born on the afternoon of May 25, 1803. Like many a Gemini, Emerson combined his lively and eloquent interest in change with a versatile playfulness that strikes some readers as evasive.

In this book I have relied primarily on (not astrology, but) Stanley Cavell as a guide to Emerson, and Jacques Lacan as a guide to Nietzsche. Cavell is the heir of Wittgenstein as well as Emerson; Lacan, the heir of Freud. It is useful at this point to define what the difference between these two traditions means for my sense of individualism—the Emersonian individualism described so well by Cavell, and the ascetic, obsessive individualism that Nietzsche, after several major twists and turns, finally incarnates in his work of the 1880s (especially the *Genealogy of Morals* and *Ecce Homo*).[2]

It may not be possible—it may not even be desirable—to eradicate the ascetic's negative way, his engrained mistrust of the objects of passion and his determination to avoid their grip. In depicting Nietzsche as a thinker who finally gives in to such asceticism in the *Genealogy of Morals,* after resisting it in earlier works like *Daybreak* and *The*

Gay Science, I have tried to make it clear that this development was not inevitable; that Nietzsche's career opens various pathways, some of them remarkably similar to Emerson's. Emerson himself remains uninterested in ascetic self-discipline, not so much opposed to it as untouched by it.

My understanding of Nietzschean asceticism is derived from Lacan's intuition, which is in turn derived from Freud's death drive, that human identity is based not on the desirability of a sovereign good, as in Aristotle, but rather on the irresistible pull of a "nothing" that takes a concrete form, the object *a*.[3] The object *a*, for Lacan, is the sign of a world that constantly testifies to the gap between desire and act. As Lacan says in his eighth seminar (1960–61): "One needs to ask oneself how one can operate honestly with one's desires. That is, how one can preserve the desire in the act, the relation of the desire to the act. Desire ordinarily finds in the act its collapse rather than its realization, and, at best, the act only presents to the desire its exploit, its heroic flourish. How to preserve, I'm saying, from the desire to this act, something that one could call a simple or healthy relation?"[4]

Quite a bit of Lacan is compressed into this passage: most notably, his resistance to the ethical hygiene he associates both with American ego psychology and with Aristotle, his refusal of the wish to establish a healthy relation between desire and behavior. We also see in Lacan's statement his rejection of what one might call, on the model of false modesty, a false honesty, determined to ignore our entanglement in trickery and self-deception. Lacan's words also convey his strong sense that desire gets abandoned or exposed, rather than fulfilled, in its enactment; and, finally, his suggestion that desire seeks its own failure or collapse, rather than its success. Lacan follows Freud's comment that it is impossible to define success in the erotic realm, since there is for us, in this region at least, no satisfaction in satisfaction: since *eros* seems fundamentally devoted, or indebted, to frustration rather than to satisfaction.

The stranding of desire at the hands of enactment is a special theme of Lacan, one that Zizek picks up and elaborates. The grotesqueness of a gesture that remains a mere gesture, part of the realm of repetition, or the dumb automatism that can reduce sex to a mere, and merely stupid, act, can discourage — collapse — desire. In the Lacanian view, all quests, all idealizations, risk such a collapse into the brute Real. The courtly lover is suddenly confronted with the excremental foulness of the beloved (a crucial example from the Provençal tradition that Lacan elaborates in his seventh seminar is Arnaut Daniel's poem in which he reports his lady's command that he put his mouth to her "trumpet," presumably her anus).[5]

What Nietzsche refers to in *Ecce Homo* as the final objection to eternal return, the presence of mother and sister, forecasts a realm of repetition-as-death. In Lacan, language is the evidence of repetition, since words only work, only achieve the status of words, by being repeated. Language as repetition is the engine of symbolic action, but it also marks the Real as what is left out of symbolization, because words merely circle repeatedly around the object they point to, citing themselves rather than it. Poetic speech generates in its self-citation a way of gesturing toward the essence that must be left out of speech. But this speech itself tends to become a congealed essence, the mark of the Real. For example, the reduction of the beloved to a mere sign or hint in the troubadour poets, and later in Petrarch, elevates her into the Symbolic realm by showing her power in, or as, her absence.[6] In this way the beloved, as a Symbolic character, is like the father, the state, or God himself, effective because absent. But the signs of the beloved that the poet indicates in his work, her eyes or hair or lips, can revert to mere marks of the Real. The blazon threatens to become a grotesque, fetishistic image, and the courtly lover's poetic efforts, as a result, risk the sheer dumb repetition of custom (the lover "sighing like furnace," with a "sonnet made to his mistress's eyebrow," as the melancholy Jacques puts it in *As You Like It*).

In Lacan, then, repetition is an "always-already" that hollows out the integrity of any deed, any moment, by reminding us that we can only ever refer to our desires, never enact or embody them truly. For this mood of Franco-theoretical ennui, every mistress is a cliché, and she becomes remarkable only when the cliché hardens into absurdity.

Cavell, in contrast to Lacan, describes a difference between living and dead repetition and suggests that the difference is subject to individual decision. Decision, for Cavell, is essentially linked to the acknowledging of others. In the process of acknowledgment, which is an inescapable support of life, even the continual regaining of life, as Cavell will describe it, things fall into place; they are established as lost to or separate from the desiring self so that the self can recover them. In this way, repetition serves life rather than death. Cavell writes in "The Uncanniness of the Ordinary" that

> There is a repetition necessary to what we call life, or the ani-
> mate, necessary for example to the human; and a repetition nec-
> essary to what we call death, or the inanimate, necessary for
> example to the mechanical; and there are no marks or features
> or criteria or rhetoric by means of which to tell the difference
> between them. From which, let me simply claim, it does not fol-
> low that the difference is unknowable or undecidable. On the
> contrary, the difference is the basis of everything there is for
> human beings to know, or say decide (like deciding to live), and
> to decide on no basis beyond or beside or beneath ourselves.[7]

"What is to be acknowledged," Cavell writes later in the essay, "is th[e] existence [of the world and others in it] as separate from me, as if gone from me . . . the world must be regained every day, in repetition, re-gained as gone."[8] For Cavell, the repetition required of us is living repe-tition, a working-through of thought and action. This project contrasts with Lacanian repetition, in which another person first appears to us as a being whose actions are (as Zizek writes) "wholly incommensurable with our needs and desires," and therefore as "a kind of automaton, a machine which utters meaningless demands at random."[9]

Cavell's "Uncanniness of the Ordinary" is an important essay for my purposes because it shows that for Cavell, in radical contrast to Lacan, it is the ineluctably different position of the other person that is primary for us, rather than, as in Lacan, the other person's way of em-bodying a threatening meaninglessness. (This meaninglessness is re-vealed by Lacan in the form of sexual difference, a fact that cannot be made sense of, since gender is definitive without ever being descrip-tive.)[10] The Lacanian specter of a seemingly infinite, or indefinite, realm of repetition presents a death-in-life that must be broken by something radically other: the central Freudian notion of the wish, which inexplicably allows the nothing to become something.[11]

Emerson does not suffer such a bad infinity, the death-in-life of meaningless repetition described in Lacan. This is to say that he is not a purgatorial or ascetic thinker; Nietzsche, like Lacan, is. What this difference implies for the Emerson-Nietzsche connection, and for our conversation about that connection, is the subject of this book. Emerson and Nietzsche offer two separate, forceful visions, each with its own promise and limits. It is important that we resist the tempta-tion to combine them, and lean instead on their *distinct* powers. Their difference signals an irreconcilability in our experience that demands attention.

It is tempting, but mistaken, to see Nietzsche as committed to an Emersonian thankfulness for existence. Laurence Lampert, in *Nietzsche and Modern Times,* suggests that Nietzsche seeks "a human way of being on the earth that permits all beings to be what they are . . . the will to eternalize out of love and gratitude." For Lampert, Nietzsche is a philosopher who embraces limits: "Nietzsche understands freedom as an always problematic obedience to what is given as one's own fate, a historical as well as a natural givenness among whose imperatives one finds oneself or comes to oneself."[12] In a similar vein, Tyler Roberts writes in *Contesting Spirit* that Nietzsche (and here Roberts invokes Emerson as well) "cultivates the passionate, eternal affirmation of life through a certain—both affirmative and critical—practice of the limit of the human."[13] Lampert and Roberts eloquently express Nietzsche's ideal, a model of careful, controlled aspiration that I have called architectonic, and that relies on one of Nietzsche's major inspirations, the late Emerson of *The Conduct of Life.* But the final reality of Nietzsche's work and life is rather less optimistic, less affirmative, than this Emersonian architecture of freedom, precisely because the wished-for freedom proved, for him, unattainable, because he remained bound to asceticism and the object *a*.

Nietzsche, unlike Emerson, suffers the effects of the object *a*, the thing that cannot be disciplined and that always disrupts, even as it sustains, our dream of a world. Zizek refers to the basic ethical attitude of psychoanalysis as an acknowledging of "the distance we are obliged to assume toward our most 'authentic' dreams, toward the myths that guarantee the very consistency of our symbolic universe."[14] If this acknowledgment sounds like the ideal of critical history Nietzsche wished for in "On the Use and Disadvantage of History for Life," Nietzsche's actual development after this text suggests that the distance we take from our necessary myths cannot be a proper distance, that we risk ruin by thinking aggressively about the pieties that sustain us. And yet we have no real choice but to do that thinking. While Emerson invites us, hosting our hopes for a newly realized individuality, Nietzsche dares us to see what this individuality might look like, and what it might cost. This is an offer "we ascetics" can't—so it seems—refuse.

Notes

INTRODUCTION

1. Gianni Vattimo's "Nietzsche and Heidegger," in *Nietzsche in Italy,* ed. Thomas Harrison (Stanford, Calif.: ANMA Libri, 1988), 23, cites Dilthey's *Essence of Philosophy* to this effect.

2. George Stack, *Nietzsche and Emerson: An Elective Affinity* (Athens: Ohio University Press, 1992), 12.

3. Ibid., 14.

4. Ibid., 51, 61.

5. See Lawrence Lampert, *Leo Strauss and Nietzsche* (Chicago: University of Chicago Press, 1996), 47n.

6. Harold Bloom, *Omens of Millennium* (New York: Riverhead, 1996), 234.

7. Heidegger frequently uses architectural images to describe Nietzsche's project, as when he comments that, on "the statement that the essence of human life is justice," "Such grounding, which clears the way and decisively erects, grounds a height that opens onto a vista." Martin Heidegger, *Nietzsche,* trans. D. F. Krell (San Francisco: Harper and Row, 1979 [1st German ed. 1961]), 3:145.

8. See Jean Granier, "Nietzsche's Conception of Chaos," in *The New Nietzsche,* ed. David Allison (Cambridge, Mass.: MIT Press, 1985 [1st ed. 1977]), 138, 141.

9. For a portrait of a divided Nietzsche that is somewhat similar to my own, and that stands in contrast to a version like Granier's, see Henry Staten, *Nietzsche's Voice* (Ithaca, N.Y.: Cornell University Press, 1990), 4: "[Nietzsche's] reiterated championing of authenticity and critique of the actor alternates with a love of irony, concealment, and masks." Staten persuasively explores the contrast between the "exploding" Nietzsche who disappears into his roles and the one who consolidates and authenticates himself. See also Daniel Conway, *Nietzsche and the Political* (New York: Routledge, 1997).

10. Slavoj Zizek, *The Ticklish Subject* (London: Verso, 1999), 216.

11. Charles Altieri, *Postmodernisms Now* (University Park: Penn State University Press, 1998), 35.

12. J. S. Mill, "On Liberty," in *The Six Great Humanistic Essays of J. S. Mill* (New York: Washington Square Press, 1963), 184–85.

13. Ibid., 180–81, italics added.

14. It is, needless to say, the very plausibility of comparing China to Microsoft that renders the comparison appealing, distracting us from the far less convincing analogy between Apple and Tibet. In the ad's terms, buying a Mac is almost a spiritual act, uniting the buyer with other consumers who care less

about the cold capitalist bottom line, efficiency and price, than about aesthetic possibility (the Mac is generally preferred by graphic designers and artistic or "visual people").

15. John Rawls, *A Theory of Justice* (Cambridge, Mass.: Harvard University Press, 1971), 526. Although there is a similarity between Rawls's defense of free markets (271-74) and his statement of the desirability of a society in which individuals recognize various, freely chosen moral goods (447-48), a passage like the one I have quoted indicates that he also resists the consumerist model.

16. Alexander Nehamas's influential *Nietzsche: Life as Literature* (Cambridge, Mass.: Harvard University Press, 1985) shares many of Rorty's impulses in this regard. See Rorty, *Contingency, Irony and Solidarity* (Cambridge: Cambridge University Press, 1989). It is true that Rorty violates his own public-private division by endowing the private ironist with public weight, but only by taming the ironist's ironies. So according to Rorty Nabokov shows us like a good liberal that cruelty is "the worst thing we do," but in order to read him this way Rorty must deny the cruelty of Nabokov's own practice, the way he dissects or torments his protagonists.

17. Alain Finkielkraut, *In the Name of Humanity* [*L'Humanité perdue*], trans. Judith Friedlander (New York: Columbia University Press, 2000 [1st French ed. 1996]), 92. For a similar critique of charity for the anonymous masses, see Alain Badiou, *L'Éthique: Essai sur le conscience du mal* (Paris: Hatier, 1993), 12-17.

18. Stack, *Emerson and Nietzsche*, discusses the two major earlier studies of the relation between the two thinkers: Eduard Baumgarten, *Das Vorbild Emersons im Werk und Leben Nietzsches* (Heidelberg: Karl Winter Verlag, 1957) and Stanley Hubbard, *Nietzsche und Emerson* (Basel: Verlag für Recht und Gesellschaft, 1958). Stanley Cavell, in *Conditions Handsome and Unhandsome* (Chicago: University of Chicago Press, 1990), 33-63, makes a case for Emerson's influence on Nietzsche (and Heidegger).

19. See Bloom, *Kabbalah and Criticism* (New York: Seabury Press, 1975), 115.

20. For a thoughtful survey of Nietzsche's effort to transform tragedy into comedy in his work, see Bernd Magnus, Jean-Pierre Mileur, and Stanley Stewart, "Reading Ascetic Reading," in *Nietzsche, Genealogy, Morality*, ed. Richard Schacht (Berkeley: University of California Press, 1994).

21. Such irony, it could be argued, remains a step beyond the Heideggerian tendency to identify the subject with the event of Being (see Zizek's analysis of Heidegger in *The Ticklish Subject*, 19-22).

22. Gianni Vattimo, *The Adventure of Difference*, trans. Cyprian Blamires and Thomas Harrison (Baltimore: Johns Hopkins University Press, 1993), 87.

23. Vattimo discusses this *Nachlass* fragment in *Adventure of Difference*, 107.

24. Emerson is here closer to the creativity of the Freudian unconscious, which is simultaneously both ours and not ours, whereas Nietzsche remains a thinker of the antithetical, of meaning that either disrupts or confirms us. On this difference between Freud and Nietzsche, see Eric Santner, *On the Psychotheology of Everyday Life* (Chicago: University of Chicago Press, 2001).

25. This remark was made in Strauss's unpublished lectures on *Zarathustra*, delivered at the University of Chicago in the 1950s.

26. Adam Phillips, *Terrors and Experts* (Cambridge, Mass.: Harvard University Press, 1996), xvii.

27. See Rorty, *Contingency, Irony and Solidarity;* Nehamas, *Nietzsche: Life as Literature;* and Nehamas, *The Art of Living* (Berkeley: University of California Press, 1998).

28. Altieri, *Postmodernisms Now,* 35-36.

CHAPTER 1

1. Thomas Carlyle, cited in Oliver Wendell Holmes, *Ralph Waldo Emerson* (Boston: Houghton Mifflin, 1895), 163; Quentin Anderson, *The Imperial Self* (New York: Knopf, 1971), vii.

2. Cornel West, *The American Evasion of Philosophy* (Madison: University of Wisconsin Press, 1990), 12-13, 19, 36, and *passim.*

3. See Cavell's discussions of Emerson in *Conditions Handsome and Unhandsome* (Chicago: University of Chicago Press, 1990) and *This New Yet Unapproachable America* (Albuquerque, N.M.: Living Batch Press, 1989).

4. The most persuasive account of Emerson's desire for wholeness as a prospect is L. Rust Brown, *The Emerson Museum* (Cambridge, Mass.: Harvard University Press, 1997), 21-42.

5. Henry David Thoreau, *Walden,* ed. J. Lyndon Shanley (Princeton, N.J.: Princeton University Press, 1971), 92.

6. Stanley Cavell, *The Senses of Walden,* expanded edition (San Francisco: North Point Press, 1981).

7. Thoreau, *Walden,* 321.

8. Michel de Montaigne, "Apology for Raymond Sebond," in Montaigne, *Complete Essays,* trans. Donald Frame (Stanford, Calif.: Stanford University Press, 1958), 331.

9. Perhaps the most sophisticated critique of the way Emerson shies away from liberal definitions of personal interest and social identity is Sharon Cameron, "The Way of Life by Abandonment: Emerson's Impersonal," *Critical Inquiry* 25, no. 1 (1998): 1-31. Yet Cameron's suggestion of a grand narrative in which Nietzsche's self-incarnation, the autobiographical *Ecce Homo,* sublates Emerson's impersonality by introducing the personal into philosophy (Cameron, 28n) supposes the necessity of Emersonian impersonality as it reappears in such early Nietzsche works as "On Truth and Lie in the Extra-Moral Sense." Accordingly, I suggest that Emersonian impersonality is not a mistake or failing, as Cameron argues, but rather preparation for a view of personal heroism that it also undermines—and that this peculiar debate itself has lasting political significance.

10. Harold Bloom, *The Ringers in the Tower* (Chicago: University of Chicago Press, 1971), 222. On Emerson's difference from Wordsworth, see Myra Jehlen, *American Incarnation* (Cambridge, Mass.: Harvard University Press, 1986), 96-105.

11. Carlyle, cited in Holmes, *Emerson,* 163.

12. Holmes, *Emerson,* 191.

13. Stephen Whicher, *Freedom and Fate,* 2d ed. (Philadelphia: University of Pennsylvania Press, 1961), 63.

14. Anderson, *Imperial Self*, 5, 7, 11, 14, 19. Anderson refines and expands his argument in his later *Making Americans* (San Diego: Harcourt Brace Jovanovich, 1992). On the motif of eating the world, and more generally on revelation in Emerson, see Joel Porte, *Representative Man*, 2d ed. (New York: Columbia University Press, 1988), 79–100.

15. George Kateb, *Hannah Arendt* (Totowa, N.J.: Rowman and Allanheld, 1983), 145.

16. Ibid., 145 and, more specifically on Emerson, 171.

17. Cavell, *Conditions Handsome and Unhandsome*, 10.

18. Interesting in this context is David Bromwich's eloquent description of Wordsworth's sense that "Property, status, function, the whole train of social and moral relations . . . between none of these and ourselves can there be the sort of happy fit that defines a human identity. To be deprived of the assurance that there is such a fit is sometimes, perhaps much of the time, a given fact of consciousness." The Wordsworthian understanding that we are dispossessed is shared by Emerson, but the sense of the dispossession as a "given fact," a reliable ground for possible reconciliation, is not. Bromwich, *Disowned by Memory: Wordsworth's Poetry of the 1790s* (Chicago: University of Chicago Press, 1999), 24.

19. See Richard Poirier, "The Question of Genius," in *The Renewal of Literature* (Cambridge, Mass.: Harvard University Press, 1987).

20. Nietzsche, *BT* 35: "the lyric poet . . . himself, completely delivered of the greed of the will, is the pure and undimmed eye of the sun."

21. I am reminded here of Cavell's reference to Heidegger's "The Thing," with its meditation on "das Gering des Ringes," "the ringing of the ring," derived from Nietzsche's Zarathustra ("The Seven Seals"). "What [Heidegger] seems to want from the word *Gering*," Cavell writes, "is both the intensification of the idea of being hooped together and at the same time the idea of this activity as slight, trivial, humble: it is the idea of diurnal devotedness." Stanley Cavell, *In Quest of the Ordinary* (Chicago: University of Chicago Press, 1988), 176.

22. Julie Ellison, *Emerson's Romantic Style* (Princeton, N.J.: Princeton University Press, 1984), 8–9.

23. Cavell, *This New Yet Unapproachable America*, 93.

24. John Lloyd Stephens, *Incidents of Travel in Egypt, Arabia Petraea, and the Holy Land* (Norman: University of Oklahoma Press, 1970), 188–90.

25. Similarly, Emerson in "The Method of Nature" notes that "Empedocles undoubtedly spoke a truth of thought, when he said, 'I am God'; but the moment it was out of his mouth . . . the world revenged itself for the seeming arrogance, by the good story about his shoe" (*E* 85; Mt. Etna supposedly threw back Empedocles' sandals when he tried to test his claim of divinity by hurling himself into it).

26. So in "Self-Reliance": "The way, the thought, the good shall be wholly strange and new" (*E* 271). In a journal entry, Emerson wishes that Garrison, Phillips, and others might wake up one day as unexpectedly different selves (*Emerson in his Journals*, ed. Joel Porte [Cambridge, Mass.: Harvard University Press, 1982], 451). See also Cavell on "abandonment" in Emerson, in *The Senses of Walden*, 138, 158; and B. L. Packer, *Emerson's Fall* (New York: Continuum, 1982), 136–47.

27. Schopenhauer and Emerson, like Shakespeare in *The Taming of the Shrew* (1.1.37–41), draw on what is apparently a folktale motif, the drunken beggar treated as a prince. For Thoreau, however, the transformation is real, not illusory. He responds to the sot-prince tale of "Self-Reliance" in *Walden*, when he relates a Hindu parable of the awakened soul as a king's son raised in the woods whose royal identity is revealed by "one of his father's ministers," and who then "knew himself to be a prince" (*Walden*, 96).

28. Cavell, *This New Yet Unapproachable America*, 101–3.

29. Ibid., 107. Sharon Cameron, in "Representing Grief: Emerson's 'Experience,'" *Representations* 15 (1986): 15–41, proposes that Emerson's emphasis on the obliquity or consistent dissociation of the self from, and in, its world finally accomplishes a preservation of the world (Cameron, 36–41). I would argue that Cameron's statement of Emerson's goal stands in implicit accord with Cavell's idea of overcoming skepticism.

30. Cavell, *This New Yet Unapproachable America*, 107.

31. See Jacques Derrida, *The Ear of the Other*, trans. Christie McDonald (Lincoln: University of Nebraska Press, 1985).

32. As I explain at the end of chapter 4, Nietzsche's idea of eternal return does not advocate the self-enclosed permanence here associated with joy. In the terms of the Zarathustra passage, eternal return is a way of uniting suffering and joy by valuing the imperfection of life (suffering) as worthy of repetition (joy).

33. Jean-Luc Nancy, *The Inoperative Community*, trans. Peter Connor et al. (Minneapolis: University of Minnesota Press, 1991). For an acute study of some ironies *not* under Emerson's control, see David Bromwich, *A Choice of Inheritance* (Cambridge, Mass.: Harvard University Press, 1989), 133–44.

34. Charles Bernstein, *Content's Dream* (Los Angeles: Sun & Moon, 1986), 31.

35. Susan Howe, *My Emily Dickinson* (Berkeley: North Atlantic Books, 1985), 13. Howe argues a radical voiding of tradition to make way for her version of Emersonian abandonment: "Categories and hierarchies suggest property. My voice formed from my life belongs to no one else. What I put into words is no longer my possession. Possibility has opened. The future will forget, erase, or recollect and deconstruct every poem."

CHAPTER 2

1. Lacan in his account of Freud draws a key distinction between desire and drive. Desire is tied to the negotiation of a specific situation, and is frustrated and allured by a particular object. Drive overrides such specificity, its true aim is its own perpetuation, rather than any particular object.

2. Gianni Vattimo provides a version of the transition from the *Birth of Tragedy* to the *Untimely Meditations* in his important book *Il soggetto e la maschera* (Milan: Bompiani, 1974). For Vattimo, in the *Untimely Meditations* historicism plays the role that Socratic rationalism played in the *Birth of Tragedy*, as the source of a decadent rigidity based on a fixed distinction between truth and falsehood (62). In both cases, Vattimo argues, Nietzsche counterposes this rigidity to the fluid play of the Dionysian mask, which creates liberating fictions

rather than imprisoning truths. In *Il soggetto e la maschera,* Vattimo tends to overestimate the security of this Dionysian fiction-making in Nietzsche, crediting it with the capacity to give the self a kind of perfect liberty; he overlooks the danger of the Dionysian, its capacity to dissolve the self. In the terms I am relying on here, Vattimo endows the Dionysian with an architectonic solidity it does not, to my mind, have.

3. Malcolm Bowie, *Freud, Proust and Lacan: Theory as Fiction* (Cambridge: Cambridge University Press, 1987), 107.

4. Joan Copjec, *Read My Desire: Lacan against the Historicists* (Cambridge, Mass.. MIT Press, 1994), 131.

5. Renata Salecl, *(Per)versions of Love and Hate* (London: Verso, 1998), 15–16.

6. See ibid., 13.

7. On the difference between the (Imaginary) ideal ego and the (Symbolic) ego ideal, see Lacan's *The Seminar of Jacques Lacan, Bk. I: Freud's Papers on Technique* (1953–1954), ed. Jacques-Alain Miller, trans. John Forrester (New York: Norton, 1991), 129–42.

8. Slavoj Zizek, "Four Discourses, Four Subjects," in Zizek, ed., *Cogito and the Unconscious* (Durham, N.C.: Duke University Press, 1998), 76.

9. Lacan, *Encore: The Seminar of Jacques Lacan, Bk. XX,* ed. Jacques-Alain Miller, trans. Bruce Fink (New York: Norton, 1998), 138.

10. Nietzsche, *Twilight of the Idols,* 2d ed., trans. R. J. Hollingdale (Harmondsworth: Penguin, 1990), 50. For a very different reading of the Nietzsche-Wagner relation as a pure Imaginary rivalry, see René Girard, "Strategies of Madness—Nietzsche, Wagner, and Dostoevski," in his *"To Double Business Bound"* (Baltimore: Johns Hopkins University Press, 1978).

11. Nietzsche, "Fatum und Geschichte," in *Frühe Schriften,* ed. Hans Joachim Mette (Munich: C. H. Beck Verlag, 1994), 59, my translation.

12. For Schopenhauer, the role of the captivation exerted by the object *a* is as a principle of inevitability, a mere part of his energic system, and therefore s a thing whose identity must remain indifferent. Schopenhauer does not allow the object *a* to disrupt the universal economy he visualizes, whereas Freud does. To put it another way: psychoanalysis is born when the hysteric's desire—the object *a* for the early Freud—becomes an orienting factor for knowledge, its crucial place, rather than the mere and merely typical site of a fall into the sickness of impossible desire (as hysteria would have appeared to Schopenhauer).

13. See Martha Nussbaum, "The Transfigurations of Intoxication: Nietzsche, Schopenhauer and Dionysus," in *Arion* (3d series) 1, no. 2 (May 1991): 75–111, reprinted in Salim Kemal, Ivan Gaskell, and Daniel Conway, eds., *Nietzsche, Philosophy and the Arts* (Cambridge: Cambridge University Press, 1998). Nussbaum's very sympathy with this Nietzschean project makes her, in this article at least, accept it as literally true, a revelation or "discover[y]" rather than a projection (108). Nussbaum's sympathy with Nietzsche's overcoming of Schopenhauer makes her overlook the fault that persists within it; she believes in Nietzsche's vision of tragedy. *Contra* Nussbaum, Nietzsche's transfiguration of Schopenhauerian will is a fantasy that continues, however subliminally, to be afflicted by the traumatic kernel of the Real that it must leave out

14. Schopenhauer, *Die Welt als Wille und Vorstellung,* Band 1, in *Sämtliche Werke,* vol. 1 (Frankfurt am Main: Suhrkamp, 1986), 481. For an interesting commentary on this passage in relation to Nietzsche see John Sallis, *Crossings: Nietzsche and the Space of Tragedy* (Chicago: University of Chicago Press, 1991), 39–41.

15. Schopenhauer, *Die Welt als Wille und Vorstellung,* 482.

16. Salecl, *(Per)versions,* 63. Salecl, I should note, does not discuss Schopenhauer in her book. Bruce Fink, in *The Lacanian Subject* (Princeton, N.J.: Princeton University Press, 1995), aligns the Real with the object *a,* the cause of desire and spur of the subject's *jouissance* (83, 92). Neil Hertz's well-known essay "Freud and the Sandman" associates Freud's notion of the uncanny with that of repetition-compulsion (Hertz, "Freud and the Sandman," in Josué V. Harari, ed., *Textual Strategies* [Ithaca, N.Y.: Cornell University Press, 1979]). See also the discussion in Lacan's second seminar on the difference between Platonic reminiscence and Freudian repetition, in *The Seminar of Jacques Lacan, Bk. II: The Ego in Freud's Theory and the Technique of Psychoanalysis, 1954–1955,* ed. Jacques-A Miller, trans. Sylvana Tomaselli (New York: Norton, 1991), 100–101.

17. On the priority of the musical metaphor in the *Birth,* see Sarah Kofman, "Metaphor, Symbol, Metamorphosis," in *The New Nietzsche,* ed. David Allison (Cambridge, Mass.: MIT Press, 1985). I find puzzling Kofman's claim that the importance Nietzsche gives to music in the *Birth,* in contrast to his later works, is "strategic" (208). If Kofman means that the priority of music in the *Birth* is *merely* strategic, rather than fundamental, she fails to say why and how this is so.

18. Lacan, *Encore: Seminar, Bk. XX,* 127.

19. Slavoj Zizek, *The Ticklish Subject* (London: Verso, 1999), 265, 309.

20. One is reminded of the joke about Hindu cosmology: the elephant whose back supports the universe rests on another elephant, but what supports that elephant? The answer: "Elephants all the way down." Similarly, Nietzsche's vision suggests "tigers all the way down."

21. See Stanley Cavell, *Conditions Handsome and Unhandsome* (Chicago: University of Chicago Press, 1990), 38–39, for a discussion of the hand in this passage from "Experience."

22. Owen Barfield, *Speaker's Meaning* (Middletown, Conn.: Wesleyan University Press, 1967), 58. See also the well-known discussion in Paul de Man, *Allegories of Reading* (New Haven, Conn.: Yale University Press, 1979), 79–131.

23. Nietzsche, in other words, resists belief in imaginary entities. Similarly, Nietzsche in his discussions of the will to power resists yielding to the temptation of anthropomorphism, which would make the will to power the property of certain "powerful" humans. Instead of identifying with such pretensions to mastery, Nietzsche, like Emerson, questions the motives behind them, asking why we are interested in the personal imposition of power or value. Heidegger's opposition to what he sees as Nietzsche's fundamental investment in the imposition of value through power ignores the diagnostic aspect of Nietzsche's interest—which to be sure is marked by an iconoclastic sympathy for powerful individuals, but which nevertheless is also able to see through their simplified belief in their power, in Emersonian fashion.

24. Cavell, *A Pitch of Philosophy* (Cambridge, Mass.: Harvard University Press, 1994), 87–88.

25. David B. Allison, in "This is Not a Christ," in *Why Nietzsche Still?* ed. Alan Schrift (Berkeley: University of California Press, 2000), 87–88, notes that in this passage Nietzsche seems to identify the floating figure in Raphael's *Transfiguration* as, not Christ, but Apollo. Allison relates this misidentification to Burckhardt's discussion of the *Transfiguration* in his *Cicerone* as Apollonian in Nietzsche's terms, as the "brilliant self-contained illumination of the form" (88).

26. Zizek, *Tarrying with the Negative* (Durham, N.C.: Duke University Press, 1993), 196.

27. Lacan, *The Four Fundamental Concepts of Psychoanalysis: Seminar Bk. XI,* trans. Alan Sheridan (New York: Norton, 1978), 101.

28. Zizek, *Tarrying with the Negative,* 197.

29. See William Kerrigan's persuasive defense of Ernest Jones's Freudian reading of Hamlet in *Hamlet's Perfection* (Baltimore: Johns Hopkins University Press, 1994), 75–77.

30. Sallis, *Crossings,* 44n, cites Vernant and Vidal-Naquet on the fact that the first word of the *Bacchae* is *hēkô,* "I arrive," Dionysus's proud announcement of his sudden coming to Thebes. See also Walter F. Otto, *Dionysus: Myth and Cult,* trans. Robert Palmer (Bloomington: Indiana University Press, 1965), 79–85, 196; along with Charles Segal's excellent book on the Bacchae, *Dionysiac Poetics and Euripides' Bacchae,* 2d ed. (Princeton, N.J.: Princeton University Press, 1997), 7–26.

31. Zizek, *Tarrying with the Negative,* 116.

32. Edward Snow, *A Study of Vermeer* (Berkeley: University of California Press, 1979), 21: "It is well to remember that Plato banished the poets from his ideal state not just because they trafficked in falsehoods and created only images of things, but also (as if there were a connection) because they dwelt on sorrow and went out of their way to keep loss fresh."

33. Plato, *Symposium,* trans. Paul Woodruff and Alexander Nehamas (Indianapolis: Hackett, 1989).

34. Quotations of Plato's *Republic* are from the translation by G.M.A. Grube, revised by C.D.C. Reeve (Indianapolis: Hackett, 1992).

35. The eclipsing of the empirical self by the rhetorical construct of art is Nietzsche's claim in the *Birth,* as it is Paul de Man's in *Allegories of Reading,* but in Nietzsche the difference is curative as it is not in de Man. Rolf Grimminger notes that for Nietzsche, "in seinem empirischen Dasein ist das Subjekt keine Kunstfigur; und als Kunstfigur hat es kein empirisches Dasein." De Man, Grimminger continues, "radikalisiert den Riss aber derart, dass er unüberbrückbar wird, fundamental." Grimminger, "Offenbarung und Leere, oder: Nietzsche, Freud und Paul de Man," in *Ästhetik und Rhetorik: Lektüren zu Paul de Man,* ed. Karl Heinz Bohrer (Frankfurt am Main: Suhrkamp, 1993), 317.

36. Lacan, *Seminar, Bk. I: Freud's Papers on Technique,* 171.

37. See Frye, *A Natural Perspective* (New York: Columbia University Press, 1965), 112.

38. Arthur Schopenhauer, *The Will to Live: Selected Writings,* ed. Richard Taylor (New York: Frederick Ungar, 1962), 1. The passage is from chapter 17 of the Supplements to Book 1 of *The World as Will and Idea.*

39. It is a sign of Nietzsche's early divergence from Schopenhauer that even

in the *Birth*, his most Schopenhauerian book, the near-equivalent to Schopenhauer's will, the Dionysian impulse, almost nowhere appears without being endowed with the grace of image and formal structure, without being married to the Apollonian.

40. See Leo Strauss, "Note on the Plan of Nietzsche's *Beyond Good and Evil*," in *Studies in Platonic Political Philosophy* (Chicago: University of Chicago Press, 1983), 181.

41. See Laurence Lampert's discussion of this point in *Nietzsche's Teaching: An Interpretation of* Thus Spake Zarathustra (New Haven, Conn.: Yale University Press, 1986), 271–86.

42. Richard Wagner, *Tristan and Isolde*, with translation by Andrew Porter, English National Opera Guide Series 6 (London: John Calder, 1983), 92.

43. Nietzsche taught the *Alcestis* at Basel in 1875 and again in 1876 (see Karl Schlechta, *Nietzsche Chronik* [Munich: Carl Hanser Verlag, 1975], 50, 54) — one of his rare excursions into Euripides in his teaching, though he taught the *Bacchae* in 1870 (Schlechta, 34).

CHAPTER 3

1. Walter Pater, Conclusion to *The Renaissance*, in *Selected Writings of Walter Pater*, ed. Harold Bloom (New York: Signet/New American Library, 1974), 61.

2. See Michel Haar, *Par-delà le nihilisme* (Paris: Presses Universitaires Françaises, 1998), 123–50.

3. Sheridan Hough, *Nietzsche's Noontide Friend* (University Park: Penn State University Press, 1997), xxiii.

4. James Conant presents a persuasive defense of Nietzsche's individualism against Rawls and others who assume that Nietzsche advocates the differential distribution of material resources in an economy of scarcity so as to favor those who have proven themselves superior in intellect and creativity. For Nietzsche, as Conant correctly states, such proof of superiority can only come within a relation of exemplarity: the superior human being shows his (or her) superiority through the influence that will turn any member of his audience toward being exemplary him/herself. In such an economy, which is primarily and finally concerned with a (perfectionist) relation to one's self on the part of *each* individual, there can be no question of an officially administered mechanism for judging and rewarding superiority (or punishing inferiority). See James Conant, "Nietzsche's Perfectionism," in *Nietzsche's Postmoralism*, ed. Richard Schacht (Cambridge: Cambridge University Press, 2000).

5. See George Kateb, *Emerson and Self-Reliance* (Thousand Oaks, Calif.: Sage Publications, 1995), for the opposition between commitment and experiment in Emerson.

6. On this question, see my account of Renaissance literary theory in *The Limits of Moralizing: Pathos and Subjectivity in Spenser and Milton* (Lewisburg, Pa.: Bucknell University Press, 1994), 27–38.

7. See Conant, "Nietzsche's Perfectionism."

8. See Joel Porte, *Representative Man*, 2d ed. (New York: Columbia University Press, 1988), 16–31.

9. John Jay Chapman, *Emerson and Other Essays* (Boston: Moffat, Yard, 1909), 72-73.

10. On the hermeneutic implications of this detachment, see my essay "Kermode on the Outside Looking In," *Gulf Coast* 8, no. 2 (summer/fall 1996), 90-96.

11. Stanley Cavell, *Philosophical Passages* (Cambridge, Mass.: Blackwell, 1995), 21.

12. Ibid., 25.

13. Ibid., 31.

14. Jacques Derrida, *Specters of Marx*, trans. Peggy Kamuf (New York: Routledge, 1994).

15. Ibid., 97.

16. Derrida, *The Politics of Friendship*, tr. George Collins (London: Verso, 1997), 24.

17. Derrida, *Specters of Marx*, 109.

18. Ibid., 114.

19. I am thinking not only of Nietzsche's Emersonian interest, in *Untimely Meditations*, in a form of thought that would serve life, but also of the emphasis on life that characterizes all of Emerson's and Nietzsche's works. In one of his lectures on early Greek philosophy given in the early 1870s in Basel, Nietzsche called Socrates "the first philosopher of *life* [*Lebensphilosoph*]," because for Socrates "thinking serves life, while among all previous philosophers life had served thought and knowledge." Friedrich Nietzsche, *The Pre-Platonic Philosophers*, ed. and trans. Greg Whitlock (Urbana: University of Illinois Press, 2001), 145.

20. Derrida's sense that the "philosophy of life" implies "a pure identity to itself" or "assured inside" on the part of the subject does not seem to me to apply to the thought of Nietzsche or Emerson, even if it is true of Marx. Here as elsewhere, Husserl appears to be Derrida's main precursor and antagonist in philosophical tradition, and this fact reduces Derrida's usefulness for the reading of thinkers like Emerson and Nietzsche. The notion of the subject that Derrida attributes to Western metaphysics is basically Husserlian, in that it aims at a clarity or self-presence that Nietzsche and Emerson, for example, do not esteem as Husserl does.

21. Yet David Farrell Krell accurately remarks on Derrida's resistance to such indefinition, his "redoubled desire to remain truly true to the memory of the other," an insistence in which "one may descry the most powerful possibilities of *promise* and *affirmation*." Krell, *The Purest of Bastards* (University Park: Penn State University Press, 2000), 19. The question here is how to define the singularity of the individual, since Derrida also remains committed to such singularity.

22. Derrida, *Specters of Marx*, 170.

23. Zizek, *The Ticklish Subject* (London: Verso, 1999), 208-12. This impossibility is, in turn, according to Zizek, related to the "bar of impossibility" that "crosses *the big Other itself,* the socio-symbolic 'substance' that confronts the subject and in which the subject is embedded," and that therefore opens a "radical . . . freedom whose space is sustained by the Other's inconsistency and lack." Zizek, "Da Capo Senza Fine," in Judith Butler, Ernesto Laclau, and Slavoj Zizek, *Contingency, Hegemony, Universality* (New York: Verso, 2000), 258.

24. Cavell, *Philosophical Passages,* 74.

25. See Derrida, *Limited INC,* trans. Samuel Weber (Evanston, Ill.: Northwestern University Press, 1988), 132: "A red light is not repressive" (see also 150-51). Compare Heidegger's discussion of automobile turn signals in *Being and Time,* trans. J. Macquarrie and E. Robinson (New York: Harper, 1962), 108-9.

26. On Nietzsche as a mole or tunneler, see David Farrell Krell's essay "Der Maulwurf," in *Why Nietzsche Now?* ed. Daniel O'Hara (Bloomington: Indiana University Press, 1985), 155-86.

27. See Allen Grossman and Mark Halliday, *The Sighted Singer* (Baltimore: Johns Hopkins University Press, 1992), 257.

28. Conant, "Nietzsche's Perfectionism," 230.

29. See ibid., 236.

30. Kenneth Gross writes of monumental statues that they "become the relics (also victims) of history reduced to a few admirable attitudes, a history thus more fully accessible to appropriation or neglect." Gross, *The Dream of the Moving Statue* (Ithaca, N.Y.: Cornell University Press, 1992), 17.

31. Werner Hamacher, "'Disgregation of the Will': Nietzsche on the Individual and Individuality," in *Reconstructing Individualism,* ed. Thomas Heller, Morton Sosna, and David Wellbery (Stanford, Calif.: Stanford University Press, 1986), 119.

32. Lacan, "Desire and the Interpretation of Desire in *Hamlet,*" in *Literature and Psychoanalysis,* ed. Shoshana Felman (Baltimore: Johns Hopkins University Press, 1982), 43.

33. Ibid., 51.

34. On this transformation, see William Kerrigan, *Hamlet's Perfection* (Baltimore: Johns Hopkins University Press, 1994), 122-51.

35. See the sketches for the *Birth of Tragedy* from 1869-70 (*KSA* 1.515-640) cited by Michel Haar in "La rupture initiale de Nietzsche avec Schopenhauer," in his *Schopenhauer et la force du pessimisme* (Paris: Editions du Rocher, 1988), 100.

36. "Wozu die Menschen da sind, wozu 'der Mensch' da ist, soll uns gar nicht kümmern, aber wozu Du da bist, das frage dich" (KSA 7.651). In "History for Life": "Aber wozu du Einzelner da bist, das frage dich" (KSA 1.319). Both passages are cited in Gerhardt, *Pathos und Distanz* (Ditzingen: Reclam, 1988), 58, 69.

37. There is a contrast here with the role of the fishermen in section #302 of *The Gay Science,* discussed in chapter 4. In #302, the fishermen's riddle frustrates the aesthete Homer's wish for a complete, cosmic embrace, but #337's "god full of power and love" accommodates "even the poorest fisherman," who becomes the necessary accompaniment to this god's happiness.

38. For a commentary on *The Gay Science*'s *cogito* passage, see William Beatty Warner, *Chance and the Text of Experience* (Ithaca, N.Y.: Cornell University Press, 1986), 130-48.

39. Cavell, *In Quest of the Ordinary* (Chicago: University of Chicago Press, 1988), 108.

40. Ibid., 128.

41. Ibid.

42. For the contrast, see Harold Bloom, *The Anxiety of Influence* (London: Oxford University Press, 1973), 132.

43. Laurence Lampert, *Nietzsche's Teaching: An Interpretation of* Thus Spake Zarathustra (New Haven, Conn.: Yale University Press, 1986), 26.

44. For the notion of imitatio in its full-fledged Renaissance form, see Thomas Greene, *The Light in Troy* (New Haven, Conn.: Yale University Press, 1982), on Quintilian and Seneca, and Richard Peterson, *Imitation and Praise in the Poems of Ben Jonson* (New Haven, Conn.: Yale University Press, 1981), 1–40.

45. Friedrich Hölderlin, *Hyperion*, vol. 2, book 2 (Berlin: Pawlak, n.d.), 272. Graham Parkes cites the Hölderlin and the Emerson passages along with *Zarathustra*'s book 2, chapter 20 and the *Birth of Tragedy*, chapter 10, in *Composing the Soul* (Chicago: University of Chicago Press, 1994), 69–70. The ultimate source for this topos of disunited limbs is Empedocles' fragment 443: "Here sprang up many faces without necks, arms wandered without shoulders, unattached, and eyes strayed alone, in need of foreheads." G. S. Kirk and J. E. Raven, *The Presocratic Philosophers* (Cambridge: Cambridge University Press, 1957), 336.

46. "Eyes without feeling, feeling without sight, / Ears without hands or eyes, smelling sans all, / Or but a sickly part of one true sense / Could not so mope" (*Hamlet* 3.4.79–82).

47. Quoted in Zizek, *The Ticklish Subject*, 29–30.

48. In a wild attempt to convince Hans von Bülow of the merits of Peter Gast's opera *The Lion of Venice*, Nietzsche in a letter of August 1888 scorns Wagner (in contrast to Gast) as a creator of fragments rather than unity. Gast, Nietzsche writes to von Bülow, has "die Fähigkeit, aus dem Ganzen zu gestalten, fertig zu werden und nicht zu fragmentarisiren (vorsichtiger Euphemismus für 'wagnerisiren')." Nietzsche, *Sämtliche Briefe*, ed. G. Colli and M. Montinari (Berlin: de Gruyter, 1986), 8:384.

49. Later, in Nietzsche's books of the 1880s, Wagner will at times have the reckless, decentered actor-like qualities of Mime, the corrupt, hyperenergetic dwarf who both raises up from childhood and plots against Siegfried in the third of the *Ring* operas, *Siegfried*. Nietzsche's later turn from Wagner, which he expresses by picturing Wagner as a decadent mimic who has abandoned himself to the roles he plays, suggests Nietzsche's own worry about becoming the masks he has adopted in his work.

50. Wagner's "great deed" of artistic founding, as Nietzsche pictures it, carries a note of sheer wish-fulfillment. Nietzsche accordingly describes art as a refuge, a "refreshing dream," "something holy that outweighs all [man's] struggle and all his distress" (*UM* 212–13).

51. Lacan, *The Four Fundamental Concepts of Psychoanalysis: Seminar Bk. XI*, ed. Jacques-Alain Miller, trans. Alan Sheridan (New York: Norton, 1978), 73.

52. Béatrice Han, in her essay on Nietzsche's *Tragic Age*, emphasizes the architectonic, integral character of Nietzsche's portraits of the pre-Socratics. See Han, "Nietzsche and the 'Masters of Truth,'" in *Heidegger, Authenticity, and Modernity*, ed. Mark Wrathall and Jeff Malpas (Cambridge, Mass.: MIT Press, 2000), 183–86.

53. Compare *PTAG* 84, where Nietzsche argues against the quasi-Cartesian "I breathe, therefore I exist."

54. For the Fichtean concept of *Anstoss,* see Daniel Breazeale, "Check or Checkmate? On the Finitude of the Fichtean Self," in *The Modern Subject,* ed. Karl Ameriks and Dieter Sturma (Albany: State University of New York Press, 1995), 96-102.

Chapter 4

1. J.-A. Miller, "Commentary on Lacan's Text," in *Reading Seminars I and II,* ed. Bruce Fink, Richard Feldstein, and Maire Jaanus (Albany: State University of New York Press, 1996), 425-26. This passage is quoted in Fink, *A Clinical Introduction to Lacanian Psychoanalysis* (Cambridge, Mass.: Harvard University Press, 1997), 208.

2. One might also remember Hesiod's injunctions in *Works and Days*: "Do not piss as you stand and face the sun. . . . Never piss into springs. / Never cross the fair waters of ever-flowing rivers / Before you wash your hands," and so on and on. Hesiod, *Works and Days,* 727-37, in *Theogony, Works and Days, Shield,* trans. Apostolos N. Athanassakis (Baltimore: Johns Hopkins University Press, 1983).

3. On this subject, see René Girard's *Violence and the Sacred,* trans. Patrick Gregory (Baltimore: Johns Hopkins University Press, 1977).

4. Trophonius was an underground, oracular god, and reputed son of Apollo; before his death and deification he was a master builder whose works included the lower parts of Apollo's temple at Delphi. See the *Oxford Classical Dictionary,* 3d ed., ed. Simon Hornblower and Antony Spawforth (New York: Oxford University Press, 1996), 1556.

5. Zizek writes that "the very duality of desire and drive can be conceived as the libidinal correlative of the duality of modern and traditional society," with the traditional society being oriented by drive, "a circular movement around the Same." Zizek, "'In His Bold Gaze My Ruin Is Writ Large,'" in Zizek, ed., *Everything You Always Wanted to Know About Lacan . . . But Were Afraid to Ask Hitchcock* (London: Verso, 1992), 232.

6. Derrida, *Of Grammatology,* trans. Gayatri Chakravorty Spivak (Baltimore: Johns Hopkins University Press, 1976), 188. Rousseauan imagination, remarks Derrida, "is the power that allows life to affect itself with its own representation" (184) — a representation that contains a hollowness or death.

7. Ibid., 276, and see also 203.

8. Ibid., 205.

9. Georg Simmel, *Schopenhauer and Nietzsche,* trans. H. Loiskandl, D. Weinstein, and M. Weinstein (Amherst: University of Massachusetts Press, 1986), 169-72.

10. For a reflection on the link between fantasy and envy, see Slavoj Zizek, "The Seven Veils of Fantasy," in *Key Concepts of Lacanian Psychoanalysis,* ed. Dany Nobus (New York: Other Press, 1998).

11. The invention of a new Symbolic whose superiority lies in its insubstantial nature bears some resemblance to Claude Lefort's definition of democracy, discussed in my Preface, as a system centered on the emptiness or provisional character of the Symbolic order, which can be filled by any content

whatever. See Lefort, *Democracy and Political Theory*, trans. David Macey (Cambridge: Polity Press/Blackwell, 1988), 1–40.

12. Paul Verhaeghe, "The Lacanian Subject," in *Key Concepts of Lacanian Psychoanalysis*, ed. Dany Nobus (New York: Other Press, 1998), 168. Lacan remarks in the third seminar that "in this discourse of the other what I take to be me is no longer a subject but an object. It's a function of mirage, in which the subject refinds himself only as misrecognition and negation." Lacan, *The Seminar of Jacques Lacan, Bk. III: The Psychoses*, ed. J.-A. Miller, trans. Russell Grigg (New York: Norton, 1993), 240.

13. Lacan, *Seminar, Bk. III*, 241.

14. Verhaeghe, "The Lacanian Subject," 168.

15. Heinrich Heine, *Briefe aus Berlin* (Göttingen: Steidl Verlag, 1997), 60.

16. Another of Emerson's rather spectacular answers to Plato's cave occurs in his "Lecture on the Times" of 1841: "We are the representatives of religion and intellect, and stand in the light of Ideas, whose rays stream through us to those younger and more in the dark" (*E* 157).

Saul Bellow's novel *The Dean's December* ends with the protagonist's visit to the Mt. Palomar observatory, and a similar (Emersonian) reflection: "And what he saw with his eyes was not even the real heavens. No, only white marks, bright vibrations, clouds of sky roe, tokens of the real thing, only as much as could be taken in through the distortions of the atmosphere. Through these distortions you saw objects, forms, partial realities. . . . Rocks, trees, animals, men and women, these also drew you to penetrate further, under the distortions (comparable to the atmospheric ones, shadows within shadows), to find their real being with your own. This was the sense in which you were drawn." Bellow, *The Dean's December* (New York: Penguin, 1982), 311.

17. See L. Rust Brown's reflections on the economic model of the psyche in Emerson, in *The Emerson Museum* (Cambridge, Mass.: Harvard University Press, 1997), 53, 58.

18. See Nietzsche, *Der Wille zur Macht* (Stuttgart: Kröner Verlag, 1930), #808. For a commentary that uses this passage and others to distinguish Nietzsche from Schopenhauer, see Nussbaum, "The Transfigurations of Intoxication," *Arion* (3d series) 1, no. 2 (May 1991): 75–111.

19. Richard Foreman's astonishing play *Bad Boy Nietzsche* (produced in 1999 at Foreman's Ontological-Hysterical Theatre in New York) conveys the torment of such immediacy, and Nietzsche's effort to escape it, during his madness. In Foreman's play, Nietzsche is constantly being teased and tormented by the figures of his work, from which he, in his insanity, can no longer protect himself: a vaguely military and sadistic officer-type, an aloof *femme fatale*, and a questioning child.

20. For this point see Gerhardt, *Friedrich Nietzsche* (Munich: C. H. Beck Verlag, 1995), 46.

21. Lacan, *Seminar, Bk. III*, 241.

22. Stendhal, *Scarlet and Black*, trans. Margaret Shaw (Harmondsworth: Penguin, 1953), 100.

23. Lesley Chamberlain's *Nietzsche in Turin* reflects on Nietzsche's "feminized" manner as the product of not just his family situation of being surrounded

by women, but also the family's three generations of Lutheran pastors. Chamberlain, *Nietzsche in Turin* (New York: Picador/St. Martin's, 1996), 29.

24. See Cacciari, *Krisis* (Milan: Feltrinelli, 1976), 105.

25. Nietzsche's image of us as childlike in our performance of this task has a near-endless resonance when we consider the many images of the child in his work. In addition, the image of a *child* carrying a goddess seems a way of avoiding sexual ramifications like those that characterize the most important relation between a god and a human in Nietzsche, that of Dionysus and Ariadne.

26. Nietzsche, in comparing himself to a wave, implicitly refuses the conventional image of the rocklike Stoic battered but unmoved by the world. Also relevant as a contrast to Nietzsche is Marcus Aurelius's injunction, in *Meditations* 4.49, "Be like the headland against which the waves break and break." Marcus Aurelius, *Meditations*, trans. Maxwell Staniforth (Harmondsworth: Penguin, 1964), 75.

27. "Aus einem ziemlich alltäglichen Vorfall." Schopenhauer, *Aphorismen zur Lebensweisheit*, in *Sämtliche Werke* (Frankfurt am Main: Suhrkamp, 1986), vol. 4, Part 1, 378.

28. Schopenhauer, *Aphorismen*, 380.

29. "Wie der Wanderer erst, wann er auf einer Höhe angekommen ist, den zurückgelegten Weg mit allen seinen Wendungen und Krümmungen im Zusammenhange überblickt und erkennt; so erkennen wir erst am Ende einer periode unsers Lebens oder gar des ganzen den wahren Zusammenhange unsrer Taten, Leistungen und Werke, die genaue Konsequenz und Verkettung, ja auch den Wert derselben." Schopenhauer, *Aphorismen*, 494.

30. Ibid., 499.

31. See Daniel O'Hara's reading of this passage in his introduction to O'Hara, ed., *Why Nietzsche Now?* (Bloomington: Indiana University Press, 1985), 11-12.

32. Nietzsche in letters to his mother in the late 1880s frequently refers to himself as "das alte Geschöpf," "the old creature." See, *inter alia*, Nietzsche, *Sämtliche Briefe*, ed. G. Colli and M. Montinari (Berlin: de Gruyter, 1986), 8:432, 445, 455, 543 (all letters from 1888).

33. Compare also Emerson's "Worship," from the *Conduct of Life:* "Every man takes care that his neighbor shall not cheat him," but this suspicion is replaced gradually by our admitting "in another man a higher degree of moral sentiment than our own,—a finer conscience, more impressionable, or, which marks minuter degrees" (*E* 1063). Again, Emerson's Gnostic argument overcomes the envious dynamic to which Nietzsche remains unwillingly loyal.

34. Jorge Luis Borges, "Funes el memorioso," in *Ficciones* (Madrid: Alianza Emece, 1971 [1st ed. 1956]).

35. Eudemus of Rhodes's rendition of the Pythagoreans' doctrine of recurrence is as follows: "Everything will eternally return in the self-same numerical order, and I shall converse with you staff in hand, and you will sit as you are sitting now, and so it will be in everything else." Cited in Bernd Magnus, *Nietzsche's Existential Imperative* (Bloomington: Indiana University Press, 1978), 60. Nietzsche refers to, and keeps his distance from, the Pythagorean version of eternal return near the beginning of "The Use and Disadvantage of History for Life."

36. For an illuminating discussion of the difference between Lacan and

Aristotle on the nature of time, see Joan Copjec, *Read My Desire: Lacan against the Historicists* (Cambridge, Mass.: MIT Press, 1994), 46–49.

37. Lacan's second seminar addresses the notion of automatism extensively.

38. My reading of the eternal return draws on Bernd Magnus's *Nietzsche's Existential Imperative.* I agree with Magnus that Nietzsche is unable to succeed in formulating a convincing empirical or descriptive account of the eternal return, in showing that the moments and circumstances of our lives will recur in the future (or that they have recurred in the past). Nietzsche's failure to publish his empirical speculations on eternal return indicates that he was unsatisfied with them (Magnus, 74, 86). Instead, Magnus argues, Nietzsche's published references to the eternal return all take a "normative" form. Instead of trying to discern an empirical pattern of recurrence in cosmic time, Nietzsche challenges us to think of our lives *as if* they were to recur eternally, and to embrace this recurrence—the "normative" reading (154). (Magnus does not say why Nietzsche was interested in trying to develop an empirical account of eternal return, but presumably in his reading the empirical represents an attempt to evade the challenge of the normative sense of the return.) I agree with Magnus that Nietzsche's eternal return is a normative dare rather than an empirical hypothesis, but I would add that Magnus's account does not explain why accepting the return as normative is such a daunting idea. Why not embrace one's life? The reason, I argue, can only be found in Nietzsche's perception of the automatism or senselessness of the recurring object *a*, the secret and unacceptable cause of desire.

Chapter 5

1. Bloom, *Figures of Capable Imagination* (New York: Seabury Press, 1976), 55. What Bloom means by the daemon is what Yeats called personality, with its impossibly ambitious demands, in contrast to the habitual, relaxed satisfactions of character. Yeatsian personality signifies an antithetical mask or persona that the strong artistic creator reaches out for as a riposte to his everyday, customary self (which Yeats named "character").

2. Pater, Conclusion to *The Renaissance,* in *Selected Writings of Walter Pater,* ed. Harold Bloom (New York: Signet/New American Library, 1974), 61.

3. Kenneth Burke, *Attitudes toward History* (New York: New Republic, 1937), 20.

4. Ibid., 41.

5. Burke, *The Philosophy of Literary Form* (Berkeley: University of California Press, 1973), 206.

6. Nietzsche, *"Fatum und Geschichte,"* in *Frühe Schriften,* ed. Hans-Joachim Mette (Munich: C. H. Beck Verlag, 1994), 58.

7. Ibid., 57. Nietzsche also seems to have remembered a passage from Heine's *Ideen. Das Buch Le Grand* (1827): "Die Welt . . . ist der Traum eines weinberauschten Gottes, der sich aus der zechenden Götterversammlung à la francaise fortgeschlichen, und auf einem einsamen Stern sich schlafen gelegt, und selbst nicht weiss, dass er alles das auch erschafft, was er träumt . . . aber es wird nicht lange dauern, und der Gott erwacht, und reibt sich die verschlafenen

Augen, und lächelt—und unsre Welt ist zerronnen in Nichts, ja, sie hat nie existiert." Heinrich Heine, *Ideen. Das Buch Le Grand* (Stuttgart: Reclam, 1972), 10.

8. On the image of eating the world, see Joel Porte, *Representative Man*, 2d ed. (New York: Columbia University Press, 1988), 80. Porte cites Emerson's dream, recorded in his journals, of October 1840: "I ate the world."

9. Cavell juxtaposes these lines from Emerson's and Nietzsche's respective essays on fate in *Philosophical Passages* (Cambridge, Mass.: Blackwell, 1995), 40.

10. Nietzsche, "Fatum und Geschichte," 59.

11. Ibid.

12. Girard, "Strategies of Madness—Nietzsche, Wagner, and Dostoevski," in *"To Double Business Bound"* (Baltimore: Johns Hopkins University Press, 1978), 76.

13. See chapter 2, 105-7, for a brief discussion of Schopenhauer and the uncanny.

14. For a comment on the topos of the *Frau-Welt* see Zizek, *The Plague of Fantasies* (New York: Verso, 1997), 66.

15. Lacan, in *Seminar, Book VII: The Ethics of Psychoanalysis,* trans. Dennis Porter (New York: Norton, 1997), 253, makes this point, I take it, in reference to Fellini's *La Dolce Vita* (it is not the disgusting sea creature at the film's end that is an image of the Real, but rather the jet-setters' movement, on the beach, toward an invisible goal).

16. See also Terence's comedy ("proxumus sum egomet mihi" *Andria* 4.1.12, along with Matthew 6:19 ("where your treasure is, there will your heart be also"). See Terence, *Andria,* ed. G. P. Shipp (London: Oxford University Press, 1960), 95.

17. Pippin, "Morality as Psychology, Psychology as Morality: Nietzsche, Eros, and Clumsy Lovers," in *Nietzsche's Postmoralism,* ed. Richard Schacht (Cambridge: Cambridge University Press, 2000), 87.

18. Heine, "The Romantic School," in *The Romantic School and Other Essays,* ed. Jost Hermand and Robert C. Holub (New York: Continuum, 1985), 4-5. For an acute discussion of Heine the cultural critic as a precursor to Nietzsche, particularly in the way both writers use oppositions (for example, Heine's Nazarene/Hellene, Nietzsche's Apollo/Dionysus), see Herwig Friedl, "Heinrich Heine und Friedrich Nietzsche," in *Heinrich Heine im Spannungsfeld von Literature und Wissenschaft,* ed. Wilhelm Gössmann and Manfred Windfuhr (Essen: Reimar Hobbing, 1990), 195-214, esp. 199-200.

19. Heine, "Concerning the History of Religion and Philosophy in Germany," in *The Romantic School and Other Essays,* 133.

20. Geoffrey Galt Harpham, *The Ascetic Imperative in Culture and Criticism* (Chicago: University of Chicago Press, 1987), 210.

21. Ibid. Harpham also writes that in the third essay of the *Genealogy* (3.18) asceticism "is rehabilitated as an instinctual activity, even a necessary antidepressant for savages. Primitive men feel an habitual heaviness, even a self-revulsion, which the ascetic priest 'cures' by prescribing 'cautious doses' of the will to power in 'mechanical activity'" (215).

22. See Bernard Williams, "Nietzsche's Minimalist Moral Psychology," in *Nietzsche, Genealogy, Morality,* ed. Richard Schacht (Berkeley: University of California Press, 1994), 245.

23. Foucault's recourse in his later work to the ancient "care of the self" as an ideal indicates that he too desired an escape from the modern alliance between the therapeutic and the punitive.

24. "Breaking on the wheel . . . impaling, ripping apart and trampling to death by horses . . . boiling of the criminal in oil or wine . . . the popular flaying . . . cutting out strips from the breast. . . . and, of course, coating the wrong-doer with honey and leaving him to the flies in the scorching sun . . . how much blood and horror lies at the basis of all 'good things'!" (*GM* 2.3).

25. Paul Valadier notes that without the reversal that generates bad conscience "the human animal would remain within the incoherence of his affects and would be unable to achieve self-mastery [l'animal humain resterait dans l'incoherence de ses affects et serait impuissant à accéder à la maîtrise de soi]." Valadier, *Nietzsche: Cruauté et noblesse de droit* (Paris: Michalon, 2000), 63. "Only through bad conscience does man become a profound, interesting, even beautiful animal," Nietzsche emphasizes (*GM* 2.16, 2.18).

26. See Zizek, *The Metastases of Enjoyment: Six Essays on Women and Causality* (New York: Verso, 1994), 216: the Other as an inaccessible subject of desire seems to encroach upon my enjoyment, to threaten my "way of life," as Freud suggested with his theory of the narcissism of minor differences in *Civilization and Its Discontents*.

27. Chapter 20 of the second essay claims to detect a reversal of this process, "a considerable decline in the consciousness of human guilt," and the resulting birth of an atheist freedom, a "second innocence." But in the following chapter, Nietzsche admits that this vision was overly optimistic, that "the facts diverge from this in a terrible way," that the redemption from guilt he dreamed of has been "foreclosed." In the *Genealogy*, the interminability of ascetic guilt constantly seems to overshadow the proposal, perhaps most memorably made in *GM* 2.16 and 2.18, that asceticism is only a transition, a bridge to something higher (a new freedom from guilt).

28. See Alexander Nehamas, "The Genealogy of Genealogy," in *Nietzsche, Genealogy, Morality*, ed. Richard Schacht (Berkeley: University of California Press, 1994), 278.

29. Tyler Roberts, *Contesting Spirit: Nietzsche, Affirmation, Religion* (Princeton, N.J.: Princeton University Press, 1998).

30. Daniel Conway, *Nietzsche and the Political* (New York: Routledge, 1997).

31. For the image of the "exploding self" see Staten, *Nietzsche's Voice* (Ithaca, N.Y.: Cornell University Press, 1990), 122–44; as well as Gary Shapiro's *Nietzschean Narratives* (Bloomington: Indiana University Press, 1989).

32. Nietzsche, *Der Wille zur Macht* (Stuttgart: Kröner Verlag, 1930), 48, translation modified.

33. Perhaps Julia Lupton and Kenneth Reinhard identify something analogous to the Nietzschean concept of the comedian of an ideal when they write that for Lacan a genuine act is neither a free choice, which involves an overestimation of the ego's powers, nor a submission to the determined, to fate, but rather "a transgression of the symbolic order delimited though not determined by its commandments." Lupton and Reinhard, *After Oedipus: Shakespeare in Psychoanalysis* (Ithaca, N.Y.: Cornell University Press, 1993), 197.

34. Zizek, *The Fragile Absolute* (New York: Verso, 2000), 49.

35. Sarah Kofman, *Explosion I* (Paris: Galilée, 1992), 47–50.

36. Ibid., 51–52.

37. In the last sentence quoted, the verb should be *ist* but has mutated into *sind:* it has left Nietzsche's control, trespassed from Nietzsche's thought of his mother and sister to the mother and sister themselves.

38. We can perhaps hear Wagnerian alliteration in the phrase "gegen giftiges Gewürm [against a poisonous serpent]": is Nietzsche staging himself as Siegfried here?

39. Hollingdale does not give this passage in his translation.

CONCLUSION

1. For an examination of the architectural image in Nietzsche, see Sarah Kofman, "Metaphoric Architectures," in *Looking after Nietzsche,* ed. Laurence Rickels (Albany: State University of New York Press, 1990), as well as Peter Sedgwick's remarks in his Introduction to *Nietzsche: A Critical Reader* (Oxford: Blackwell, 1995), which references a section from *Twilight of the Idols,* "Skirmishes of an Untimely Man."

2. The difference between Nietzsche's and Freud's respective uses of concepts like *Trieb* (drive) and *Instinkt* has been very usefully described by Paul-Laurent Assoun in his *Freud et Nietzsche* (Paris: Presses Universitaires de France, 1980). I have been less concerned in this book, however, with the difference between, say, Nietzsche's notion of drives that refine themselves and Freud's account of repetitive, dumbly insistent drives (see Assoun, 127–46), than with detecting Nietzsche's final vulnerability to Freudian drive. Assoun accurately reflects Nietzsche's sometimes rather more idealizing view of the matter, which can be understood as an attempt to escape the brutality of (Freudian) drive. See also the comments on Lampert at the end of this Conclusion; and for a rather different but stimulating approach to these matters, Daniel Chapelle, *Nietzsche and Psychoanalysis* (Albany: State University of New York Press, 1993).

3. Lacan, *Le Séminaire, Livre VIII: Le transfert,* ed. Jacques-Alain Miller (Paris: Editions du Seuil, 1991), 13–15.

4. "On doit se demander par quels moyens opérer honnêtement avec les désirs. C'est-à-dire—comment préserver le désir dans l'acte, la relation du désir à l'acte? Le désir trouve ordinairement dans l'acte plutôt son collapsus que sa réalisation, et, au mieux, l'acte ne présente au désir que son exploit, sa geste héroïque. Comment préserver, dis-je, du désir à cet acte, ce que l'on peut appeler une relation simple, ou salubre?" Ibid., 14.

5. Lacan, *Seminar, Bk. VII: The Ethics of Psychoanalysis,* trans. Dennis Porter (New York: Norton, 1997), 161–64. The best commentary on this motif in Lacan is the concluding chapter of Henry Staten, *Eros in Mourning: Homer to Lacan* (Baltimore: Johns Hopkins University Press, 1995), in which see esp. 175, 180.

6. See the discussion of courtly love in Lacan's *Seminar, Bk. VII* (139–54). As Zizek writes, in Lacan courtly love is paradigmatic for all erotic life because the object of desire is always an "inhuman partner" first of all, "a radical Otherness which is wholly incommensurate with our needs and desires" (Zizek, *The*

Metastases of Enjoyment: Six Essays on Woman and Causality [New York: Verso, 1994], 90). As such, the object of desire needs to be sublimated or idealized so that (in the form of the recalcitrant Lady or *domna*, for example), "*the Object of desire itself coincides with the force that prevents its attainment*—in a way, the object 'is' its own withdrawal, its own retraction" (Zizek, *Metastases*, 96).

7. Cavell, "The Uncanniness of the Ordinary," in *In Quest of the Ordinary* (Chicago: University of Chicago Press, 1988), 158.

8. Ibid., 172.

9. Zizek, *Metastases*, 90.

10. See Verhaeghe, *Does the Woman Exist?* (New York: Other Press, 1999), 205–47, on sexual difference.

11. On the wish in Freud as "a supplement, a beyond of the logic of reality with its substitutions," and on the psychoanalytic theory of love as a "wish that one be given something for nothing," see John Forrester, *Truth Games* (Cambridge, Mass.: Harvard University Press, 1997), 158–59.

12. Laurence Lampert, *Nietzsche and Modern Times* (New Haven, Conn.: Yale University Press, 1993), 405, 431. For a more detailed account of Lampert's version of Nietzsche's project, see the conclusion to his *Leo Strauss and Nietzsche* (Chicago: University of Chicago Press, 1996), 166–86.

13. Tyler Roberts, *Contesting Spirit: Nietzsche, Affirmation, Religion* (Princeton, N.J.: Princeton University Press, 1998), 12.

14. Zizek, *Metastases*, 88.

Works Cited

Primary Sources

Emerson, Ralph Waldo. *Emerson in His Journals*. Ed. Joel Porte. Cambridge, Mass.: Harvard University Press, 1982.

———. *Essays and Lectures*. Ed. Joel Porte. New York: Library of America, 1983.

Nietzsche, Friedrich. *The Birth of Tragedy*. Trans. Shaun Whiteside. London: Penguin, 1993.

———. *Daybreak*. Trans. R. J. Hollingdale. Cambridge: Cambridge University Press, 1982.

———. *Ecce Homo*. Trans. R. J. Hollingdale. Intro. by Michael Tanner. London: Penguin, 1992.

———. *Frühe Schriften*. Ed. Hans-Joachim Mette. Munich: C. H. Beck Verlag, 1994.

———. *The Gay Science*. Trans. Walter Kaufmann. New York: Vintage Books, 1974.

———. *On the Genealogy of Morality*. Trans. Carol Diethe. Cambridge: Cambridge University Press, 1994.

———. *Philosophy in the Tragic Age of the Greeks*. Trans. Marianne Cowan. Washington, D.C.: Regnery Gateway, 1962.

———. *The Pre-Platonic Philosophers*. Ed. and trans. Greg Whitlock. Urbana: University of Illinois Press, 2001.

———. *Sämtliche Briefe (Kritische Studienausgabe)*. Ed. Giorgio Colli and Mazzino Montinari. 8 vols. Berlin: de Gruyter, 1986.

———. *Sämtliche Werke (Kritische Studienausgabe)*. Ed. Giorgio Colli and Mazzino Montinari. 15 vols. Berlin: de Gruyter, 1967–77.

———. *Thus Spake Zarathustra*. Trans. R. J. Hollingdale. Harmondsworth: Penguin, 1961.

———. *Twilight of the Idols*. Trans. R. J. Hollingdale. 2d ed. Harmondsworth: Penguin, 1990.

———. *Untimely Meditations*. Trans. R. J. Hollingdale. Cambridge: Cambridge University Press, 1983.

———. *The Will to Power*. Trans. Walter Kaufmann and R. J. Hollingdale. New York: Vintage/Random House, 1968.

———. *Der Wille zur Macht*. Stuttgart: Kröner Verlag, 1930.

Secondary Sources

Allison, David. "This Is Not a Christ." In *Why Nietzsche Still?* ed. Alan Schrift. Berkeley: University of California Press, 2000.

Altieri, Charles. *Postmodernisms Now*. University Park: Penn State University Press, 1998.

Anderson, Quentin. *The Imperial Self*. New York: Knopf, 1971.

————. *Making Americans*. San Diego: Harcourt Brace Jovanovich, 1992.

Assoun, Paul-Laurent. *Freud et Nietzsche*. Paris: Presses Universitaires de France, 1980.

Badiou, Alain. *L'Éthique: Essai sur la conscience du mal*. Paris: Hatier, 1993.

Barfield, Owen. *Speaker's Meaning*. Middletown, Conn.: Wesleyan University Press, 1967.

Baumgarten, Eduard. *Das Vorbild Emersons im Werk und Leben Nietzsches*. Heidelberg: Karl Winter Verlag, 1957.

Bellow, Saul. *The Dean's December*. New York: Penguin, 1982.

Bernstein, Charles. *Content's Dream*. Los Angeles: Sun & Moon, 1986.

Bloom, Harold. *The Anxiety of Influence*. London: Oxford University Press, 1973.

————. *Figures of Capable Imagination*. New York: Seabury Press, 1976.

————. *Kabbalah and Criticism*. New York: Seabury Press, 1975.

————. *Omens of Millennium*. New York: Riverhead, 1996.

————. *The Ringers in the Tower*. Chicago: University of Chicago Press, 1971.

Borges, Jorge Luis. "Funes el memorioso." In *Ficciones*. Madrid: Alianza Emece, 1971 [1st ed. 1956].

Bowie, Malcolm. *Freud, Proust and Lacan: Theory as Fiction*. Cambridge: Cambridge University Press, 1987.

Breazeale, Daniel. "Check or Checkmate? On the Finitude of the Fichtean Self." In *The Modern Subject*, ed. Karl Ameriks and Dieter Sturma. Albany: State University of New York Press, 1995.

Bromwich, David. *A Choice of Inheritance*. Cambridge, Mass.: Harvard University Press, 1989.

————. *Disowned by Memory: Wordsworth's Poetry of the 1790s*. Chicago: University of Chicago Press, 1999.

Brown, L. Rust. *The Emerson Museum*. Cambridge, Mass.: Harvard University Press, 1997.

Burke, Kenneth. *Attitudes toward History*. New York: New Republic, 1937.

————. *The Philosophy of Literary Form*. Berkeley: University of California Press, 1973.

Cacciari, Massimo. *Krisis*. Milan: Feltrinelli, 1976.

Cameron, Sharon. "Representing Grief: Emerson's 'Experience.'" *Representations* 15 (1986): 15–41.

————. "The Way of Life by Abandonment: Emerson's Impersonal." *Critical Inquiry* 25, no. 1 (1998): 1–31.

Cavell, Stanley. *Conditions Handsome and Unhandsome*. Chicago: University of Chicago Press, 1990.

————. *Philosophical Passages*. Cambridge, Mass.: Blackwell, 1995.

————. *A Pitch of Philosophy*. Cambridge, Mass.: Harvard University Press, 1994.

————. *In Quest of the Ordinary*. Chicago: University of Chicago Press, 1988.

————. *The Senses of Walden*. Expanded edition. San Francisco: North Point Press, 1981.

————. *This New Yet Unapproachable America*. Albuquerque, N.M.: Living Batch Press, 1989.

Chamberlain, Lesley. *Nietzsche in Turin*. New York: Picador/St. Martin's, 1996.

Chapman, John Jay. *Emerson and Other Essays*. Boston: Moffatt, Yard, 1909.

Chapelle, Daniel. *Nietzsche and Psychoanalysis.* Albany: State University of New York Press, 1993.

Conant, James. "Nietzsche's Perfectionism." In *Nietzsche's Postmoralism,* ed. Richard Schacht. Cambridge: Cambridge University Press, 2000.

Conway, Daniel. *Nietzsche and the Political.* New York: Routledge, 1997.

Copjec, Joan. *Read My Desire: Lacan against the Historicists.* Cambridge, Mass.: MIT Press, 1994.

De Man, Paul. *Allegories of Reading.* New Haven, Conn.: Yale University Press, 1979.

Derrida, Jacques. *The Ear of the Other.* Trans. Christie McDonald. Lincoln: University of Nebraska Press, 1985.

———. *Of Grammatology.* Trans. Gayatri Chakravorty Spivak. Baltimore: Johns Hopkins University Press, 1976 [1st French ed. 1967].

———. *Limited INC.* Trans. Samuel Weber. Evanston, Ill.: Northwestern University Press, 1988.

———. *The Politics of Friendship.* Trans. George Collins. London: Verso, 1997.

———. *Specters of Marx.* Trans. Peggy Kamuf. New York: Routledge, 1994.

Ellison, Julie. *Emerson's Romantic Style.* Princeton, N.J.: Princeton University Press, 1984.

Fink, Bruce. *A Clinical Introduction to Lacanian Psychoanalysis.* Cambridge, Mass.: Harvard University Press, 1997.

———. *The Lacanian Subject.* Princeton, N.J.: Princeton University Press, 1995.

Finkielkraut, Alain. *In the Name of Humanity* [*L'Humanité perdue*]. Trans. Judith Friedlander. New York: Columbia University Press, 2000 [1st French ed. 1996].

Forrester, John. *Truth Games.* Cambridge, Mass.: Harvard University Press, 1997.

Friedl, Herwig. "Heinrich Heine und Friedrich Nietzsche." In *Heinrich Heine im Spannungsfeld von Literatur und Wissenschaft,* ed. Wilhelm Gössmann and Manfred Windfuhr. Essen: Reimar Hobling, 1990.

Frye, Northrop. *A Natural Perspective.* New York: Columbia University Press, 1965.

Gerhardt, Volker. *Friedrich Nietzsche.* Munich: C. M. Beck Verlag, 1995.

———. *Pathos und Distanz.* Ditzingen: Reclam, 1988.

Girard, René. "Strategies of Madness—Nietzsche, Wagner, Dostoevski." In *"To Double Business Bound."* Baltimore: Johns Hopkins University Press, 1978.

———. *Violence and the Sacred.* Trans. Patrick Gregory. Baltimore: Johns Hopkins University Press, 1977.

Granier, Jean. "Nietzsche's Conception of Chaos." In *The New Nietzsche,* ed. David Allison. Cambridge, Mass.: MIT Press, 1985 [1st ed. 1977].

Greene, Thomas. *The Light in Troy.* New Haven, Conn.: Yale University Press, 1982.

Grimminger, Rolf. "Offenbarung und Leere, oder: Nietzsche, Freud und Paul de Man." In *Ästhetik und Rhetorik: Lektüren zu Paul de Man,* ed. Karl Heinz Bohrer. Frankfurt am Main: Suhrkamp, 1993.

Gross, Kenneth. *The Dream of the Moving Statue.* Ithaca, N.Y.: Cornell University Press, 1992.

Grossman, Allen, and Mark Halliday. *The Sighted Singer*. Baltimore: Johns Hopkins University Press, 1992.

Haar, Michel. *Par-delà le nihilisme*. Paris: Presses Universitaires Francáises, 1998.

———. "La rupture initiale de Nietzsche avec Schopenhauer." In *Schopenhauer et la force du pessimisme*. Paris: Editions du Rocher, 1988.

Hamacher, Werner. "'Disgregation of the Will': Nietzsche on the Individual and Individuality." In *Reconstructing Individualism*, ed. Thomas Heller, Morton Sosno, and David Wellbery. Stanford, Calif.: Stanford University Press, 1986.

Han, Béatrice. "Nietzsche and the 'Masters of Truth.'" In *Heidegger, Authenticity, and Modernity*, ed. Mark Wrathall and Jeff Malpas. Cambridge, Mass.: MIT Press, 2000.

Harpham, Geoffrey Galt. *The Ascetic Imperative in Culture and Criticism*. Chicago: University of Chicago Press, 1987.

Heidegger, Martin. *Being and Time*. Trans. J. Macquarrie and E. Robinson. New York: Harper, 1962 [1st German ed. 1927].

———. *Nietzsche*. 4 vols. Trans. David Farrell Krell. San Francisco: Harper and Row, 1979 [1st German ed. 1961].

Heine, Heinrich. *Briefe aus Berlin*. Göttingen: Steidl Verlag, 1997 [1st ed. 1822].

———. *Ideen. Das Buch Le Grand*. Stuttgart: Reclam, 1972 [1st ed. 1827].

———. *The Romantic School and Other Essays*. Ed. Jost Hermand and Robert C. Holub. New York: Continuum, 1985.

Hertz, Neil. "Freud and the Sandman." In *Textual Strategies*, ed. Josué V. Harari. Ithaca, N.Y.: Cornell University Press, 1979.

Hesiod. *Works and Days*. In *Theogony, Works and Days, Shield*. Trans. Apostolos N. Athanassakis. Baltimore: Johns Hopkins University Press, 1983.

Hölderlin, Friedrich. *Hyperion*. Berlin: Pawlak, n.d.

Holmes, Oliver Wendell. *Ralph Waldo Emerson*. Boston: Houghton Mifflin, 1895.

Hornblower, Simon, and Antony Spawforth, eds. *Oxford Classical Dictionary*. 3d ed. New York: Oxford University Press, 1996.

Hough, Sheridan. *Nietzsche's Noontide Friend*. University Park: Penn State University Press, 1997.

Howe, Susan. *My Emily Dickinson*. Berkeley: North Atlantic Books, 1985.

Hubbard, Stanley. *Nietzsche und Emerson*. Basel: Verlag für Recht und Gesellschaft, 1958.

Jehlen, Myra. *American Incarnation*. Cambridge, Mass.: Harvard University Press, 1986.

Kateb, George. *Emerson and Self-Reliance*. Thousand Oaks, Calif.: Sage Publications, 1995.

———. *Hannah Arendt*. Totowa, N.J.: Rowman and Allanheld, 1983.

Kemal, Salim, Ivan Gaskell, and Daniel Conway, eds. *Nietzsche, Philosophy and the Arts*. Cambridge; Cambridge University Press, 1998.

Kerrigan, William. *Hamlet's Perfection*. Baltimore: Johns Hopkins University Press, 1994.

Kirk, G. S., and J. E. Raven. *The Presocratic Philosophers*. Cambridge: Cambridge University Press, 1957.

Kofman, Sarah. *Explosion I*. Paris: Galilée, 1992.

———. "Metaphor, Symbol, Metamorphosis." In *The New Nietzsche,* ed. David Allison. Cambridge, Mass.: MIT Press, 1985 [1st ed. 1977].

———. "Metaphoric Architectures." In *Looking after Nietzsche,* ed. Laurence Rickels. Albany: State University of New York Press, 1990.

Krell, David Farrell. "Der Maulwurf." In *Why Nietzsche Now?* ed. Daniel O'Hara. Bloomington: Indiana University Press, 1985.

———. *The Purest of Bastards.* University Park: Penn State University Press, 2000.

Lacan, Jacques. "Desire and the Interpretation of Desire in *Hamlet.*" In *Literature and Psychoanalysis,* ed. Shoshana Felman. Baltimore: Johns Hopkins University Press, 1982.

———. *Le Séminaire, Livre VIII: Le transfert.* Ed. Jacques-Alain Miller. Paris: Editions du Seuil, 1991.

———. *The Seminar of Jacques Lacan.* Ed. Jacques-Alain Miller. Trans. Alan Sheridan, Sylvana Tomaselli, John Forrester, Russell Grigg, Bruce Fink, et al. New York: Norton, 1981–.

Lampert, Laurence. *Leo Strauss and Nietzsche.* Chicago: University of Chicago Press, 1996.

———. *Nietzsche and Modern Times.* New Haven, Conn.: Yale University Press, 1993.

———. *Nietzsche's Teaching: An Interpretation of* Thus Spake Zarathustra. New Haven, Conn.: Yale University Press, 1986.

Lefort, Claude. *Democracy and Political Theory.* Trans. David Macey. Cambridge: Polity Press/Blackwell, 1988.

Lupton, Julia, and Kenneth Reinhard. *After Oedipus: Shakespeare in Psychoanalysis.* Ithaca, N.Y.: Cornell University Press, 1993.

Magnus, Bernd. *Nietzsche's Existential Imperative.* Bloomington: Indiana University Press, 1978.

Magnus, Bernd, Jean-Pierre Mileur, and Stanley Stewart. "Reading Ascetic Reading." In *Nietzsche, Genealogy, Morality,* ed. Richard Schacht. Berkeley: University of California Press, 1994.

Marcus Aurelius. *Meditations.* Trans. Maxwell Staniforth. Harmondsworth: Penguin, 1964.

Mikics, David. "Kermode on the Outside Looking In." *Gulf Coast* 8, no. 2 (summer/fall 1996): 90–96.

———. *The Limits of Moralizing: Pathos and Subjectivity in Spenser and Milton.* Lewisburg, Pa.: Bucknell University Press, 1994.

Mill, John Stuart. "On Liberty." In *The Six Great Humanistic Essays of J. S. Mill.* New York: Washington Square Press, 1963.

Miller, J.-A. "Commentary on Lacan's Text." In *Reading Seminars I and II,* ed. Bruce Fink, Richard Feldstein, and Maire Jaanus. Albany: State University of New York Press, 1996.

Milton, John. *Paradise Lost.* Ed. Alastair Fowler. London: Longman, 1998.

Montaigne, Michel de. *Complete Essays.* Trans. Donald Frame. Stanford, Calif.: Stanford University Press, 1958.

Nancy, Jean-Luc. *The Inoperative Community.* Trans. Peter Connor et al. Minneapolis: University of Minnesota Press, 1991.

Nehamas, Alexander. *The Art of Living*. Berkeley: University of California Press, 1998.

———. "The Genealogy of Genealogy." In *Nietzsche, Genealogy, Morality*, ed. Richard Schacht. Berkeley: University of California Press, 1994.

———. *Nietzsche: Life as Literature*. Cambridge, Mass.: Harvard University Press, 1985.

Nussbaum, Martha. "The Transfigurations of Intoxication." *Arion* (3d series) 1, no. 2 (May 1991): 75–111.

O'Hara, Daniel, ed. *Why Nietzsche Now?* Bloomington: Indiana University Press, 1985.

Otto, Walter F. *Dionysus: Myth and Cult*. Trans. Robert Palmer. Bloomington: Indiana University Press, 1965.

Packer, B. L. *Emerson's Fall*. New York: Continuum, 1982.

Parkes, Graham. *Composing the Soul*. Chicago: University of Chicago Press, 1994.

Pater, Walter. Conclusion to *The Renaissance*. In *Selected Writings of Walter Pater*. ed. Harold Bloom. New York: Signet/New American Library, 1974.

Peterson, Richard. *Imitation and Praise in the Poems of Ben Jonson*. New Haven, Conn.: Yale University Press, 1981.

Phillips, Adam. *Terrors and Experts*. Cambridge, Mass.: Harvard University Press, 1996.

Pippin, Robert. "Morality as Psychology, Psychology as Morality: Nietzsche, Eros, and Clumsy Lovers" In *Nietzsche's Postmoralism*, ed. Richard Schacht. Cambridge: Cambridge University Press, 2000.

Plato. *Republic*. Trans. G.M.A. Grube. Revised by C.D.C. Reeve. Indianapolis: Hackett, 1992.

———. *Symposium*. Trans. Paul Woodruff and Alexander Nehamas. Indianapolis: Hackett, 1989.

Poirier, Richard. *The Renewal of Literature*. Cambridge, Mass.: Harvard University Press, 1987.

Porte, Joel. *Representative Man*. 2d ed. New York: Columbia University Press, 1988.

Rawls, John. *A Theory of Justice*. Cambridge, Mass.: Harvard University Press, 1971.

Roberts, Tyler. *Contesting Spirit: Nietzsche, Affirmation, Religion*. Princeton, N.J.: Princeton University Press, 1998.

Rorty, Richard. *Contingency, Irony and Solidarity*. Cambridge: Cambridge University Press, 1989.

Salecl, Renata. *(Per)versions of Love and Hate*. London: Verso, 1998.

Sallis, John. *Crossings: Nietzsche and the Space of Tragedy*. Chicago: University of Chicago Press, 1991.

Santner, Eric. *On the Psychotheology of Everyday Life*. Chicago: University of Chicago Press, 2001.

Schacht, Richard, ed. *Nietzsche's Postmoralism*. Cambridge: Cambridge University Press, 2000.

Schlechta, Karl. *Nietzsche Chronik*. Munich: Carl Hansen Verlag, 1975.

Schopenhauer, Arthur. *Sämtliche Werke*. Frankfurt am Main: Suhrkamp, 1986.

———. *The Will to Live: Selected Writings*. Ed. Richard Taylor. New York: Frederick Ungar, 1962.

———. *The World as Will and Idea*. 2 vols. Trans. E.F.J. Payne. New York: Dover, 1958.

Sedgwick, Peter, ed. *Nietzsche: A Critical Reader*. Oxford: Blackwell, 1995.

Segal, Charles. *Dionysiac Poetics and Euripides' Bacchae*. 2d ed. Princeton, N.J.: Princeton University Press, 1997.

Shapiro, Gary. *Nietzschean Narratives*. Bloomington: Indiana University Press, 1989.

Simmel, Georg. *Schopenhauer and Nietzsche*. Trans. H. Loiskandl, D. Weinstein, and M. Weinstein. Amherst: University of Massachusetts Press, 1986.

Snow, Edward. *A Study of Vermeer*. Berkeley: University of California Press, 1979.

Stack, George. *Nietzsche and Emerson*. Athens: Ohio University Press, 1992.

Staten, Henry. *Eros in Mourning: Homer to Lacan*. Baltimore: Johns Hopkins University Press, 1995.

———. *Nietzsche's Voice*. Ithaca, N.Y.: Cornell University Press, 1990.

Stendhal [Henri Beyle]. *Scarlet and Black*. Trans. Margaret Shaw. Harmondsworth: Penguin, 1953 [1st French ed. 1830].

Stephens, John Lloyd. *Incidents of Travel in Egypt, Arabia Petraea, and the Holy Land*. Norman: University of Oklahoma Press, 1970.

Strauss, Leo. "Note on the Plan of Nietzsche's *Beyond Good and Evil*." In *Studies in Platonic Political Philosophy*. Chicago: University of Chicago Press, 1983.

———. On Nietzsche's Zarathustra. Unpublished lecture series.

Thoreau, Henry David. *Walden*. Ed. J. Lyndon Shanley. Princeton, N.J.: Princeton University Press, 1971.

Valadier, Paul. *Nietzsche: Cruauté et noblesse de droit*. Paris: Michalon, 2000.

Vattimo, Gianni. *The Adventure of Difference*. Trans. Cyprian Blamires and Thomas Harrison. Baltimore: Johns Hopkins University Press, 1993 [1st Italian ed. 1980].

———. "Nietzsche and Heidegger." In *Nietzsche in Italy*, ed. Thomas Harrison. Stanford, Calif.: ANMA Libri, 1988.

———. *Il soggetto e la maschera*. Milan: Bompiani, 1974.

Verhaeghe, Paul. *Does the Woman Exist?* New York: Other Press, 1999.

———. "The Lacanian Subject." In *Key Concepts of Lacanian Psychoanalysis*, ed. Dany Nobus. New York: Other Press, 1998.

Wagner, Richard. *Tristan and Isolde*. Trans. Andrew Porter. English National Opera Guide Series 6. London: John Calder, 1983.

Warner, William Beatty. *Chance and the Text of Experience*. Ithaca, N.Y.: Cornell University Press, 1986.

West, Cornel. *The American Evasion of Philosophy*. Madison: University of Wisconsin Press, 1990.

Whicher, Stephen. *Freedom and Fate: An Inner Life of Ralph Waldo Emerson*. 2d ed. Philadelphia: University of Pennsylvania Press, 1961.

Williams, Bernard. "Nietzsche's Minimalist Moral Psychology." In *Nietzsche, Genealogy, Morality*, ed. Richard Schacht. Berkeley: University of California Press, 1994.

Zizek, Slavoj. "Da Capo Senza Fine." In Judith Butler, Ernesto Laclau, and Slavoj Zizek, *Contingency, Hegemony, Universality.* New York: Verso, 2000.

———. "Four Discourses, Four Subjects." In *Cogito and the Unconscious,* ed. Slavoj Zizek. Durham, N.C.: Duke University Press, 1998.

———. *The Fragile Absolute.* New York: Verso, 2000.

———. "In His Bold Gaze My Ruin Is Writ Large." In *Everything You Always Wanted to Know about Lacan, but Were Afraid to Ask Hitchcock.* New York: Verso, 1992.

———. *The Metastases of Enjoyment: Six Essays on Women and Causality.* New York: Verso, 1994.

———. *The Plague of Fantasies.* New York: Verso, 1997.

———. "The Seven Veils of Fantasy." In *Key Concepts of Lacanian Psychoanalysis,* ed. Dany Nobus. New York: Other Press, 1998.

———. *Tarrying with the Negative.* Durham, N.C.: Duke University Press, 1993.

———. *The Ticklish Subject.* London: Verso, 1999.

Index